D0065079

Social Security:
Beyond the Rhetoric of Crisis

STUDIES FROM THE PROJECT ON THE FEDERAL SOCIAL ROLE

FORREST CHISMAN AND ALAN PIFER, SERIES DIRECTORS

The Politics of Social Policy in the United States
Edited by Margaret Weir, Ann Shola Orloff, and Theda Skocpol

Democracy and the Welfare State
Edited by Amy Gutmann

Social Security: Beyond the Rhetoric of Crisis
Edited by Theodore R. Marmor and Jerry L. Mashaw

Social Security: Beyond the Rhetoric of Crisis

EDITED BY

THEODORE R. MARMOR

JERRY L. MASHAW

PRINCETON UNIVERSITY PRESS

Copyright © 1988 by Princeton University Press

Published by Princeton University Press, 41 William Street, Princeton, New Jersey 08540
In the United Kingdom: Princeton University Press, Guildford, Surrey

This book has been composed in Linotron Sabon

Clothbound editions of Princeton University Press books are printed on acid-free paper,
and binding materials are chosen for strength and durability. Paperbacks, although
satisfactory for personal collections, are not usually suitable for library rebinding

Printed in the United States of America by Princeton University Press,
Princeton, New Jersey

Designed by Laury A. Egan

Library of Congress Cataloging-in-Publication Data

Social security: beyond the rhetoric of crisis / edited by Theodore R. Marmor,
Jerry L. Mashaw.
p. cm.—(Studies from the Project on the Federal Social Role)
Includes bibliographical references and index.
ISBN 0–691–07776–2 (alk. paper)   ISBN 0–691–02285–2 (pbk.)
1. Social security—United States.   I. Marmor, Theodore R.   II. Mashaw, Jerry L.
III. Series.
HD7125.S5992   1988   368.4'3'00973—dc19
88–10238   CIP

To the Memory of Wilbur J. Cohen and Robert M. Cover

CONTENTS

PART IV.

LIST OF TABLES AND FIGURES

Tables

Figures

LIST OF ABBREVIATIONS

AIME	Adjusted Indexed Monthly Earnings
ALJ	Administrative Law Judge
AMA	American Medical Association
CODA	Cash or Deferred Arrangement
CPI	Consumer Price Index
CDI	Continuing Disability Investigation
DDS	Disability Determination Service
DRG	Diagnosis Related Group
EITC	Earned Income Tax Credit
ERISA	Employee Retirement Income Security Act of 1974
FICA	Federal Insurance Contributions Act, commonly referred to as the Social Security payroll tax
GDP	Gross Domestic Product
GNP	Gross National Product
HCFA	Health Care Financing Administration
HEW	Department of Health, Education and Welfare (in 1978, with the creation of a separate Department of Education, became Department of Health and Human Services)
HHS	Department of Health and Human Services
IRA	Individual Retirement Account
MCPI	Medical Care Price Index
NHS	National Health Service (Britain)
OASI	Old Age and Survivors Insurance (Social Security from 1935 until the addition of disability insurance in the 1950s)
OASDI	Old Age, Survivors, and Disability Insurance
OASDHI	Old Age, Survivors, Disability, and Health Insurance (includes the Medicare program, added in 1965)
OECD	Organization for Economic Cooperation and Development (see note 8.6)
OHA	Office of Hearings and Appeals
OPEC	Oil Producing Energy Cartel
PCE	Personal Consumption Expenditures
PIA	Primary Insurance Amount
SERPS	State Earning-Related Pension Scheme (Britain)
SRA	Supplemental Retirement Account
SSA	Social Security Administration
SSI	Supplemental Security Income

FOREWORD

This book is one of several volumes based on activities sponsored by the Project on the Federal Social Role. The Project was a nonprofit, nonpartisan enterprise established in 1983 to stimulate innovative thinking about the future directions of federal social policy.

Americans are doubtless more preoccupied than any other people with questions about the fundamental purposes and directions of their national government. In part this concern reflects a healthy political culture. We are always searching for better ideas about government and always disagreeing about which ideas are best. In part, too, our concern reflects a longstanding ambivalence about the value of national institutions. We still honor the tradition of Thomas Jefferson, which presumes against an active federal role, in an era when programs and policies emanating from Washington permeate every aspect of our lives.

But while Americans never seem to tire of arguing about the proper role of national government, systematic thinking on this subject has been neglected in recent years. Scholars have produced a great deal of excellent research about specific policies and programs. But there has been too little careful study of what effect those measures, considered as a whole, have on the American people.

This neglect of the larger issue of public policy is deeply troubling. The federal social role is more than the sum of its parts. The various policies and programs that constitute it interact with each other in a great many ways. Collectively they have a far greater impact on our future as a nation than the study of particular issues can reveal.

More importantly, the specific measures of government are all parts of a broader commitment by the American people to employ their common resources toward achieving common goals. Only a strong sense of what those goals are and what overall directions of policy are required to achieve them can ensure that so large and diverse an enterprise as the federal government serves the general welfare.

The problems that arise when basic issues of purpose and direction are neglected have been vividly demonstrated in recent years. For half a century Americans supported an almost continual expansion of the federal social role. But the growth of federal activism slowed in the late 1970s and early 1980s, and there were dire predictions that national government had exhausted its possibilities as an instrument for social betterment. A period of reassessment followed. For over a decade, virtually every aspect of the social role was closely scrutinized by politicians, scholars, and the press.

As an exercise in public education, this reassessment was undoubtedly a success. But as an exercise in policy development it was a disappointment. No clear directions for the future emerged. The federal role was neither greatly augmented nor diminished; nor was it set on any new course. The nation remained locked in political stalemate.

Although periods of national stock-taking are often healthy, prolonged stalemate is a luxury that the United States cannot afford. While national policy has been standing still, major forces of change have been at work in our social and economic life. Transformations in the nature of our economy, evolving personal lifestyles, societal aging and worsening conditions for many of the poor are the largest and most visible developments. We are no longer the nation that we were a few decades ago, and because government pervades so many aspects of our lives, we need new measures to suit our new circumstances.

The recent reassessment of public policy failed to come to grips with the forces of social and economic change in large part because it proceeded in a piecemeal fashion. Debate was confined primarily to the merits and demerits of policies and programs already in place. As a result, the nation artificially constrained its options. We failed to examine carefully enough the need for major new initiatives by the federal government and ways to make them work.

In this static and backward-looking environment, destructive myths and misunderstandings found fertile ground—most notably the myth that there are severe limits to what activist government can achieve. This idea takes various forms, and in most of those forms it is seriously misleading. If our national history teaches us anything, it is that each generation is capable of accomplishing far more through the use of government than previous generations would have dreamed possible. History also teaches that we *must* accomplish more: that effective government is a never-ending process of responding to new needs and opportunities. This requires breaking with the ideas and patterns of the past. As often as not, the social role has evolved through large measures that defied past skepticism and cut across the categories of previous thought.

Washington, D.C   Forrest Chisman
                                                                 Alan Pifer

PREFACE

This volume grew out of an interdisciplinary reexamination of Social Security by Yale University faculty in law, economics, and political science. The Yale Project on Social Security, as it came to be known, began as a faculty seminar within the Institution for Social and Policy Studies in 1984–1985. With funds from both Alan Pifer and Forrest Chisman's Project on the Federal Social Role and the Ford Foundation, we broadened our effort to include faculty and student seminars and two major conferences. At its core was the group of faculty members whose papers are represented in this volume. Rudolf Klein and Michael O'Higgins of the University of Bath and Paul Starr of Princeton also gave lectures at our 1985 conference that, with revision, became chapters for this book. Bob Ball inaugurated both our faculty seminar and the conference lecture series.

The fiftieth anniversary of the Social Security Act of 1935 itself provided an occasion for discussion of how change and stability in the features of this now venerable institution might inform thought about its future. Our reexamination of Social Security programs, however, had sources other than the occasion of that important anniversary. In both seminars and conferences we explored what America's social insurance programs have meant historically, socially, economically, politically, and legally. Our aim was to understand and assess the possibilities and prospects for Social Security over the decades ahead, for Social Security is both a prominent and a puzzling feature of the American version of the welfare state.

Social insurance pensions—for retirement, disability, unemployment, and premature death—are crucial to the economic security of Americans but not well understood by them. As we began our studies, more than a decade of stagflation had prompted much commentary about America's welfare state. But a comparison of "informed" commentary, by both supporters and critics, with general public opinion revealed a paradox. Overall, Americans regarded Social Security programs as desirable but fiscally endangered. By contrast, the insiders' debate among policy professionals, academics, and political commentators revealed much less concern about impending financial disaster than about the proper form of American social insurance for the future. Moreover, a slightly harder look suggested that this simple, if paradoxical, disjunction overlay a much more variegated discussion with a shifting programmatic and political focus.

We began, thus, with puzzles and questions about a complex set of institutions operating in an even more complex polity. The essays that follow reveal some of that complexity. They also reveal a rather common vision. Optimistic if not quite congratulatory, that vision sees remarkable strengths in these obviously imperfect New Deal institutions and opportunities for further improvement as Americans move beyond the rhetoric of crisis that has in recent years surrounded, and to some degree obscured, them.

Enterprises of this kind inevitably generate complicated administrative tasks for which academic editors are hopelessly unsuited. We are fortunate to have the dedicated and ever competent assistance of Elizabeth Auld, and we warmly thank her for getting and keeping us organized. We also have a special debt to our financial benefactors, particularly Alan Pifer and Forrest Chisman, philanthropoids of social conviction, scholarly accomplishment, and personal grace. Alan and Forrest believed (sometimes more than we) that our partnership had something serious to say and gave us the time and the freedom to formulate what that was. We wish also to acknowledge general financial support from the Kaiser Family Foundation throughout the early stages of this project, and from the Rockefeller Foundation, in the final stages of manuscript editing and production.

Other scholars commented on these essays in generous detail; we acknowledge our considerable debt to them. They include: Henry Aaron, Bruce Ackerman, Jim Blumstein, Fay Cook, Martha Derthick, Sandy Jencks, Larry Mead, Jim Lorenz, Robert Morris, Alicia Munnell, Deborah Stone, and Michael Taussig. Felicity Skidmore's and Deborah Chassman's careful readings of the original papers and of the final manuscript, respectively, prevented needless errors, while Paul Pierson's research assistance both enriched our understanding and stimulated us to clarify and refine our views.

Finally, this book is dedicated to the memory of Robert Cover, whose premature death cut short the scholarly life of one of the nation's most imaginative students of public affairs, past and present, and to Wilbur Cohen, partner with our coauthor Ball in the shaping of Social Security institutions over the past fifty years. We only regret that neither were able to read the final product of our labors—the first as a major participant in its writing, the second as one who was intensely interested in our efforts and who understood our reasons for persisting.

Theodore R. Marmor and Jerry L. Mashaw
New Haven, Connecticut
December 1987

Social Security:
Beyond the Rhetoric of Crisis

INTRODUCTION

For fifty years America has lived with the legacy of New Deal debates over American social policy. The report of the Committee on Economic Security in 1935 symbolized the terms of disagreement for a half-century of programmatic initiatives, funding disputes, and partisan clashes. Crudely put, the Democratic party championed the New Deal's paradigm of governmental responsibility for the maintenance of America's welfare state and celebrated the welfare state's expansion fiscally and programmatically. The Republican party's conservatives often attacked these New Deal premises but, until recently, reluctantly continued social welfare programs and financing in practice. In fact this partisan rhetoric obscured two other divisions of equal importance: on the one hand, the split between conservatives and liberals of whatever party and, on the other, the differences within the liberal camp between social insurance enthusiasts and those preoccupied with what is currently called the problem of the "underclass." The passage of Medicare in 1965, for instance, symbolized the triumph of social insurance liberals over the conservative coalition of Republicans and southern Democrats. The War on Poverty, like the Civil Rights Act of the same period, illustrated the priorities of those more preoccupied with the bottom of the income distribution than with expanding social insurance.

The complicated currents and countercurrents of the welfare state debate have often been suppressed precisely at the stage of programmatic innovation. In the New Deal, economic catastrophe held the reform coalition together despite intense conflict about the federal government's proper role. Postwar prosperity and the extraordinary majorities of the early Johnson administration blurred the divisions of creed, emphasis, and constituency between the social insurance advocates and the trustees for the poor. A common enemy like Barry Goldwater makes the Social Security Administration (SSA) and the Office of Economic Opportunity seem like joint ventures.

In the wake of the stagflation of the 1970s, however, the reform coalition has come apart. Just as the Social Security retirement system was more generously funded in 1972, the optimistic economic assumptions of its expansion were about to be undermined. And, with the Reagan election of 1980, a full-scale Republican assault on the New Deal legacy rekindled debate over the fundamental premises that support a generous and wide-ranging federal role in social policy. The particular struggles of the 1970s—Social Security pensions and their growth, hospital cost-containment, welfare reform, day care, regulation of private pensions, and the like—spilled over into a broad critique of American social policy. In the familiar language of American politics, there was a "crisis" and a concentrated demand for rethinking the structure of the American welfare state.

Politically, the prospects for thoughtful considerations of these issues are not encouraging. Our governmental institutions fragment attention in an already diverse polity, making regular incremental adjustment difficult and thoughtful reassessment nearly impossible. Legally, there is considerable flexibility for adjustments in the major spending programs, but socially, there is rigidity about, and resistance to, tinkering with the New Deal legacy. Thus those who want action, particularly reductions in benefits, resort to cries of "crisis" to prompt action. This familiar move elicits stubborn resistance among those determined to forestall what they view as inhumane dismantling of America's social insurance programs.

Moreover, only since the mid-1970s has the need for retrenchment been a plausible item on the programmatic agenda. At its outset and for some fifteen years thereafter, Social Security was a very small program. Indeed, until well after World War II, Social Security was in one sense an insurance company's ideal: a program with many contributors but few recipients of monthly checks. The major struggles about the program in its infancy had nothing to do with deficit anxieties but rather with the control of embarrassingly large surpluses. The solution, confirming the supremacy of the New Deal political coalition, was to broaden and expand benefits.

From the perspective of these early years, the growth of Social Security in the two decades after 1950 is particularly striking. Increases in Social Security's tax rate, numbers of beneficiaries, and employees between 1950 and 1970 concretely suggest the scale of change. In 1950, combined employer-employee contributions to Old Age and Survivors Insurance (OASI) amounted to 3 percent of the first $3,000 of income; two decades later, the figure was 8.4 percent on a taxable base of $7,800. By 1950, ten years after Social Security's first payments were made, only 16 percent of Americans over sixty-five were eligible for retirement benefits; in 1960 this figure had climbed to 70 percent, and by 1970 it was more than 90 percent.[1] Similarly dramatic changes are evident in the size of the Social Security Administration (SSA). In 1950, some twelve thousand persons

[1] Joseph A. Pechman, Henry J. Aaron, and Michael K. Taussig, *Social Security: Perspectives for Reform* (Washington, D.C.: Brookings Institution, 1968), Table B-8, and Peter J. Ferrara, *Social Security: The Inherent Contradiction* (San Francisco: Cato Institute, 1980), Tables 1 and 2. Robert M. Ball, *Social Security: Today and Tomorrow* (New York: Columbia University Press, 1978), p. 107.

worked for the ssa, split between the central office in Baltimore and the extended network of field offices. By 1970, this number had grown to slightly more than fifty thousand.[2] And, of course, these employees were now administering disability and medical insurance programs that had not existed two decades earlier. The postwar years had indeed provided an extended and happy adolescence for America's growing programs of social insurance.

But the decade of the 1970s was unkind to mature welfare states, and American Social Security programs were not exempt from the anxieties of maturity. Rapid inflation during the Vietnam War brought pressure to increase benefits. Amendments in 1972 to the original Social Security Act both increased benefits 20 percent across the board and automatically indexed future payments to inflation. But two developments brought unexpected controversy to this historically conventional expansion of social insurance benefits. Stagflation, which produced revenue losses simultaneously with benefit increases, ignited fears of financial insolvency and gave evidence of trust fund shortfalls by the mid-1970s. And a technical feature in the formula for indexing unexpectedly exacerbated the pressures by producing higher benefits than planned. The pressure of stagflation—highlighted and worsened by the oil shocks of 1973–1974 brought increased media attention to Social Security, hitherto generally ignored by the nation's political reporters. The potential "bankruptcy" of the system became a major news story.[3] By 1977 Congress had remedied the technical problem, but only after four years of persistent criticism that Social Security would, without change, "go broke." The 1977 amendments presumed that raising the level of worker income subject to Social Security taxes and the rate of those taxes (in 1981, 1985, and 1990)— along with some other technical but important adjustments—the Social Security system would remain "financially sound until the end of the century."[4]

The early 1980s, however, were years of further economic turmoil and heightened anxiety in American politics generally. The strains of the

[2] Of the 12,000 employees in 1950, just over 5,000 worked in Baltimore; of the 50,000 working for the ssa in 1970, almost 40 percent were in the central office. Social Security Administration, personal communication, June 1986.

[3] Publications ranging from *Time* magazine to *The New York Review of Books* treated the impending crisis in Social Security with such headlines as "What the Nation Can Afford: A Debt-threatened Dream" (*Time*, May 24, 1982) and "Social Security: The Coming Crash" (Peter G. Peterson, *The New York Review of Books*, Dec. 2, 1982. Ferrara, in *Social Security: The Inherent Contradiction*, devotes all of chapter 5 to the topic of Social Security and bankruptcy.

[4] Ben W. Heineman, Jr., and Curtis A. Hessler, *Memorandum for the President: A Strategic Approach to Domestic Affairs in the 1980s* (New York: Random House, 1980), p. 354.

1970s had not been removed by financial adjustments to Social Security in 1977. By the time of Reagan's election in 1980, fears for the solvency of American pensions were again quite widespread. Reagan's initial program of reform—retrenchment and increased military preparedness—brought Social Security back on the public agenda with a vengeance. His proposals for sharp reductions in future pensions were met with howls of protest, but the question of how to deal with the anticipated shortfall in Social Security receipts nevertheless mobilized action. Amid looming deficits and voter outrage, a special bipartisan Commission on Social Security (often referred to as the Greenspan Commission after its chairman, Alan Greenspan) was charged with bringing to the Congress and the President a plan to remove the specter of bankruptcy from Social Security. The result in 1983 was yet another fiscal reform—proposed by the Commission and rapidly passed by the Congress—brought the Social Security "trust funds" into balance for the foreseeable future.

By the mid-1980s, Social Security was once again immune from annual retrenchment. This shift was evident in the presidential election of 1984, when Ronald Reagan finally embraced Social Security with a clarity previously reserved to legatees of the New Deal. For all the uproar, the Social Security loyalists could rest content that the most fearful scenarios of disruption were averted. Yet a decade of crisis rhetoric—much of it focused on the fiscally modest but morally controversial welfare programs—had undeniably affected public perceptions.

The adjustments of 1982–1983 seemed to have had little impact on Americans' general sense of uneasiness about Social Security's future. The reform legislation made large changes in the present and future balance of revenues and outlays. Through the combination of tax increases and benefit reductions the commission's reforms will raise a projected $166 billion over the period from 1983 to 1989 and eliminate two-thirds of the projected seventy-five-year trust fund deficit.[5] But, as public opinion polls continue to show, the confidence of the citizenry in Social Security's future was hardly bolstered even as the financial strain of the system was reduced.[6] The rhetoric of crisis had made Social Security seem an endan-

---

[5] Alicia H. Munnell, "The Current Status of Social Security Financing." Paper presented at the Yale Faculty Seminar on Social Security, November 19, 1984. Revised version, December 19, 1984.

[6] Confidence in Social Security's future has fallen sharply in recent years. Among those aged 55 to 64 in 1984, 44 percent expressed confidence "in the future of the social security system," down sharply from the 74 percent expressing the same opinion in 1975. For those aged 18 to 24, there has been an even more dramatic diminution of confidence. In 1975, 45 percent were confident in the system's future, whereas in 1984 only 31 percent expressed that same confidence. Put another way, the number of people of all ages who expressed a lack of confidence in the future of Social Security increased from 37 percent in 1975 to

gered institution. It remains broadly, indeed overwhelmingly, supported, fiscally sound for the foreseeable future but still shrouded in fearfulness.[7]

Social Security Reform: Beyond the Rhetoric of Crisis

The inquiry that resulted in this volume began in the immediate aftermath of the Greenspan Commission's report of 1983 and the subsequent 1983 Amendments to the Social Security Act. These conventional adjustments in benefits and taxes seemed to us not only to have failed to quell a decade-long national anxiety about the impending "collapse" of the Social Security system, but they also appeared to herald the emergence or reemergence of a more fundamental debate about the basic fairness and efficacy of the New Deal's social insurance vision. Some critics worried that Social Security pensions were depressing savings and reducing the share of capital investment in the economy. The advent of the Individual Retirement Account (IRA) had rekindled enthusiasm in some quarters for private, individual provision for old age. This was particularly true for the generations that would participate in a mature Social Security scheme with fewer contributing workers per elderly beneficiary. They would, therefore, not enjoy the extraordinarily generous benefits, compared to their contributions, that had been available through Social Security to their parents.

Nor was the specter of fiscal crisis fully expunged, even for the experts, by the 1983 amendments and the Greenspan Commission's projections. Some attacked these long-run projections as unrealistic. Others noted that explosive growth of the federal government's medical and disability programs might produce fiscal crisis even if Social Security retirement pension funds were solvent.

Neoconservative critics of Social Security, emboldened perhaps by the first Reagan victory and the public's apparent shift to the right on social policy issues, had begun to attack the basic structure of Social Security as an essentially fraudulent device to provide "welfare" under the guise of "social insurance." These critics attempted to expose Social Security both

---

almost 68 percent in 1984 ("Social Security: Young and Old View the System's Prospects," *Public Opinion*, April–May 1985, p. 22).

[7] Quite a number of books written in the 1980s have addressed the question of how this came to be and what it means for the sensible discussion of the place of social insurance in American life. See, for example, W. Andrew Achenbaum, *Social Security: Visions and Revisions* (New York: Cambridge University Press, 1986); Paul Light, *Artful Work: The Politics of Social Security Reform* (New York: Random House, 1985); Michael J. Boskin, *Too Many Promises: The Uncertain Future of Social Security* (Homewood, Ill.: Dow Jones-Irwin, 1986); Peter J. Ferrara, ed., *Social Security: Prospects for Real Reform* (Washington, D.C.: Cato Institute, 1985).

as a bad bargain for the ordinary wage earner and as having no more political legitimacy than the always-morally-controversial needs-tested welfare programs. And on both the left and the right arguments were used to criticize the profligacy of a program that failed to "target" restricted social welfare resources on the worst off in the society.

Yet the impression of political trouble, anxiety, and loss of legitimacy that these fiscal events and criticisms suggest was in some ways belied by the 1984 presidential elections. On the way to a humiliating defeat, Walter Mondale made one issue salient for the nation: Ronald Reagan's alleged antipathy to Social Security. In the process Reagan transformed himself, at least publicly, into the staunchest of Social Security's defenders. This lesson was hardly lost on the Congress. In budgets starved for fiscal protein, Social Security remains in the late 1980s a sacred cow. Social Security seems at once deeply troubled and politically untouchable.

Against this backdrop of contemporary concerns and events Social Security policy presents to the interested analyst a series of questions, indeed puzzles: Does Social Security as originally conceived and subsequently changed have a coherent and defensible ideology? If so, is that set of principles and beliefs adequate to the demands of a contemporary political environment that, during the Reagan years, seems to emphasize the privatization of many roles adopted by the modern welfare state? What explains the peculiarly feverish quality of recent Social Security politics—a politics that seems to consist of periodic bouts of high anxiety, claims of doom and crisis, rigid resistance to any alteration, eventual marginal adjustment, and continuing uncertainty about the future? What is the role of the "entitlement" or "social insurance" idea in this political dynamic? Is that idea a myth, an impediment to constructive change, or a valuable source of legitimacy and stability?

What is the relationship of Social Security policy to broader issues of fiscal and economic policy? Is Social Security a drain on the economy? Can compulsory social insurance be justified economically, politically, or philosophically? How do Social Security payroll taxes (FICA) fit into the general fabric of tax policy? Does tax policy with respect to IRAS and private pension plans, combined with Social Security OASI pensions, add up to a coherent retirement policy? Finally, how should we locate our concerns and debates about Social Security in the broader world of social welfare policy? Are our concerns necessarily parochial—born of unique political, economic and cultural circumstances? Or do the questions that arise for us correspond to those raised in other developed, democratic, welfare states?

These were the sorts of questions we debated in seminars, addressed in conferences, and treated in the papers that follow. We do not have answers for all of them, and some of the answers given are perhaps more tentatively held than expressed. Yet a sense of confidence about the basic structure of American Social Security and a sense of optimism about its future possibilities is discernable in these pages. Indeed, this overall perception is quite striking given the gloomy, if not misanthropic, view of American Social Security now fashionable in some circles.

The Organization of this Book

Thematically, the essays in this volume can be grouped into four general categories. The first group (Ball, Tobin, and Cover) addresses issues of the structure and legitimacy of Social Security from three different perspectives: historical, contemporary, and constitutional. The second set of commentators (Graetz and Starr) focuses on the oldest and fiscally most substantial of Social Security's programs, retirement insurance, and assesses that program in the context of contemporary retirement policy and politics. In a third brace of chapters, Mashaw and Marmor address the development of two of the other major Social Security programs, disability insurance and medical insurance, both of which were included within the original New Deal conception of social insurance but which were added a quarter century or more after the Social Security Act of 1935. Finally, in the Klein and O'Higgins chapter, we step back from peculiarly American concerns to compare our recent preoccupations with developments in other western democracies. We cannot here do complete justice, of course, to the richness, persuasiveness, and insight of the essays that follow; however, we can describe in brief compass the general character of their arguments.

Robert Ball's historical treatment of the development of Social Security policy (Chapter 1) makes plain that the current Social Security system is not a hodge-podge of loosely connected programs incrementally developed over the past fifty years. The system instead responds in broad outline and much concrete detail to that envisioned in the 1930s blueprint for a comprehensive social insurance scheme. American social insurance has its own unique historical features, but it is also broadly similar to regimes established in almost all western democracies. The system has worked much as planned, and it seems to have retained its overwhelming political support precisely because the basic conception was politically sound. The risks insured against—retirement, death, disability, unemployment, and illness—are universal, and entitlement through earnings empowers rather than degrades. The program was and is premised on fundamental commitment to individual or family self-sufficiency and a market economy. To say that the redistributive features of Social Security make social insurance the same as welfare payments, as some recent articles have done, is about as sensible as saying that motels and airlines who give senior citizen and family discounts do not operate as private enterprises.

Although Ball celebrates the success of the original understanding of Social Security, he recognizes both the inevitability of change and the peculiar tensions generated by demographic shifts, fiscal strain, and the maturing of the system itself. However, he recommends an organizational rearrangement rather than a substantive policy response to these stresses. He favors relocating and reconstituting the Social Security Administration as a bipartisan board reporting directly to the President. In his view such a structure would facilitate the management of change, while simultaneously rebuilding public confidence in the system itself.

James Tobin's contribution (Chapter 2) addresses the economic justifications for current programs and their macroeconomic effects. Although he finds the basic scheme both economically sound and normatively appropriate, Tobin emphasizes the demographic strains on Social Security pensions that will materialize in the next century. The major problem, as Tobin sees it, is that a retirement program that is intentionally redistributive within generations is becoming unintentionally more redistributive across generations. Tobin's essay recommends not only marginal changes that will ameliorate some of these emerging problems, but also urges that, contrary to the planning horizons usual in American politics, we begin to debate soon how to deal with the fiscal crunch of the mid-twenty-first century. Do the coming generations wish to maintain the replacement ratio of pensions to earnings by raising payroll tax contribution rates or give up some benefits to avoid tax increases? Should we move further than is now planned to fund future benefits instead of relying mainly on "pay-as-you-go," as in the past? Should we credit individual participants with entitlements earned by their contributions, in "personal security accounts"? Some of these possible changes would require long transitions—as much as fifty years.

The discussion of substantial change in Social Security programs raises issues of both political feasibility and legal legitimacy. The very idea of social *security* entails entitlement—a concept of obvious political salience but uncertain legal import. Robert Cover's essay (Chapter 3) reveals, however, that notwithstanding the political rigidities that entitlement holders interject into any policy process, the constitutional position of Social Security policymaking is both secure and flexible. Having surmounted initial fears that the scheme was unconstitutional, Social Security now operates within a constitutional regime that provides Congress with capacious powers to alter the system. Although Social Security is a major element in the financial planning of every working family, the constitutional protections for the basic framework of economic security are less fulsome than for private pension or annuity benefits making significantly smaller contributions to the protection of their beneficiaries' stand-ard of living. Cover argues that the constitutional jurisprudence has em-phasized flexibility to a degree that may impair the public's sense of security and reinforce political resistance and rigidity whenever there is talk of change. Ironically, a less flexible, and therefore more legally se-cure, constitutional posture might contribute to a more flexible politics.

Michael Graetz (Chapter 4) begins Part II of the volume by addressing two often neglected features of Social Security pensions—their fit with what might be called a general retirement security policy and the relation-ship of Social Security financing to overall tax policy. From both perspec-tives Graetz finds the existing structure incoherent and possibly perverse. The redistributive features of Social Security retirement benefits are sup-ported by a regressive tax structure and may be overwhelmed by the ma-jor benefits provided high income households through the tax treatment of private pensions, IRAs, and SRAs. Legal structure also affects retirement politics. It is not surprising to find, for example, that private provision of retirement security through IRAs grew rapidly at the very time Social Se-curity pensions generated fiscal concern. FICA taxes are explicitly revealed on every pay stub while substantial IRA "tax expenditures" remain con-cealed even in national budgetary documents. And, of course, no part of FICA payments is deductible from ordinary income. Focusing on these and other anomalies, Graetz elaborates a significant reform agenda for retire-ment security policy that goes well beyond the conventional analyses of Social Security pensions themselves.

Paul Starr's Chapter 5 takes up the political theme introduced by Graetz and generalizes the challenge of "privatization" implicit in Graetz's discussion of IRAs. Ranging broadly across other policy do-mains, Starr sees the ideology of privatization as the major challenge to the philosophy of social insurance in the decades ahead. Starr then places this challenge within a political and fiscal context that goes beyond the historical message of Bob Ball's analysis—major changes in the Social Se-curity system are the more likely product of surplus rather than fiscal strain. Starr regards the privatization challenge as particularly acute in the next two decades, since the 1983 reforms will produce significant sur-pluses in Social Security trust fund accounts. Starr's essay thus reinforces Tobin's view that the coming decade may be the most significant since the 1930s for purposes of long-range Social Security planning.

Acknowledging that this "window of opportunity" might be used for a gradual move toward a more "private-like," if not "privatized" system, however, Starr argues forcefully for the retention of what he calls the "public household" features of Social Security. In his view a public pay-as-you-go system financed from long-term economic growth and pecul-iarly attentive to the needs of the least well-off income earners is superior to privatization proposals when judged by both the economic security and distributive justice dimensions of the policy debate. He predicts, therefore, that the basic structure will survive the challenge of the privatization movement; it is consistent with both our needs and our beliefs.

In the third section of the book Professors Mashaw and Marmor examine two different portions of the Social Security scheme—disability pensions and Medicare payments. Mashaw (Chapter 6) finds disability politics a distinctive subset of Social Security politics generally. Entitlements ideology, social insurance ideals, the work ethic, and fiscal crisis all play a role, as they do in Social Security pensions. But critical to understanding the disability program is a set of legal institutions—administrative law judges and federal courts—which strongly protect entitlements, shape public perceptions, and set legislative agendas. Disability politics is preeminently a politics of "rights" in which policy flexibility at the administrative level is sharply constrained whenever the policy direction is toward limiting expenditure, for stringency is easily equated with lawlessness. The disability program thus has the expansionist tendencies evident in Ball's and Tobin's discussions of pensions, but for reasons that have as much to do with institutional structure as with continuous public support.

Marmor's discussion of Medicare (Chapter 7) emphasizes the differences between its legislative enactment in the mid-1960s and its environment two decades later. Medicare, like disability coverage, was an unfinished item from the social insurance blueprint of the New Deal. Its politics involved fundamental struggles over both governmental legitimacy and fiscal commitments. Medicare's original objective was to keep the economic burden of illness from overwhelming old people and their children while avoiding basic changes in American medicine.

Twenty years later, the costs of the program and the inflationary and organizational problems of medical care make Medicare, unlike retirement and disability pensions, a troubled program. The politics of Medicare's implementation have diverged from those of pensions, partly because of differences in administering a program of third-party payment instead of pension checks, and partly because of the pace of change in the medical care world and the fiscal strain of medical inflation. Medicare is now more vulnerable to changes than other parts of Social Security. It is more confusing in operation than social insurance cash programs and, with the advent of the Health Care Financing Administration (HCFA), it is administratively divorced from the social insurance roots that gave it its early legitimacy. The problems of Medicare are not really programmatic, they are the problems of American medicine generally. Correspondingly, effective remedial policies for Medicare are substantially broader than the modest adjustments within Social Security's cash programs that this book suggests are possible and desirable.

In the final section and essay, Rudolf Klein and Michael O'Higgins (Chapter 8) comparatively analyze fiscal crises and policy responses in modern welfare states during the past decade. All western democracies have faced similar problems of stagflation and now confront similar demographic trends. Whether the problem is characterized as a short-term economic problem, a fundamental shift in political commitment, or the final emergence of the internal contradictions of capitalism, they, like the United States, must rethink and adjust their social welfare policies in the light of new environmental factors. As Klein and O'Higgins reveal, this rethinking and adjustment has gone on apace in the OECD countries, and many have made more radical adjustments than has the United States. But overall European adjustments reveal a pattern of incremental change grounded in a recognition of the welfare state as a set of mature social welfare programs that define the status quo and that cannot be either shrunk or expanded radically without massive economic and political dislocation. Klein and O'Higgins thus return us to a theme with which Ball's essay and this volume began. Just as the United States was a laggard in developing a relatively complete social insurance system, it has also been slow to develop mechanisms of adjustment for its maturing welfare state that combine policy flexibility with the maintenance of the public confidence essential to social security—and the principal purpose of Social Security.

I

1

The Original Understanding on Social Security: Implications for Later Developments

ROBERT M. BALL

Social Security did not spring full blown from the minds of New Deal advisers in the 1930s. Part of the "original understanding" of the role, purpose, and nature of Social Security in the United States was based on what had developed in Europe.[1] Those who designed the American system studied foreign experience intensely, and although the details were American inventions, the concepts were not.[2] America borrowed the idea of a government-sponsored, independently financed, contributory and compulsory program protecting against the loss of earned income arising

---

[1] Germany set up the first old-age, survivors, and disability insurance program in 1889, and well before 1935 when the American Social Security system was established, in one form or another, governments were providing protection against these risks in Austria, Belgium, Bulgaria, Czechoslovakia, Denmark, France, Hungary, Ireland, Italy, Luxembourg, the Netherlands, Poland, Romania, Russia, Spain, Sweden, and the United Kingdom. There were also systems in many countries outside Europe. Social Security Administration, *Social Security Programs Throughout the World—1983*, Research Report No. 59 (Washington, D.C.: Government Printing Office, 1983), p. 19.

[2] In the staff reports to the Committee on Economic Security, the cabinet committee responsible for making the original recommendations for a Social Security program, the foreign experience is carefully described. See *Social Security in America, The Factual Background of the Social Security Act as Summarized from Staff Reports to the Committee on Economic Security* (Washington, D.C.: Government Printing Office, 1937).

Also the staff working on what was to become the old-age benefits section of the Social Security Act were fully familiar with the European precedents. One staff member, Barbara Nachtrieb Armstrong, had produced a major work on social insurance: *Insuring the Essentials: Minimum Wage, Plus Social Insurance* (New York: Macmillan, 1932). The other two professionals working on this part of the study were economics professor J. Douglas Brown of Princeton, an industrial relations expert, and Murray W. Latimer, who had written the monumental study of private pensions, *Industrial Pension Systems in the United States and Canada*, 2 vols. (New York: Industrial Relations Counselors, 1932).

when people retire from work in old age, when people become totally disabled, or when a wage earner dies. By now, most countries around the world have such systems.

The Origin and Nature of Social Insurance

The origins of social insurance are very old. The principles upon which modern government systems are based were applied in nongovernment plans centuries before Germany set up the first state program in 1889. Social insurance grows out of a long tradition of people banding together to help themselves. Formal benefit plans, for example, were established by the guilds of the Middle Ages. These plans required predetermined contributions from each member while working and paid specified benefits in the event of disability or death.[3] Another forerunner of social insurance is the "customary fund" found in the mining districts of Austria and other central European countries; some funds date back to the sixteenth century.[4] Later, fraternal orders and friendly societies were organized by the hundreds for the central purpose of providing insurance protection for their members.[5] Trade unions throughout the world developed protection plans, and commercial insurance covering some of the same risks of income loss became widely available.[6]

[3] For example, the Gild of the Blessed Virgin Mary founded in 1357 at Kingston-Upon-Hull in England collected annually two shillings and twopence in silver from each married couple and from each single man and woman. Benefits are described as follows:

If it happen that any of the gild becomes infirm, bowed, blind, dumb, deaf, maimed, or sick whether with some lasting or only temporary sickness, and whether in old age or in youth, or be so borne down by any other mishap that he has not the means of living, then, for kindness' sake, and for the souls' sake of the founders, it is ordained that each shall have, out of the goods of the gild, at the hands of the wardens, sevenpence every week; and every one so being infirm, bowed, blind, dumb, deaf, maimed or sick, shall have the sevenpence every week as long as he lives. If any of these poor and infirm folks should get so low in the world that he cannot pay the before-named yearly charge of two shillings and twopence, and has no goods on which it may be levied, then part of the weekly payment of sevenpence shall be set aside, so that the quarterly payments towards the two shillings and twopence shall be fully made, and so that on no account shall that yearly payment be released.

Toulmin Smith, Esq., *English Gilds*, published for the Early English Text Society (London: N. Trubner & Co., 1870), pp. 155–57.

[4] For a brief authoritative account of the forerunners of social insurance see John Graham Brooks, *Compulsory Insurance in Germany, Fourth Special Report of the Commissioner of Labor* (Washington, D.C.: Government Printing Office, 1895), pp. 29–44.

[5] For a considerable discussion of the origin and nature of these orders and societies in England and the United States see: Terence O'Donnell, *History of Life Insurance in Its Formative Years* (Chicago: American Conservation Co., 1936), pp. 612–77.

[6] Ibid.

The origins and tradition of social insurance are clear. It is a nearly universal response of wage economies to the fact that most people are dependent on earnings and grows out of the efforts of workers to protect themselves and their families from loss of those earnings. This self-help approach is greatly preferred by workers throughout the world to the alternative of relief and assistance. One does not have to seek far for the reason. In insurance, applicants demonstrate something positive—that they have worked sufficiently to be eligible and thus have an earned right to the payment—then they receive payment based on their past earnings from funds to which they have contributed. There is no test of individual need, and the beneficiaries can add income from savings or private pensions to their social insurance benefits. In relief and assistance, applicants prove something negative—that they do not have enough to get along on. They are then given a grant unrelated to their previous level of living and designed only to bring them up to some community-determined minimum. If they have other income it is subtracted from their grant; all recipients are reduced to the same low level of living.

Neither the form of government nor the economic system seems to make much difference in the approach taken. Social insurance systems following nearly identical principles are found in market-oriented economies, in highly-planned economies, and in economies where the state is the main owner and operator of industry. The common element is the need to make up for wage loss.

Social Security Accomplishments

When the American Social Security program reached its fiftieth year in 1985, we celebrated one of the major achievements of the century. When the program was enacted, only about six million persons, 15 percent of those employed, held jobs covered by any sort of retirement system; only a tiny handful—perhaps 300,000 to 400,000—actually were receiving a pension.[7] The poorhouse toward the end of life, with all its horrors, was a very real part of America.[8]

Social Security changed all that. It has gradually brought about a peaceful revolution in the way older people, totally disabled people, widows, and orphans live. It has been largely responsible for the fact that the proportion of those 65 and over who are desperately poor is now about the

[7] In 1932, Murray Latimer estimated that there were about 160,000 recipients of private industrial pensions to which must be added civil service and military retirees, ministers, and teachers. Murray W. Latimer, *Industrial Pension Systems in the United States and Canada*, 2 vols. (New York: Industrial Relations Counselors, 1932), p. 852.

[8] See Abraham Epstein, *Insecurity: A Challenge to America* (New York: Harrison Smith and Robert Haas, 1933).

same as for the rest of the population, instead of more than twice as high, as it was as recently as 1959. Without Social Security, more than half the elderly would have incomes below the federal government's rock bottom definition of poverty; instead, 12.4 percent are in that category today. Even though eliminating much of the outright poverty among the elderly, Social Security has not moved them very far up the income scale. At the end of 1984, average retirement benefits were only $460.60; and yet 62 percent of the over-65 beneficiaries received more than half and one-fourth received more than 90 percent of their income from Social Security.[9]

But Social Security is much more than an antipoverty program. In 1986, 125 million earners contributed to the program. It has become a base on which practically all families build protection against the loss of earned income. Every private pension is planned on the assumption that the pensioner will also receive Social Security, and individuals who save on their own rely on Social Security as a base for their efforts.[10] Today over 37 million people, retired or disabled workers and their dependents, widows, and motherless and fatherless children—one in seven Americans—get Social Security payments every month.

The Original Understanding

In broad outline, then, the original understanding of Social Security was defined by the nature of the institution borrowed from abroad: insurance against wage loss, compulsory, contributory, independently financed, without a test of need, and with eligibility and benefits based on past earnings. But the more specific understanding in America was embodied in three reports and the legislation that followed: the report of the Committee on Economic Security[11] and the 1935 Social Security Act;[12] the report of the Advisory Council of 1937–1938[13] and the 1939 amend-

[9] From the March 1985 *Current Population Survey of the Bureau of the Census*, quoted in A. Ycas Martynas and Susan Grad, "Incomes of Retirement-Aged Persons in the United States," Paper delivered at a meeting of the International Social Security Association, Baltimore, May 6–8, 1986.

[10] For a more extended discussion of the integration of Social Security with private pensions, see Chapters 4 and 5 of this volume.

[11] *Committee on Economic Security, Report to the President.* Washington, D.C.: Government Printing Office, 1935.

[12] The detailed provisions of the Old-Age, Survivors and Disability Insurance program can be traced in summary form from the original Act through all successive amendments by reference to *The Social Security Bulletin, Annual Statistical Supplement, 1984–85* (Washington, D.C.: Government Printing Office, 1985), pp. 2–34.

[13] *Advisory Council on Social Security of 1937–1938, Final Report* (Washington, D.C.: 1939).

ments; and the reports of the Advisory Council of 1947–1949[14] and the 1950 amendments.

Advisory councils on Social Security, with their representation of leaders in industry and labor, actuaries, economists, and other Social Security experts, and members of the public have frequently renewed the original understanding on Social Security as the program has developed. In addition to those already mentioned, a 1953 advisory group was very important in gaining further extension of program coverage and in winning support for Social Security principles from the first Republican administration to have responsibility for the program's management.[15] The 1959 Advisory Council reviewed the program and strongly endorsed the financing method.[16] The 1965 council contributed importantly to the 1965 amendments.[17] The 1971 council was important in the development of the 1972 amendments, which made the system inflation proof.[18] And the Advisory Council of 1975 was the first to recommend stabilizing replacement rates through wage indexing, the major change brought about by the 1977 amendments.[19] The 1979 council was the first to recommend income taxation of Social Security benefits and to explore thoroughly the treatment of women under Social Security.[20] The National Commission on Social Security Reform, appointed by President Reagan early in 1982, was the key to the 1983 amendments.[21] Several other citizens' councils and advisory groups had less but still important influence. All, whether appointed by Republican or Democratic administrations, after months of study and debate, reaffirmed the basic philosophic underpinnings of the original understanding. For example, the first recommendation of the 1983 commission reads:

[14] Advisory Council on Social Security of 1947–1949, *Recommendations for Social Security Legislation, Reports to the Senate Committee on Finance* (Washington, D.C.: Government Printing Office, 1949).

[15] Consultants on Social Security, *A Report to the Secretary of HEW on Extension of OASI to Additional Groups of Current Workers* (Washington, D.C.: Government Printing Office, 1953).

[16] Advisory Council on Social Security Financing, *Financing Old-Age, Survivors and Disability Insurance, A Report* (Washington, D.C.: Government Printing Office, 1959).

[17] Advisory Council on Social Security of 1965, *The Status of the Social Security Program and Recommendations for Its Improvement* (Washington, D.C.: Government Printing Office, 1965).

[18] Advisory Council on Social Security of 1971, *Reports of the 1971 Council on Social Security* (Washington, D.C.: Government Printing Office, 1971).

[19] Quadrennial Advisory Council on Social Security, *Report of the Council* (Washington, D.C.: Government Printing Office, 1975).

[20] Advisory Council on Social Security of 1979–1980, *Report of the Council* (Washington, D.C.: Government Printing Office, 1980).

[21] National Commission on Social Security Reform, *Report of the Commission* (Washington, D.C.: Government Printing Office, 1983).

The members of the National Commission believe that the Congress, in its deliberations on financing proposals, should not alter the fundamental structure of the Social Security program or undermine its fundamental principles. The National Commission considered, but rejected, proposals to make the Social Security program a voluntary one, or to transform it into a program under which benefits are a product exclusively of the contributions paid, or to convert it into a fully-funded program, or to change it to a program under which benefits are conditioned on the showing of financial need.[22]

The American System: Its Origin and History

How did the United States finally get around to joining the other industrial nations of the world in establishing a contributory social insurance system? The answer lies in the crisis atmosphere produced by the worst depression this country has ever known.

With nearly a third of the work force out of jobs and with millions and millions of families in desperate straits in the mid-1930s, the nation was open to new ideas as never before. In 1934 and 1935, President Roosevelt used this great national crisis as an opportunity to create permanent institutions dealing with persistent and fundamental problems of economic security. He was not at all content to deal only with the emergencies of the moment; rather, he used those emergencies to change permanently the role of the federal government in the lives of ordinary people. This was a watershed period in the history of America,[23] and no other legislative enactment of the New Deal has had such an enduring effect on American families as the Social Security Act. The old-age benefit provisions of the act, signed into law on August 14, 1935, have grown into our old-age, survivors, and disability insurance system, which most Americans think of as Social Security, and our nationwide system of health insurance for the elderly and the long-term totally disabled, Medicare.

The 1935 act, although very substantially amended in 1939, was important in defining the kind of old-age, survivors, and disability insurance program we have today because it settled some of the most basic policy issues. It spelled out many parts of the original understanding on Social

---

[22] Ibid., chap. 2, p. 2

[23] Much of the material that follows is based on the author's essay, "The 1939 Amendments to the Social Security Act and What Followed," in *The Report of the Committee on Economic Security of 1935 and Other Basic Documents Relating to the Developments of the Social Security Act, Fiftieth Anniversary Edition*, ed. Alan Pifer and Forrest Chisman (Washington, D.C.: National Conference on Social Welfare, 1985), pp. 161–72. See also Robert M. Ball, *Social Security: Today and Tomorrow* (New York: Columbia University Press, 1978).

Security. The 1935 act established a system that was nationwide, federally administered, compulsory and contributory, and, after considerable dispute, without provision for electing out by those with private pension coverage. Unlike many European plans then in effect, the system included all those working in covered occupations, not just those with low wages. Although the maximum amount of earnings counted for tax and benefit purposes was limited, all in covered occupations were included for earnings up to the maximum. The principle of paying benefits only to those substantially retired was also established in the original program. But no one was excluded from benefits because of nonwork income or because of assets; benefits were to be paid as a matter of right, related to past earnings and contributions, but weighted in favor of the lower-paid earner. The age of first eligibility for retirement benefits was set at 65. All these understandings survived the extensive revampings of 1939 and 1950. They endure to this day, although the newest set of amendments stipulates that, beginning in 2000, the age of first eligibility for full benefits will rise gradually until it reaches 67 in 2022.

But these provisions did not survive unchallenged. Controversy swirled around the old-age benefit provisions of the new Social Security act. It was a major issue in the 1936 presidential campaign. The Republican candidate, Alfred Landon, characterized the program as "unjust, unworkable, stupidly drafted and wastefully financed." The contributory feature, he said, was "a cruel hoax."[24] Critics claimed that every worker would have to wear a dog tag with his Social Security number on it. John Hamilton, the National Chairman of the Republican party, said the only indication the administration still thought of these unfortunates as human was that the tags were made of stainless steel so they would not discolor the skin of the wearers.[25] The constitutionality of the act was challenged, and it was not until May 24, 1937, that this issue was resolved by two Supreme Court decisions, *Steward Machine Co. v. Davis* and *Helvering v. Davis*.[26]

There were still other controversies. What seemed most important at the time was a continuing battle between those who favored a substantial build-up of reserves that would earn interest and thus reduce the level of later contributions and those who favored raising only the amount of money needed to pay current benefits—the "pay-as-you-go" approach. Opponents of a large fund, estimated to reach $47 billion under the 1935 act, believed the build-up had serious consequences for sound fiscal pol-

[24] Arthur M. Schlesinger, Jr., *The Age of Roosevelt: The Politics of Upheaval* (Cambridge, Mass.: The Riverside Press, 1960), p. 613.

[25] Ibid., p. 636.

[26] Supreme Court, 837 and 910, October term, 1936. For a full discussion of the constitutionality of Social Security, see chapter 3 of this volume.

icy. Investing the funds in government securities, as provided by the law, would require a large, permanent national debt they considered undesirable. Yet if the Social Security funds were invested elsewhere, new federal involvement in private economic activity would have raised the specter of socialism. They argued, too, that the reserves would encourage extravagant federal spending because Social Security would have created a ready source of federal borrowing. On the other side, many supporters of a large earnings reserve looked on it as a way to avoid an eventual general revenue contribution. A pay-as-you-go approach had the inherent problem that benefits in the early years would greatly exceed the value of contributions paid, with more of the cost for early retirees being pushed forward to later generations than in a system with large reserves. Pay-as-you-go opponents feared later contribution rates would be so high that general revenues would be called on to pay for the start-up costs that had not been funded. In fact, such an eventual government contribution was advocated by pay-as-you-go supporters. President Roosevelt personally backed a large earnings reserve to prevent later costs falling on general revenues.

But financing controversies did not reach the basic nature of social insurance. No matter how these issues were decided, benefit rights would still be based on past earnings, and substantial earmarked contributions would be made by those who were to benefit from the system.

Largely because of the impasse over financing, the chairman of the Senate Committee on Finance agreed to appoint a special subcommittee to cooperate with the Social Security Board in studying the advisability of amending the old-age benefit program. There was also to be a citizens' advisory council appointed jointly by the subcommittee and the Social Security Board.[27] Arthur Altmeyer, chairman of the Social Security Board, saw the formation of this council as an opportunity to move ahead with much more than financing changes. The council was also asked to consider whether it would be advisable to begin monthly payments earlier, to increase the amount of the monthly benefits payable in the early years, to provide benefits for the disabled and survivors, and to extend coverage to additional groups. Throughout the council's work there was cordial cooperation among Brown, the chairman of the advisory council, Altmeyer, and Senator Vandenberg, an influential Republican member of the Senate Finance Subcommittee. This cooperation and the prestige of the council

[27] Made up of six representatives each from labor and industry and thirteen representatives from the general public, the council was chaired by Professor J. Douglas Brown of Princeton. As a staff member of the Committee on Economic Security, Brown had a major role in the development of the 1935 Old-Age Benefits program. Advisory Council of 1937–1938, *Report.*

members, many of whom were nationally known, resulted in quick passage of the council's recommendations.

1937–1938 COUNCIL RECOMMENDATIONS

The 1937–1938 council was probably the most important of all the advisory councils in determining the original understanding and the continuing shape of the Social Security program. The entire history of Old Age, Survivors, and Disability Insurance (OASDI) from 1939 to the amendments of 1972 can correctly be described as rounding out the structure recommended by this council. The only major innovation this early council did not consider and take a stand on was the introduction of the various automatic provisions keeping benefits up-to-date with wages and prices, as provided in the 1972 and 1977 amendments. And even here it can well be argued that the additional protection provided is within the spirit of the 1935 and 1939 legislation. After all, the objective from the beginning was to provide continuing protection in real terms, not a benefit that would shrink as wages and prices rose.

In 1939, then, based on the council recommendations, the program was redesigned to set the pattern for all that was to follow. Social Security became a program of family protection, providing not only old-age benefits for workers but also benefits for wives, widows, and children. The benefits were weighted to favor lower-paid workers even more heavily than in 1935, and in several ways the system was made more effective sooner. The first date for the payment of monthly benefits was moved from 1942 to 1940. Higher benefits were paid in the early years by relating benefits to average monthly earnings in covered employment, rather than to total earnings over a lifetime.

The council recommended balancing the increased cost of higher early benefits, including the addition of a wife's benefit, by reducing the amount payable to single annuitants in the long run and eliminating a money-back guarantee payable under the 1935 act. Instead of the former lump-sum payments rebating contributions, it recommended a small death benefit.

All these changes made the benefits paid in the early years less directly related to past earnings and contributions. Workers with dependents were favored for the first time under the 1939 amendments, and lower-paid earners and those nearing retirement age were favored more under the 1939 act than under the original program. Thus, there were important modifications of equity principles in order to make benefits more adequate.

Although it favored total disability benefits in principle, the council did not recommend covering this risk at this stage in the development of the program because they foresaw much greater administrative difficulty in determining the ability to work than in proving age or death.[28] Council members recommended extending coverage as far as they deemed feasible at the time and established universal coverage as a goal. They recommended against building large earnings reserves and favored instead a modified pay-as-you-go system, with a contingency reserve to meet unanticipated short-term needs. They favored an eventual general revenue contribution, which in a mature system would have reached one-third of outgo; this recommendation is the only major proposal of this council consistently rejected by successive Congresses and cannot reasonably be considered part of the original understanding of Social Security.

One comes away from reading the 1937–1938 Advisory Council report astonished at the foresight shown by the developers of this most important of all American social programs. The Social Security program has endured in essentially the same form because it dealt well with an old and persistent problem—how to plan for the replacement of wages lost when a worker retires in old age, becomes totally disabled, or dies.

Later legislation has even adhered to the long-range goal for benefit levels. It just is not true, as is sometimes said, that the benefits have been greatly liberalized and that the program has departed from the modest goals of the system's founders.[29] Robert J. Myers, former chief actuary of the Social Security Administration, calculates that, under the formula adopted in 1939, a worker retiring today at 65 after earning the average wage would receive—in the absence of changes in wage and price levels—40 percent of his or her preretirement earnings, referred to as the replacement rate. The average couple's replacement rate today under the 1939 formula would be 60 percent.[30] These replacement rates for average wages—the goals of the 1939 amendments—are almost exactly the same as those established for now and the future by the automatic provisions of the 1977 amendments—41 percent and 62 percent, for a single worker and married couple, respectively.

Also, contrary to what is sometimes said, the financing of the system was planned with the expectation that the ratio of workers to beneficiaries would drop substantially as the elderly population continued to grow. The 1937–1938 council estimated that by 1980, 14 to 15 percent of the total population would be made up of persons aged 65 and over, compared to 6.3 percent at the time they were making their recommenda-

[28] For a full discussion of disability coverage, see Chapter 6 of this volume.

[29] This is a common misstatement and appeared recently in Michael J. Boskin, *Too Many Promises: The Uncertain Future of Social Security* (Homewood, Ill.: Twentieth Century Fund Report, Dow Jones-Irwin, 1986), p. 7.

[30] Robert J. Myers, *Social Security*, 3 ed. (Homewood, Ill.: Richard D. Irwin, 1985), App. 3–5: 233.

tions.[31] Current estimates are that the figure will not reach 14 percent until well after the year 2000.[32] Those who designed the 1939 amendments can hardly be accused of overlooking the burden that demographic change would cause. The notion that the system was planned for a ratio of 16 workers to 1 beneficiary (the ratio in 1950) and that the 1982 financing problems were caused by the ratio dropping to 3 to 1 (a favorite explanation of Reagan administration spokesmen in 1981 and 1982) is just plain wrong.[33] Both the 1935 act and the 1939 amendments took account of the future to a remarkable degree, and the financing provisions over the years have been designed to meet the expected shift in the ratio of beneficiaries to workers.

Developments from 1939 to 1950

Between 1939 and 1950 the Social Security system developed very slowly. The retirement features of most social insurance systems, like private pensions, take a long time to become effective because those already retired when the system begins ordinarily are not eligible for benefits. Social Security was no exception. Under the system implemented after the 1939 amendments, workers had to have been in covered employment the equivalent of half the time after 1936 in order to be eligible for Social Security benefits at age 65. Obviously no one already retired when the system started met the test, and the proportion of the aged eligible for benefits grew slowly (see Figure 1.1). In 1950, fifteen years after the passage of the original Social Security legislation, only 16 percent of those aged 65 and over were getting Social Security benefits. Today 90 percent of those aged 65 and over receive benefits, and 95 out of 100 children and their mothers are protected by the life insurance (survivors insurance) feature. Four out of five people in the age group from 21 through 64 now have protection against loss of income caused by severe disability.

The failure to keep Social Security benefits up-to-date with wage and price changes during the 1940s and the fact that few people were eligible for benefits almost proved its undoing. Social Security was simply not very important. If a senator wanted to be on record as helping older peo-

[31] Advisory Council of 1937–1938, *Report*, p. 15.

[32] *1986 Annual Report of the Federal Old-Age and Survivors Insurance and Disability Insurance Trust Funds* (Washington, D.C.: Government Printing Office, 1986), p. 82, Table A1.

[33] For example, the Portland, Maine, *Press Herald* for February 5, 1982, quoted Deputy Commissioner of Social Security Paul B. Simmons as follows: "Overriding all other difficulties—unemployment, inflation, benefit changes—'it's a demographic problem.'

"In 1950, 16 workers were paying taxes for each beneficiary. Today the ratio is 3.3 workers per beneficiary. By the turn of the century, the ratio could drop to 2-1 because the population grows increasingly older."

Population 65 & Over
In Millions

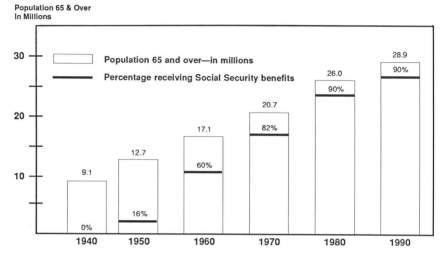

FIGURE 1.1. Population Aged 65 and Over, and Percentage of that Population Receiving Social Security Benefits, 1940–1990
  Source: Office of the Actuary, Social Security Administration.

ple, he introduced a bill to pay more old-age assistance because the federal and state means-tested program was paying many more people over age 65 than Social Security was (see Figure 1.2). Support was growing for radical alternatives to Social Security, such as the payment of flat benefits to all the elderly financed from general revenues or a vastly increased means-tested system. Once again an advisory council came to the rescue, convening in 1947 and issuing its report in 1949.[34]

This council, in addition to advocating changes to greatly hasten achievement of full program effectiveness, made statements of principle that were particularly important to the American system. Although important in all economies dependent upon a wage system, social insurance is perhaps of the very greatest importance in a dynamic economy like that of the United States, where industries rise and fall with some rapidity and new enterprises continually replace the old. In the final analysis, the economic security of the individual depends on the success of industry and agriculture in producing an increasing flow of goods and services. However, the 1949 council stated:

> ... the very success of the economy in making progress, while creating opportunities, also increases risks. Hence, the more progressive the economy, the greater is the need for protection against economic hazards. The protection should be made available on terms

[34] Advisory Council of 1947–1949, *Report*.

Recipients
In Thousands

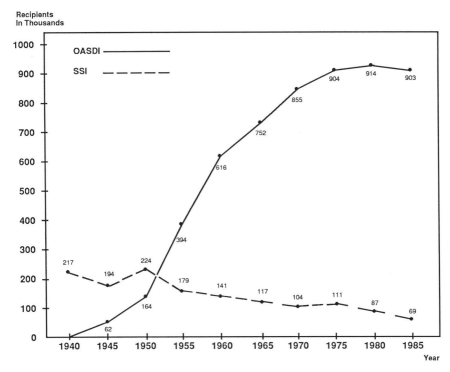

FIGURE 1.2. Persons Aged 65 and Over Receiving OASDI Benefits and SSI Payments, Number per Thousand, 1940–1985

Source: U.S. Department of Health and Human Services, Social Security Administration, *Social Security Bulletin, Annual Statistical Supplement, 1984–85*, p. 235, Table 168, updated to 1985.

Note: For 1940–1973, SSI data refer to the Old-Age Assistance Program. Beginning January 1974, the SSI program superseded the Old-Age Assistance Program in the fifty states and the District of Columbia.

which reinforce the interests of the individual in helping himself. A properly designed Social Security system will reinforce the drive of the individual toward greater production and greater efficiency and will make for an environment conducive to the maximum of economic progress.

The council continued:

Differential benefits based on a wage record are a reward for productive effort and are consistent with general economic incentives, while the knowledge that benefits will be paid—irrespective of whether the individual is in need—supports and stimulates his drive to add his personal savings to the basic security he has acquired through the insurance system. Under such a social insurance system, the individual earns a right to a benefit that is related to his contribution to production. This earned right is his best guarantee that he will receive the benefits promised and that they will not be conditioned on his accepting either scrutiny of his personal affairs or restrictions from which others are free.[35]

At a time when the future of Social Security was in doubt because of its inadequacy (benefits averaged only $25 a month and few people were getting them), the 1949 council restated the principles underlying the original understanding of Social Security and urged the extension of the system.

Opportunity for the individual to secure protection for himself and his family against the economic hazards of old age and death is essential to the sustained welfare, freedom, and dignity of the American citizen. For some, such protection can be gained through individual savings and other private arrangements. For others, such arrangements are inadequate or too uncertain. Since the interest of the whole Nation is involved, the people using the government as the agency for their cooperation should make sure that all members of the community have at least a basic measure of protection against the major hazards of old age and death.[36]

1950 AMENDMENTS

The 1950 amendments based on this council's report went a considerable way toward the original goal of universal coverage. The amendments also changed the beginning date for measuring the amount of work needed to qualify and for the computation of average earnings on which benefits were based. This was done primarily to avoid penalizing those in newly covered occupations, but it also made qualifying for benefits easier for all workers and increased benefit levels in the early years.[37]

[35] Ibid., p. 1.

[36] Ibid., p. 1.

[37] Under the 1939 law, a worker reaching age 65 in early 1955 would have had to have earnings in thirty-six calendar quarters to be eligible for retirement benefits (one-half the calendar quarters elapsing after 1936 and prior to the quarter in which the worker reached age 65). After the 1950 amendments, such a worker needed earnings in only eight quarters earned after 1936 (a number equal to one-half the calendar quarters elapsing after 1950 up to the quarter in which the worker reached age 65). Under the 1939 Act, wages on which the benefit was based were averaged from 1936 up to the quarter in which the individual became 65; but after 1950, the averaging period was from 1950 on, if that produced a higher benefit, as it usually would, since the low wages of the past were eliminated from the average.

Under the change in the benefit formula, the level of benefits promised ultimately under the old law was paid sooner but not increased. Specifically, the 1939 provision increasing benefits 1 percent for each year worked under the program was dropped, and the percentage of average wages immediately payable—the replacement rate—was increased. This followed the 1939 precedent of paying higher benefits sooner, but it balanced the higher benefits by cutting back on later costs. The various changes increased the level of benefits immediately by 77 percent. Equally important, the 1950 amendments resulted in many more people getting benefits sooner, and, as Figure 1.2 illustrates, the federal and state old-age assistance program was quickly relegated to second place.

The 1950 amendments also removed many provisions that treated women differently from men and in other ways updated the system, while continuing the basic 1939 design.[38] The 1947–1949 advisory council recommended a limited program of total disability insurance, but this branch of social insurance was not added to the old-age and survivors program until 1956.[39] Instead, in 1950, the Congress passed a federal and state disability assistance plan, based on a test of need.

The changes made by the 1950 amendments may well have preserved the system. By the time the Eisenhower administration started to evaluate the program in 1953, Social Security was a functioning institution paying significant benefits to millions of people—a real change, not in principle but in effectiveness, from the program of the 1940s. Skeptical at first, that administration over time endorsed the basic ideas underlying Social Security and worked for program improvements.[40] The task of rounding

[38] For example, benefits for surviving children of a married female worker were made generally available for the first time as were benefits for dependent husbands and widowers. Also for the first time benefits were paid to the wives of retired workers, regardless of age, if they were caring for the worker's child under age 18. Benefits for surviving divorced wives caring for eligible children were also added.

[39] Advisory Council of 1947–1949, *Report*, pp. 69–93.

[40] The early days of the Eisenhower administration was a period of considerable uncertainty for Social Security. The Democrats had been in office for twenty years, and the new administration, understandably, approached all New Deal programs and their administrators with skepticism. A Republican Congress was conducting a hostile investigation of Social Security under a Subcommittee of Ways and Means whose chairman favored scrapping OASI and substituting noncontributory flat benefits for all elderly people. See U.S. Congress, House Committee on Ways and Means, *Analysis of the Social Security System; Hearings*, 83rd Cong., 1st Sess. (Washington, D.C.: Government Printing Office, 1953).

Gradually, however, after thorough investigation involving a group of outside consultants (*A Report to the Secretary of HEW*) and after an investigation by an associate of Under Secretary Nelson Rockefeller, Roswell B. Perkins, who later became an assistant secretary of HEW, the administration endorsed Social Security.

The influence of some Social Security supporters in the administration was also of great importance. Marion B. Folsom, first under secretary of the Treasury and later secretary of

out the basic structure established in 1939 continued under the Eisenhower administration and beyond. Coverage was further extended; for example, by the end of 1965 the only major groups remaining outside the program were federal civilian employees and those nonprofit and state and local employees who had not taken advantage of the voluntary provisions applying to them. (All nonprofit employees and newly hired federal employees were covered compulsorily by the 1983 amendments. By 1984 about 70 percent of state and local employees had been covered by voluntary agreements, leaving only 4 million outside the system.)

Benefit levels were increased by amendments in 1952, 1954, 1958, 1965, 1967, 1969, and 1971 that, after a considerable lag, more or less kept pace with rising wages. Thus, the replacement rate was maintained by ad hoc legislative changes. The age of first eligibility for benefits was reduced to 62, first for women (1956) and later for men (1961), but the benefits were reduced actuarially for those who claimed benefits before age 65.

In 1954, a provision was added to prevent a reduction in old-age and survivors' protection for workers who had failed to work under the program because of total disability. In 1956, cash benefits for disability were added. The United States was much slower than other countries in providing disability protection. In most countries, long-term total disability insurance, frequently called invalidity insurance, has been considered a natural accompaniment of old-age and survivors insurance. Thus, wages are partially replaced when some permanent or long-lasting event—retirement in old age, death, or long-term total disability—reduces earnings or ends the possibility of earning. Other branches of social insurance deal with short-term risks such as unemployment, short-term illness, and the cost of acute medical care. In the United States, however, it was more than twenty years after the passage of the original Social Security Act before insurance against the loss of wages due to long-term, total disability was added to protection against the risks of retirement in old-age and death.

Passage of disability insurance was very controversial in the United States (see fuller discussion in Chapter 6). It was opposed by the organized medical profession (which saw it as a first step toward socialized medicine), by the insurance industry (which had lost money on the disability policies it sold in the 1920s), and by conservatives generally.[41] Although the Eisenhower administration opposed the program, the president signed the bill when it narrowly passed over administration protests.

HEW, was particularly important. As an official of Eastman Kodak he had been a member of the advisory councils of 1935, 1937–1938, and 1947–1949 and was a strong supporter of the system, as was Arthur Larson, the under secretary of Labor.

[41] For a summary of the arguments then made against such a program see "Memorandum of Dissent by Two Members," Advisory Council of 1947–1949, *Recommendations*, p. 85.

Because of this controversy and the legitimate concern about the difficulty of disability administration, the initial program was very conservatively designed and paid benefits only at age 50 or older. It was liberalized a few years later, however, after the Social Security Administration (SSA) demonstrated that it could do the job well.[42]

But the addition of this risk, too, was within the scope of the original understanding of the nature of social insurance as borrowed from Europe and as endorsed by the 1937–1938 council. It was not a philosophical departure but a further fulfillment of the basic design.

The history of Social Security legislation in the early 1960s was dominated by the fight to establish Medicare (for full discussion see Chapter 7). Although it was an extremely controversial piece of legislation, strongly opposed by the doctors, insurance companies, and business generally, Medicare seemed nevertheless the only way to protect the living standard of retirees. It was all well and good to provide Social Security benefits to meet the regular recurring expenses of daily living, but there was no way for Social Security recipients to budget for the extraordinary and unpredictable expenses of a costly illness, as they could for rent or food. With the elderly using three times as much hospital care as younger people and with average incomes only half as large, private insurance premiums geared to the cost of care for the elderly were just too high for most retired people to pay. Thus, hospital insurance was seen as necessary to achieve the goals of the cash benefit program. The government stepped in and, using the approach already made familiar by OASDI, required contributions over the working lifetime of those who were to have the protection. The plan included voluntary coverage of part of physician costs; premiums paid by the elderly provided half the financing, and general revenues the other half. The only important development in the OASDI system between 1958 and 1965 was the 1960 extension of disability insurance to workers of all ages along with other liberalizations in that program. Because attention during this period was concentrated largely on Medicare, not even benefit increases to keep up with the cost of living were enacted.

All in all, the period from 1950 to 1972 represents a continuation of the work of the 1937–1938 advisory council—expanding the insurance system to include additional groups of workers, ad hoc provisions to help keep pace with rising wages and prices, and broadened coverage to provide disability insurance and limited health insurance. The system gradually became more and more effective, and by 1970, although benefit lev-

---

[42] For discussion see U.S. Congress, House Subcommittee on the Administration of the Social Security Laws, *Hearing on the Administration of the Social Security Insurance Program*, 86th Cong., 1st sess., 1959.

els were still extremely modest, it was beginning to do well the job it had been designed to do.

1972 AND 1977 AMENDMENTS

Amendments in 1972 provided for further important improvements in the basic system. Benefit levels were increased by 20 percent; even more important, the Nixon administration's proposal for automatic increases in benefits tied to the cost of living was adopted, along with several other automatic provisions. As a result, the program now does automatically what used to be done by ad hoc adjustment, an uncertain method subject to long delays. Keeping pace with wages and prices was a necessary part of the original understanding, and contribution rates had previously been set at levels to allow for such adjustments as wages rose, but now the benefit changes are made automatically.[43]

Further amendments in 1977 added other automatic provisions. Because of the 1977 amendments, future benefits will be computed so as to bear the same relationship to wages current at the time of computation as is true for benefits being awarded today. In other words, the replacement rate of initial benefits will be kept the same indefinitely; for example, workers retiring in 2020 who have earned average wages will get benefits equal to roughly 41 percent of wages then payable, as do workers retiring today who have earned average wages. All these automatic provisions have greatly increased the value of Social Security to those covered by the program, gearing the system to a rising level of living in the initial computation and making it inflation-proof thereafter.

SOCIAL SECURITY SINCE 1977

Valuable as these automatic provisions are, however, they make the system more vulnerable to poor economic performance. The income of Social Security depends primarily on the size of payrolls—and thus wage levels and the rate of unemployment. But outgo, because of the automatic cost-of-living adjustment, is affected greatly by the rate of inflation. Therefore, when inflation rose rapidly in the late 1970s and early 1980s and wages did not keep pace, Social Security reserves were drawn down to dangerously low levels. As a result, throughout 1981 and 1982 there was much talk of bankruptcy and the need to cut back on benefits or to

[43] Prior to the adoption of the automatic provisions in 1972, the contribution rates were based on long-range cost estimates using level-earnings assumptions. According to the chief actuary of the Social Security Administration, the chief purpose of basing the contribution rates on estimates using such assumptions was to allow for future benefit increases "to keep the benefits up to date in the event of rising earnings levels." Myers, *Social Security*, p. 392.

borrow from general revenues. The Reagan administration and Congress could not agree on what should be done.[44]

The 1982–1983 National Commission on Social Security Reform broke this political stalemate, negotiating an agreement supported by the president and the speaker of the House and enacted into law in early 1983.[45] These 1983 amendments—making modest changes in benefits and taxes and providing safeguards against the recurrence of what caused the previous financing crisis—have restored financial stability to Social Security for both the short and the long run. The trust funds will not only be rebuilt, but huge annual surpluses are expected for decades. The present design has, in effect, moved back to the earlier goal of building a sizable earnings reserve. For example, interest on the funds is estimated to be $259 billion during the year 2010.[46]

The Understanding Today and Tomorrow

Social Security is as useful today as it was expected to be when first designed. The essence of OASDI is that while people work, they and their employers make contributions earmarked for Social Security; and when earnings are lost because of retirement in old age, long-term total disabil-

[44] The Reagan administration in May 1981 proposed benefit cuts which, when added to the cuts the administration had earlier proposed in its budget, would have amounted to a reduction of one-fourth in the future level of Social Security protection. The proposals were presented as necessary to save the system. Although the proposals were overwhelmingly rejected by the Congress, the administration continued to argue throughout 1981–1982 that cuts of this magnitude were needed to solve the system's financial problems. A liberal coalition of labor organizations, organizations representing retired and disabled persons, social welfare organizations and churches, Save Our Security (SOS) argued, on the other hand, that the difficulty was temporary (beginning in 1990 the actuarial cost estimates showed large annual surpluses for many decades) and that the program should be allowed to borrow from the general fund to tide it over. Throughout the period various groups, experts, and congressional committees joined in the argument with a variety of plans and proposals, and the papers, radio, and television were full of stories of impending doom. For further discussion of the factual background of the problem and some of the proposals made during this period see Robert M. Ball, "Social Security Today," Testimony Before the Task Force on Entitlements, Uncontrollables and Indexing, Committee on the Budget, Washington, D.C.: U.S. House of Representatives, March 1, 1982.

[45] National Commission, *Report.*

[46] For a description of the National Commission's recommendations and the 1983 amendments see Myers, *Social Security*, pp. 282–98. Annual surpluses for OASDI under the intermediate cost estimates are projected to be $16 billion in 1987, $31 billion in 1988, $41 billion in 1989, $55 billion in 1990, $61 billion in 1991, $93 billion by 1995, with the trust funds building from $44 billion at the end of 1984 to $1.3 trillion by the year 2000 and to $12.7 trillion by 2030 before starting to decline. Social Security Administration, "Long-Range Estimates of Social Security Trust Fund Operations in Dollars." Actuarial Note Number 127. Baltimore, Md., 1986.

ity, or death, benefits are paid. This was the original understanding, and it is the understanding today. This important principle of relating benefits and taxes to the amount of wages, where the higher-paid get higher benefits and also make higher contributions, supports the general incentive system of wage differentials. At the same time, if Social Security is to be effective in largely eliminating the need for means-tested supplementation for lower-paid workers, benefits must continue to be a higher proportion of past wages for those with low earnings than for those with high earnings. To pay the same percentage of wage replacement at all earning levels, with the percentage high enough to keep the minimum wage earner and his dependents from having to turn to assistance or relief, would mean that higher-paid workers would get much more than they do today. We have elected, rather, for a much less expensive system that can still do an effective job as part of a four-tier approach to adequate income in retirement: (1) a universal, compulsory social insurance system; (2) supplementary private pensions (in practice confined largely to average and above-average earners); (3) individual private savings; and (4) underlying the whole, as the last resort, a means-tested national system of Supplemental Security Income (SSI).

Except for the 1972 substitution of the federal SSI program for the federal and state assistance programs to the needy elderly, blind, and disabled, all this was included in the original understanding and envisioned by the 1937–1938 council. It has taken a long time to develop, but today the system is working well.

This does not mean the system is perfect. Undoubtedly changes will be made in the future as they have been made in the past. Certainly the goal of universal coverage should be completed by bringing in the four million state and local employees outside the system. Once the reserves have been built up to adequate contingency levels, a decision will need to be made whether to build an earnings reserve as provided by present law or return to pay-as-you-go financing. A good case can be made for either approach.[47] And perhaps during the next fifteen years further consideration will be given to whether it is wise to raise the age of first eligibility for full benefits, as planned under present law.

Many people believe it would be desirable to have Social Security administered by a bipartisan board directly under the president, as was the case in the beginning. Such a change, passed by the House of Representatives in July 1986, might help protect the system from short-term budget and political pressures. Since annual Social Security surpluses are used to

---

[47] A trust fund equal to about one and a half times the following year's outgo would be sufficient to weather a severe recession such as the one in 1981–1982 and still have sufficient funds available to provide a safety margin during the early stages of recovery.

help meet deficit reduction targets in the general budget (for all other purposes Social Security transactions are now "off-budget" as they were prior to fiscal year 1969), there is a temptation to increase the annual Social Security surpluses by either freezing cost of living adjustments or cutting back on benefits in other ways. A bipartisan board charged with protecting the separately financed Social Security system might be successful in limiting Social Security changes to those deemed desirable for reasons internal to the Social Security system. Above all, administration by a bipartisan board directly under the president would emphasize the unique trustee character of Social Security and provide an institutional setting stressing continuity and freedom from partisan political influence.

And, over time, we may want to change the system to provide higher benefits for those who are the worst off—beneficiaries now unmarried. Most elderly couples, given Social Security, can now get by (only 9 percent are below the poverty level). Poverty among the elderly is concentrated largely on single retired workers and single survivors. Unmarried male beneficiaries over age 65 have a 19 percent poverty rate; unmarried female beneficiaries, a 24 percent rate. And, of course, the proportion of the elderly made up of unmarried women, principally widows, is very large and increases dramatically at older ages. Of all family units over age 65, 57 percent are unmarried women. By age 85, out of a total of 1.8 million units, 70 percent or 1.2 million are unmarried women, with a poverty rate of 25 percent, even when total family income is considered for the 30 percent who live with friends or relatives. In the long run, it would be desirable to raise the replacement rate for both single workers and widows—the primary insurance amount (PIA)—and working couples (on equity grounds, i.e., they pay more)[48] while holding the replacement rate for couples with only one worker where it is today.[49] The treatment of homemakers who are divorced after many years of marriage also needs improvement. These changes are well within the original understanding.

Over the years of Social Security development there has been tension at the borderlines between Social Security and the other three tiers of our retirement system; this, too, will continue. Reasonable people will continue to differ on how much retirement income should come from private pensions and savings and how much from Social Security. The private insurance industry, for example, although supporting Social Security, has usually opposed increasing the benefit level and the maximum benefit and

[48] For more on the PIA, see Chapter 2, especially Figure 2.9.

[49] These goals can be accomplished, for example, by increasing the PIA by 7 percent and reducing the spouse's benefit from 50 percent to 40 percent of the PIA. Such a change would require additional financing equal to an increase in the contribution rate of about one-fourth of one percentage point for both employers and employees.

contribution base, while labor has supported such expansion of Social Security's role. And reasonable people will also continue to differ on how much of the job should be left to the means-tested system of ssi, which paid only 7 percent of the elderly in 1985.

There are more than two sides to the argument over this borderline. Some would put greatly increased emphasis on equity and for the long run relate Social Security benefits strictly to the past contributions or earnings of individual workers, leaving a much higher proportion of the elderly population with inadequate Social Security benefits and dependent on ssi. And some who support the present weighting in the benefit formula and dependents' benefits and the objective of socially adequate benefits nevertheless believe that any further modifications to give low-wage beneficiaries higher benefits is wasteful because higher benefits would go to some who are not low income people.[50] Others believe that certain modifications in this direction are desirable on grounds of both equity (couples with only one paid worker, it is argued, are treated too favorably compared to other groups) and social need, but they also agree that further weighting in the benefit formula or a high minimum benefit would be undesirable because such changes would further weaken the benefit/contribution relationship.[51] Still others, however, care little about equity considerations and would modify the tax structure (in one way or another having higher-paid people pay more and lower-paid people pay less) and reduce reliance on ssi by increasing Social Security benefits for the low paid—an approach which many believe would undermine the broad public support Social Security now enjoys.[52]

Arguments about how much each tier should do compared to the other tiers have been going on throughout the whole life of the Social Security system, and the present division of responsibilities has the appearance of an uneasy truce. But few want to emphasize only a single tier and do away with the others. Each part of the four-tier system has a role to perform, but clearly Social Security is the most important and basic tier, as expected from the beginning.

[50] The view that, in general, the remaining needs of low income persons can be met better through ssi improvements is widely held. The distinction here is that some would not change Social Security to meet even part of the remaining problem.

[51] The author of this chapter, for example, believes in a mixed system that keeps a careful eye on equity considerations while also moving toward the goal of adequate benefits for regular, full-time, low-paid earners. How to maintain the desirable balance between the two principles of equity and adequacy so that goals are met and political support maintained is matter for compromise and judgment.

[52] For example, see Congressman Roybal's proposal in 1986 that high-salaried persons pay Social Security taxes on their full salaries so that lower-paid workers could pay lower rates than scheduled, thus tilting the system still further away from a direct relationship between benefits and contributions.

The Social Security system has been remarkably stable over the years because of the conservative design of the original understanding: separate financing, workers' contributions, and the wage-related benefit structure. These principles will endure because they make sense. Modification within the original understanding will certainly continue in the future, but for the time being Social Security needs a rest. For the near term it is important to leave the program alone, build back a sizable contingency reserve, and improve public confidence in the system—a result to be expected as large annual surpluses in the trust funds build.

Social Security has changed the face of America. People who would otherwise be among our most economically vulnerable groups—the retired aged, widows, orphans, and the totally disabled—have income they can count on month after month as a matter of right. This has been accomplished with the enthusiastic acceptance of the vast majority of Americans. Although the change from the situation half a century ago is startling, the methods used have been anything but revolutionary. The program is built on traditional values and concepts—self-help, mutual aid, insurance, and incentives to work and save. These fundamental principles appeal to workers everywhere. People like to earn what they get, and they like to have other people earn what *they* get.

The founding fathers of Social Security planned well, and we are reaping the benefits of their work fifty years later through a program now soundly financed for both the short and the long run. In major outline, the Social Security system fits the future as well as the present.

2

The Future of Social Security:
One Economist's Assessment

JAMES TOBIN

To most Americans Social Security means federal pensions paid to old people, Old Age and Survivors Insurance (OASI) in technical lingo. That is my subject here. It is only one of the programs begun by the Social Security Act of 1935, which also established our federal-state systems of unemployment compensation, assistance to needy old people, and assistance to families with dependent children, as well as various social services. From the beginning, OASI differed from the other initiatives in several respects. It was to be a federal program, uniform across the nation. Like unemployment compensation, its benefits to persons eligible because of required payroll tax contributions were not conditioned on need but only on those contributions and on other personal circumstances, mainly age and substantial retirement. In several steps beginning in 1954, disability was added to those personal circumstances, and it is sometimes necessary to refer to the combined program, Old Age, Survivors, and Disability Insurance (OASDI). In 1965 health insurance for the elderly, Medicare, was added, and the comprehensive acronym became Old Age, Survivors, Disability, and Health Insurance (OASDHI). But OASI remains the giant Social Security program.

On its golden anniversary (1985) OASI was both successful, surely even beyond the dreams of its founders, and troubled. In the *1985 Economic Report of the President,* his Council of Economic Advisers credits

I am greatly indebted to many people whose comments, suggestions, and ideas improved this paper. Michael Taussig, who discussed its initial version at the April 1985 symposium, also provided very helpful detailed comments on my text. Others who helped and tried, with at least some success, to save this amateur in the field from error included Robert Ball, Merton Bernstein, Michael Boskin, Gary Fields, Ted Marmor, Alicia Munnell, Jerry Mashaw, Robert J. Myers, and John Shoven. Two undergraduates, Daphne Butler and Louis Thomas, assisted capably with data and diagrams.

OASI for the remarkably healthy economic position of the elderly. The other side of the same coin is the growth in the program's cost, a source of considerable anxiety and alarm. Panic in 1981 and 1982 about the imminent "insolvency" of the trust fund was dissipated by legislation in 1983, a bipartisan compromise package of future payroll tax increases and benefit cuts projected to keep the fund in the black for several decades.[1]

Nonetheless Social Security continues to be a candidate for federal budgetmakers seeking ways to cut deficits in the overall federal budget. Moreover, the 1983 package may not forestall another and more serious insolvency threat in the twenty-first century.

Major Issues Facing OASI

Any assessment of the future of OASI must face three interrelated issues: balancing contributions and benefits; erosion of confidence; and financing. I shall discuss each in turn.

Balancing Contributions and Benefits. The overriding long-run issue about OASI is the balance between the tax contributions of the young and the benefits of the old.[2] The system is now geared to scale up benefits automatically to maintain the ratio of benefits to contemporaneous wages, the replacement ratio, at its historical level of roughly 40 percent. Payroll tax rates are the residual balancing item in the OASI financial equation. They have been raised steadily for years, and according to current projections they will have to be raised substantially next century if the replacement ratio is to be maintained. The generations involved, however, may at some point prefer to move to or toward a different option— freezing the tax rates and adjusting future benefits instead. This would mean that in the twenty-first century the benefit-wage ratio would fall: OASI benefits would still be rising in absolute purchasing power, but they would decline relative to the wages of active workers. It is not too soon to begin serious consideration of the options.

Erosion of Confidence. The confidence of young workers in Social Security has eroded in recent years. Some are worried that the system will go broke. Others perceive that their rate of return on the payroll tax contributions they and their employers make will be quite low, in contrast to

[1] See Chapter 1, note 46.

[2] This generational conflict, so prominently publicized, is somewhat, but only slightly, mitigated by the fact that some OASI benefits go to the young, mainly indirectly. They might otherwise have to contribute to their parents' support, and they might receive smaller inheritances. Also, elderly beneficiaries who work continue to pay Social Security taxes.

the interest rates they observe in financial markets today. They wonder why participation in such a system should be compulsory. The link between the contributions of, or on behalf of, any individual participant and his or her eventual benefits is quite loose, and quite mysterious. The system is a hybrid, mixing social retirement insurance with some intragenerational redistribution in favor of workers with low earnings. This is bound to diminish the rates of return high-wage workers perceive they can earn through OASI.

Old issues return anew: Should OASI be made more purely an insurance program, letting the general federal budget handle redistribution via needs-tested transfers? Should the link between contributions and benefits be actuarially fair for individual participants? Should the benefit entitlements earned by past contributions be reported regularly and clearly to participants throughout their careers? Should compulsory participation be limited to defined levels of contributions and benefits? As Robert Ball recounts in Chapter 1 of this volume, the founders of Social Security confronted these questions and compromised. Compromises, even theirs, are not graven in stone. Times, circumstances, and attitudes change. At the end of this chapter I shall sketch, as an option worth considering, a system that links contributions and benefits more explicitly and tightly.

Financing Social Security. The issues just raised regarding the links between contributions and benefits for individual participants are related to questions about the financing of the system as a whole. Until now Social Security has been mainly a pay-as-you-go system, using its current receipts from workers' contributions to pay its current benefits. Its trust fund, as its reserves are called, has been deliberately kept small. Under the 1983 legislation, this fund will grow to unprecedented heights relative to annual outlays over the next fifteen to twenty years. Thereafter it is projected to decline, and to vanish after midcentury.

A case can be made on macroeconomic grounds for a funded system in preference to pay-as-you-go. Full funding would mean a trust fund commensurate to OASI's liabilities for the future benefits earned by the contributions previously paid in. The accumulation of such a fund, it can be argued, would add to national saving and investment enough productive capital to yield the promised benefits. That yield might well be a higher rate of return than pay-as-you-go can offer.[3]

History cannot be rerun. A shift to full funding would take nearly a half century to accomplish. Moreover, the proposal inevitably raises the

---

[3] The most prominent critic of pay-as-you-go and advocate of funding has been Martin Feldstein. His "Social Security, Induced Retirement, and Aggregate Accumulation," *Journal of Political Economy*, 82 (September–October 1974): 905–26, stated his thesis and was followed by a series of other articles he published supporting and defending it.

question of the relation between Social Security trust funds and the over-all federal budget. I shall discuss these financial issues, and in my sketch of possible reforms for the next century I shall describe how the long transition to a fully funded system might be managed.

Social Security on the Defensive

OASI has certainly done well for today's elderly: they have very little wage income, they retire earlier, and they live longer.[4] Yet the incidence of poverty among them is now no higher than in the population at large. Figure 2.1 shows the decline in poverty among the elderly, compared with the total population. OASI coverage, 60 percent in 1937, now extends to virtually the whole labor force. Of persons aged 65 and over, 94 percent receive OASI pensions, up from 16 percent in 1950. (See Figure 2.2.) OASI pensions account for 40 percent of the aggregate income of those senior citizens and provide more than half the income for 59 percent of them.[5]

The cost has risen too. Figures 2.3 and 2.4 show outlays for OASI bene-fits in percentage of the federal budget and of GNP. Benefits are not ex-pected to rise faster than GNP in the future. Social Security contributions, by both employers and employees, have risen faster than employee com-pensation; and that trend is projected to continue. (See Figure 2.5.) OASDI payroll tax rates, employer and employee combined, were 2 percent from 1937 to 1949 and are scheduled to be 12.4 percent after 1989. The pay-roll tax burden is further increased by the levy for health insurance; its history and projections are shown in Figure 2.6.

In 1983 the prospect that OASDI would run in the red and use up the small kitty previously accumulated inspired Congress and the president to patch together, with the help of a blue-ribbon commission chaired by Alan Greenspan, a bipartisan compromise of future payroll tax increases and benefit cuts. In addition, the more affluent beneficiaries must now pay personal income tax on some OASI income. This legislation is projected to keep the OASI trust fund in the black for seventy-five years, although it

---

[4] The labor force participation rate of elderly (age 65 or older) males declined from 26.8 percent in 1970 to 17.4 percent in 1983, and that of elderly females from 9.7 to 7.8 percent. Those elderly who are in the labor force are increasingly likely to work only part time; part-time elderly workers have increased from 35 in 1960 to 50 percent for males, and from 48 to 61 percent for females. See Council of Economic Advisors, *1985 Economic Report of the President* (Washington, D.C.: Government Printing Office, 1985), chap. 5. Since 1960, life expectancy at age 65 has increased by 1.4 years for white males, 2.9 years for white females, 1.2 years for other males, and 2.8 years for other females. In 1960, 33 percent of elderly males and 35 percent of elderly females were aged 75 or over; in 1983, the figures were 36 and 46 percent respectively. *Statistical Abstract of the United States*, Table 103, p. 69 and Table 33, p. 30.

[5] *1985 Economic Report*, chap. 5.

Percent below
Poverty Line

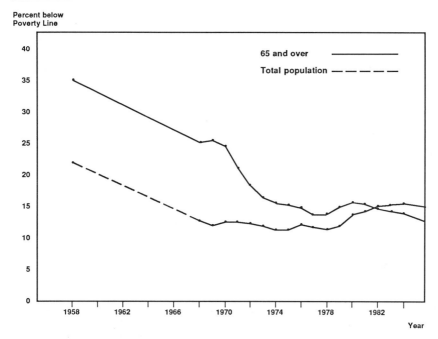

FIGURE 2.1. Percentage of Persons in Households with Poverty Incomes and Persons Aged 65 or Over Compared with the Total Population, 1958–1984.

Source: U.S. Bureau of the Census, *Current Population Reports*, Series P–60, No. 130 (1979), Table 1; No. 152 (1984), Table 3.

Note: No observations are shown for 1959–1967 because they are not available for the elderly population during those years.

will begin to dwindle about 2030.[6] Figure 2.7 shows sizes of the trust fund relative to annual benefit outlays, according to actual history and two projections, one before and one after the 1983 amendments.

This Greenspan–O'Neill–Reagan compromise did not lay the issues to rest. Cutting entitlements, especially in the politically less obvious way of suspending or limiting indexation, is regularly on the agenda as president and Congress struggle to limit or eliminate budget deficits. Thus far the political popularity of Social Security has protected OASI from cuts beyond those of the 1983 legislation. But OASI remains vulnerable to the national concern about the overall federal deficit and Reagan's determination to solve that problem without raising federal taxes.

It has long been clear that the main fiscal priority of the Reagan admin-

[6] *Report of the National Commission on Social Security Reform January 1983*. See also Federal Old-Age and Survivors Insurance and Disability Insurance Trust Funds, Board of Trustees, *Annual Report* (Washington, D.C.: Government Printing Office, 1985), Table E3, p. 123.

Percent Receiving
Benefits

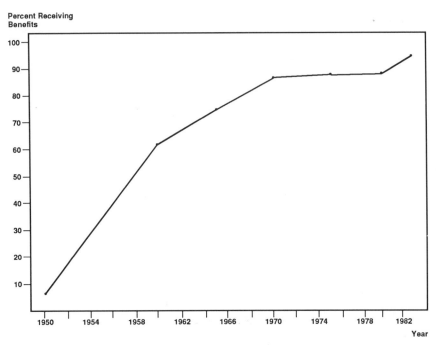

FIGURE 2.2. Percentage of Persons Aged 65 or Over in Households Receiving OASI Benefits, 1960–1983

Source: Economic Report of the President, 1985, Table 5-6, p. 174.

istration is to bring down the size of the unified federal budget relative to GNP, while sharply raising defense spending. Deficit reduction is a means to that end, not a priority in its own right. That is why tax increases are ruled out, and why indexed transfer payments are fair game while indexed adjustments of personal income tax brackets are sacrosanct. If other budget programs do not yield sufficient deficit reduction, Social Security may again be asked to "do its share," in effect channeling trust fund surpluses to defense spending and to the preservation of the 1981 income tax reductions.

The well-advertised anxieties about the finances of OASI and the political struggles they inspired have led to considerable cynicism about the program, especially among the young. Proposals to cut Social Security, coming so soon after the compromise rescue legislation of 1983 and after the solemn promises of the 1984 presidential campaign, were bound to reinforce prevalent cynicism about the sanctity of Social Security commitments. Only 18 percent of respondents in a 1981 poll thought Social Security was financially sound, and 68 percent said it was "in trouble." In another 1981 survey 54 percent of the sample, including 74 percent of those aged 18 to 29, thought the Social Security System would not have

Benefits/Budget (%)

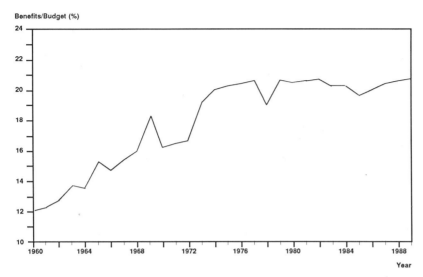

FIGURE 2.3. Aggregate OASI Benefits as Percentage of Federal Budget Outlays, 1960–1989, and as Projected, 1985–1989

Sources: Budget outlays: *Economic Report 1986*, Table B27, and Congressional Budget Office, *Economic and Budget Outlook Fiscal Years 1987–1991*, Feb. 1986, p. xiv, Table 1. Benefits: *Trustees' Report*, p. 58, Table 25; and *Social Security Bulletin, Annual Statistical Supplement 1983*, p. 76, Table 18.

the money to pay them benefits; only 30 percent of the total, including only 18 percent of the 18 to 29 group, thought it would.[7]

The young evidently expect to support their seniors by heavy payroll taxes and to get little or nothing of value in their turn. These expectations are not well informed. Both official projections and those of private experts show that despite its problems the system can deliver the promised benefits. Doubtless many people were misled by headlines about the vanishing trust fund, thinking erroneously that continuation of benefit payments depended on the fund. But the attitudes are important, even if based on misperceptions. There is an ugly intergenerational conflict beneath the recent and current political debates on Social Security finance. Many young people regard the system as bankrupt, budget-busting, and catering to the self-interest of an affluent retired middle class.

How Social Security Got Into Trouble

Why and how did so successful and popular a program run into financial difficulties and come to encounter distrust among its future benefici-

[7] American Enterprise Institute for Public Policy Research, *Public Opinion*, August–September 1981, pp. 35–37, reporting polls in 1981 by Tarrance Associates for the National Foundation of Independent Business and by CBS/*New York Times*.

Benefits/GNP (%)

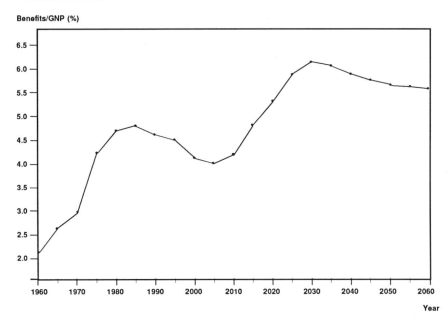

FIGURE 2.4. Aggregate OASI Benefits as Percentage of GNP, 1960–2060 (Actual before 1985, and as Projected, 1985–2060)

Source: GNP history, *Economic Report 1986*, Table B-1; projections from GNP growth rates assumed in Alternative II-A, *Trustees' Report*, p. 28, Table 10. Benefits: *Trustees' Report*, p. 58, Table 25; *Social Security Bulletin, Annual Statistical Supplement 1983*, p. 76, Table 18.

aries? There are several reasons in recent history, some related to the general economic and political environment and some intrinsic to the OASI system.

Stagflation. Along with the economies of the rest of the world, the American economy went sour beginning in 1970. The period since then has been an era of stagflation, OPEC oil shocks, four recessions, and low productivity growth. The most important symptom relevant to our topic is that real after-tax wage incomes, instead of rising at 2.5 to 3 percent per year as they had in the two previous decades, actually declined. A young man starting work in 1963 or 1973 has not experienced the progress toward the American dream that his father rightly took for granted a decade or two earlier. Indeed, from 1973 to 1983 his real wage income went down.[8] If young families nonetheless advanced their incomes during the

[8] Frank Levy and Robert Michel, "Are Baby Boomers Selfish?," *American Demographic Magazine*, April 1985.

Tax Rate

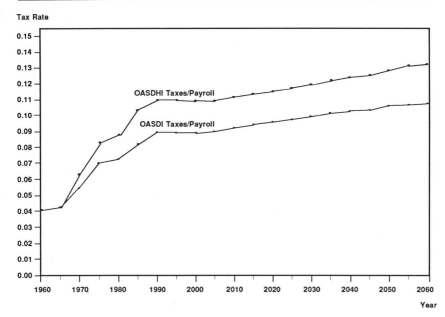

FIGURE 2.5. Aggregate Social Security Payroll Tax Contributions Relative to Total Employee Compensation, 1960–2060

Note: These ratios are not the same as the contribution rates shown in Figure 2.6. Employee compensation is larger than taxable payroll because an employee's annual wage income is not taxed above a "cap" and fringe benefits are not taxed at all. Moreover, social security coverage is not quite complete. The projections beyond 1985 assume the tax rates scheduled in current legislation shown in Figure 2.6. It is probable that HI taxes for Medicare will be increased by legislation in the next few years.

The projections are for *Trustees' Report* Alternative II-A. Projections for the variables shown here had to be inferred from other information in the *Report*. From Table 10, p. 28, it is possible to infer projected growth rates of dollar GNP and nominal wages. Table A2, p. 81, gives projections of the ratio of taxable payroll to GNP. Thus, the implied growth projected for taxable payroll can be calculated, and the scheduled tax rates (see Figure 2.6) applied to yield projected aggregate contributions. Similarly, the growth of total employee compensation, based on the 1985 figure from *Economic Report 1986*, Table B-21, can be estimated from the Trustees' Table 10, using the data there given on the growth of earnings per worker, inflation, and employment.

1970s, it was because both spouses worked and postponed or eschewed child-bearing. The commitment of today's young women to working careers in preference to motherhood also means there will be few payroll taxpayers relative to OASI beneficiaries next century.

Meanwhile, the living standards of the elderly not only escaped the economy-wide setbacks but sharply improved. From 1970 to 1980, while average monthly real wages declined by 7.4 percent, average monthly OASI benefits rose in real terms by 37 percent. Generous improvements of

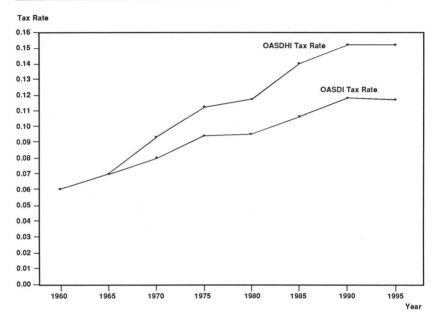

FIGURE 2.6. Social Security Tax Rates on Taxable Wages and Salaries, Employee and Employer Combined, 1960–1995

Source: *Social Security Bulletin Annual Statistical Supplement 1983*, p. 19, Table D.

Note: Current legislation schedules the tax rates shown in the figure. Official *Trustees' Report* projections assume no changes in OASDI tax rates after 1955. Further increases in hospital insurance tax rates, for Medicare, are likely to be legislated in order to keep the HI Trust Fund, legally separate, in the black.

benefits were enacted in the early 1970s, and were protected by automatic adjustment to the Consumer Price Index (CPI) beginning in 1973.[9]

The Political Climate. The contrast of the stagnant 1970s with the prosperously growing 1960s was summarized by Lester Thurow in the term zero-sum society, implying intensified conflict over the distribution of a national pie that was no longer growing. Redistributions of income of all kinds via taxes and governmental transfers waned in popularity. Tax revolts mushroomed in local, state, and national politics. General trust in government was eroded by Vietnam and Watergate. Conservative economics and ideology gained influence. The public was receptive to the conservative diagnosis of the 1970s, which attributed the disappointing economic performance to the size and growth of government—expenditures, taxes, regulations—rather than to OPEC and other external misfor-

[9] *1985 Economic Report*, chap. 5.

Coverage Ratio

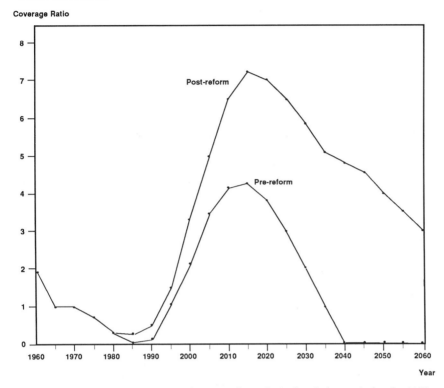

FIGURE 2.7. Ratio of OASI Trust Fund to Annual Benefit Outlays before and after the 1983 amendments to the Social Security Act: 1960–1980 and as Projected, 1985–2060.

Sources: Prereform: *Report of the National Commission on Social Security Reform* (Washington, D.C.: Government Printing Office, 1983), Appendix A, p. 165. Postreform: *Trustees' Report*, p. 70, Table 33.

Note: The reforms of the 1983 legislation will have succeeded, according to the Trustees' projections, in keeping the OASI Trust Fund in the black throughout the period, although it will be declining relative to benefits after 2010.

tunes. The last two, maybe even three, presidential elections have been won on the slogan "government is not the solution, it is the problem."

Demographic Trends. The age distribution has turned adverse to Social Security. Aged workers retire sooner and live longer. Births, low in the 1920s and 1930s, zoomed after the Second World War, began to decline in the 1960s, and now hardly suffice to replace parents. The trends are shown in Figure 2.8. The ratio of persons aged 20 to 64 to persons aged 65 and over is falling, and so, of course, is the number of workers per OASI beneficiary.

These clouds have some silver linings. Official projections have gone

Support Ratio

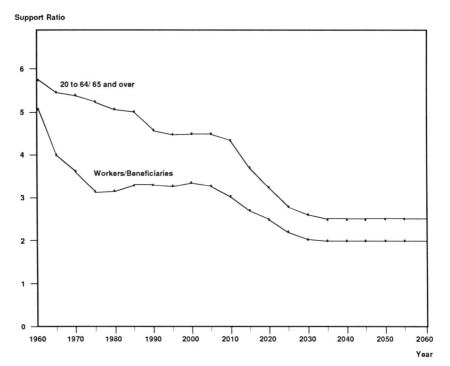

FIGURE 2.8. Ratios of Persons Ages 20 to 64 to Those Aged 65 and Over, Ratio of Covered Workers to OASI Beneficiaries, 1960–1980, and as Projected, 1985–2060
   Source: Trustees' Report, p. 77, Table A1; p. 65, Table 29.

wrong in the past, and the current ones may be unduly pessimistic. Lower natural population and labor force growth may open the doors to more legal immigrants, mostly young workers who will be paying into the trust fund. Greater scarcity of labor might lead to faster growth of real wages—though given present uncertainties about capital formation and technological progress, this is by no means a sure thing. In any case, workers with fewer children will be able to afford either higher payroll taxes or additional saving on their own retirement.

The Maturing of the System. Some difficulties endemic to the OASI system became salient in the less benign environment after 1970, especially after 1973. Even though the climate is now improving, these problems once surfaced will not go away. They have roots in the history of OASI.

OASI took a long time to reach maturity, and growing up was much easier than adulthood. The reach of the system, thus of the payroll tax, was gradually extended by legislation and economic change (for example, migration from rural self-employment to nonfarm wage labor). Ratios of persons in covered employment any time during a year to average civilian employment for the year are indicative: they were 0.82 in 1950; 1.10 in 1960; 1.13 in 1984.[10] During this long period of expanding coverage, the number of contributing active workers was growing more rapidly than the labor force, and of course the covered percentage of retired workers was always lagging behind. By the 1970s we were coming to the end of this road. The few remaining pockets of exempt private employment were being absorbed. State and local governments still have discretion; they are likely to continue successfully their resistance to compulsory inclusion.

Growth of coverage combined with growth of labor force and productivity to swell the proceeds of the payroll tax faster than the benefit payments committed by previous legislation. The surpluses might have been allowed to pile up in the OASI trust fund, the way an insurance company channels current premiums into reserves against its liabilities to future beneficiaries. But this was not done. Even so, the taxes and benefits set in the original act in 1935 would have built a substantial fund, estimated at that time to reach $47 billion in 1980 (equivalent to about 300 billion actual 1980 dollars—compared with 1980 benefit outlays of $105 billion). In fact, the trust fund was $23 billion in 1980. The 1939 amendments deliberately scaled down the fund's growth, aiming only at a modest contingency reserve. In addition, as surpluses loomed after 1950, Congress regularly increased the scope and size of benefits. The reforms were always very desirable improvements in the effectiveness and fairness of the system. Several generations of beneficiaries have, therefore, obtained excellent returns on their contributions, and I will, too. But as the system approached maturity, these enlarged benefits could be continued only by successive increases in payroll taxes. (See Chapter 1 of this volume for a detailed historical discussion.)[11]

Indexation. In 1972 another fateful decision was made, the automatic indexing of benefits. At the same time, benefits were scaled up by 20 percent. Indexation was well intended. Indeed it was an act of political abnegation by Congress. The setting of benefits (including, but in practice not confined to, adjusting them for inflation) was taken off the regular political agenda. Moreover, there was every reason in past experience to believe the move was financially prudent. OASDI revenues would grow

[10] Covered workers, Board of Trustees, *1985 Annual Report*, Table 29, p. 65; civilian workers, *1985 Economic Report*, Table B-32, p. 270.

[11] See also, Alan Pifer and Forrest Chisman, eds., *The Report of the Committee on Economic Security of 1935 and Other Basic Documents, Fiftieth Anniversary Edition* (Washington, D.C.: National Conference on Social Welfare, 1985), especially chap. 6 by Robert Ball, "The 1939 Amendments to the Social Security Act and What Followed." See also Myers, *Social Security*, pp. 357–58.

with wages, benefits with prices. Wages grow faster than prices; anyway they always had. Came the OPEC rise in oil prices and the vanishing of productivity growth, and this relationship was reversed. In this way the stagflation of the 1970s hit OASI finances very directly. The blow was compounded by an inadvertent technical error in the 1972 legislation, which under the circumstances overindexed benefits; this was corrected in 1977.

In retrospect it is easy to see that indexing by the CPI is not a good idea, even in economic times less turbulent than the 1970s. It is not a good idea for government-paid benefits, and it is not a good idea for wage contracts. Such indexing immunizes the favored individuals from losses the nation as a whole cannot escape—in 1973–1974 and 1979–1980 the big rises in the cost of imported oil—and throws their costs onto unprotected fellow citizens. Likewise indexation in effect exempts its beneficiaries from paying the increased taxes embodied in the prices that compose the index; others must bear the burdens of the public programs financed by those taxes. It would be both possible and desirable to construct an index purged of these unintended implications and mandate its use, not only in Social Security but wherever else indexed commitments are made; this should be done before the economy runs again into stormy weather like the 1970s.[12]

Social Security and National Saving

The issue of pay-as-you-go versus funding is both more basic and more difficult than correcting for inflation. At the macroeconomic level the question is how OASI financing affects national saving and capital investment and, through them, future productivity and standards of living.[13] It

[12] Indexation modified in the way described has been adopted in Austria and Sweden. For the United States, the appropriate index is conceptually a National Income and Product Accounts deflator for the personal consumption expenditures (PCE) component of Gross National *Income*. This is the deflator for the PCE component of gross national product modified to exclude changes in indirect taxes. It would measure changes in the dollar cost per unit of value added by payments of income to domestic factors of production in the making and delivery of consumption goods and services to domestic consumers. Increases and decreases in the dollar prices of imported consumption goods, or of imported materials used in making domestic consumption goods, would not be counted. Neither would changes in indirect taxes—mainly sales, excise, and payroll taxes. Although the Department of Commerce PCE "deflator" is closest conceptually to the desired index, the Bureau of Labor Statistics Consumer Price Index (CPI) could be modified to approximate these exclusions. Between 1971 and 1981, the period of import price shocks, the PCE deflator rose 10 percent less than the CPI; the difference would be somewhat greater if the deflator were purged of indirect taxes.

[13] For more discussion of the relationship between public and private provision of retirement security and national savings, see Chapters 4 and 5.

is obviously related to the similar question about overall federal fiscal policies.

Martin Feldstein has been the most prominent and insistent critic of pay-as-you-go financing. He argues that this system greatly diminishes aggregate national saving. Workers regard their payroll tax contributions as saving; the prospect of future OASI pensions spares them, at least in part, the need to provide for retirement on their own. But under pay-as-you-go, the government treats receipts from those taxes like any other revenues and spends them. They are not channeled, directly or indirectly, through the capital markets into investment in productive capital assets whose yields could pay the future pensions. Feldstein estimated the national capital stock to be trillions of dollars smaller than it would have been with a funded system.

Feldstein's argument overstates the problem, both theoretically and empirically.[14] It probably is true that OASI taxes displace some voluntary saving. For example, some private pension plans, explicitly aiming at a target ratio of total retirement income to wage or salary, offset OASI improvements by lowering their own provisions. (For more on this topic, see Chapter 4, where Michael Graetz discusses the implications of this integration of Social Security with private pension benefits.) However, many workers are so constrained by their current liquid resources that they cannot offset OASI taxes by consuming more and saving less on their own. Moreover, many elderly pensioners do not consume all their pensions during retirement, as the Feldstein scenario assumes they do. Their benefits wind up, in part, in larger bequests to their children. Middle and upper income retired individuals typically save actuarially excessive amounts against the risk of prolonged high medical and custodial expenses, knowing that any unneeded amounts will end up in their estates.[15] Empirical studies provoked by Feldstein's work are inconclusive, but they indicate that the effects of unfunded OASI on voluntary private saving are at most much smaller than Feldstein asserted.

OASI Financing and Federal Fiscal Policy

The issue turns also on the effects of OASI financing on general federal fiscal policy and of that policy on the economy and its rate of capital accumulation. Would the overall "unified" budget deficit be smaller if,

[14] For review of the controversy see Henry Aaron, *The Economics Effects of Social Security* (Washington, D.C.: Brookings Institution, 1982).

[15] Regarding the saving behavior of the elderly and its departure from Feldstein's assumptions, see Sheldon Danziger, J. van der Gaag, E. Smolensky, and Michael K. Taussig, "The life-cycle hypothesis and the consumption behavior of the elderly," *Journal of Post Keynesian Economics* 5 (Winter 1982–83): 208–27.

because of funding, OASI were in surplus? Or would the political and economic strategies that determine the budget offset the OASI surplus with a larger deficit in other transactions? A test may come in the 1990s and 2000s when, thanks to the 1983 legislation, the OASI trust fund is projected to grow to 10 to 20 percent of GNP with annual surpluses of 2 to 2.5 percent of GNP.[16] Moreover, we are about to return to the pre-1968 practice of focusing official attention on the administrative budget and deficit, thus separating the trust funds from the budget that is presumptively supposed to balance.

My guess is that in the past the federal government would have run larger administrative deficits had the trust funds been raking in surpluses. Indeed this often would have been good macroeconomic policy because fiscal stimulus was needed to avoid or overcome recessions and keep the economy close to full employment. Fund surpluses, if not offset by administrative deficits or aggressively stimulative monetary policy, would frequently have meant greater unemployment rather than more capital accumulation. If we were to assume that nowadays Federal Reserve monetary policy calls the macroeconomic tune, so that national output and employment are always what the Fed wants and permits, irrespective of fiscal policy, then the situation would correspond more closely to Feldstein's assumptions. Conditional on monetary policy, we would get more capital formation the lower the federal deficit. And funding, combined with segregated accounting, probably would lower the overall deficit, although by less than the OASI surplus.

A truly funded system could be expected to yield on average a higher rate of return on participants' contributions. A mature pay-as-you-go system cannot do better than the rate of growth of real payrolls—that is, the sum of the rates of growth of employment and real wages. In the long run the growth of real wages is the growth of labor productivity. The formulas prescribed in the 1972 and 1977 legislation approximately guarantee that real benefits will grow along with real wages (that is, with productivity). That is how earnings replacement rates are maintained. The formulas ignore trends in labor force and employment, which also determine the growth in real payrolls and thus in OASI contributions. As those growth trends decline, it will not be possible to pay the benefits the formulas generate without raising payroll tax rates. To make the same point another way, in those circumstances it will not be possible to hold tax rates constant without lowering earnings replacement rates.[17]

---

[16] On the fiscal issues posed by these projections see Alicia H. Munnell and Lynn E. Blais, "Do we want large Social Security surpluses?" *New England Economic Review* (September–October 1984): 5–21.

[17] What follows is an explanation, with some simple algebra and arithmetic, of the trade-

For the rest of the century, the growth of real payrolls should be about 3 percent per annum. Subsequently labor force growth will slow down. The baby-boomer bulge will subside, and the growth of the female labor force will decline as women's participation in the labor force approaches that of men. In official middle-range economic and demographic projections for the first half of the next century, real earnings per worker grow at about 1.8 percent per year and the covered labor force at 0.1 percent, implying growth of taxable payrolls at well below 2 percent. The major uncertainty is productivity growth. The sources of its decline in the 1970s are still a mystery to students of the subject. Should labor productivity take off next century, the returns on the contributions of younger persons currently working or entering the labor force will be much better than the estimates look now.

A funded system could in principle yield a rate of return equal to the economy's real interest rate, basically a reflection of the marginal productivity of capital. Social Security trust funds, invested in federal securities, actually earn a bit less because the federal government's borrowing rate is lower than rates on private securities. Those beneficiaries partially sub-

---

off between replacement rates and tax rates and an illustration in relation to projections well into the next century.

The trade-off between the contribution tax rate c and the replacement rate r under pay as you go is easy to see if it is assumed that every year benefits and contributions are strictly equal and that the trust fund is always zero. Such calculation also indicates starkly how the tradeoff worsens when, as will be happening next century, the number of contributing workers per contemporaneous retired beneficiary declines.

Let x be worker-support, the number of workers per beneficiary; let w be their real wage; and let b be the real benefit. The replacement rate r is by definition b/w. Pay-as-you-go implies $b = cwx$, or $r = cx$. If x is lower, it takes proportionately higher c to keep r constant, or proportionately lower r to keep c constant. This is the political-economic dilemma discussed in the text.

The following table gives some illustrative numbers.

	1984	2004	2044b	2044c
worker-support, x	3.3	3.2	2.0	2.0
replacement ratio, r	0.38	0.41	0.40	0.25
tax rate, c	0.114	0.124	0.20	0.124
real wage w (1984 = 100)	100	136	302	302
real benefit b = rw	38	56	121	75
real benefit b (1984 = 100)	100	147	318	197

Notes: Data from *Trustees Report*, projection II-A. Tax rates as now legislated in 2004. Two alternatives for 2044: 2044b holds replacement rate at present level, as will occur from automatic continuation of present benefit formulas. 2044c freezes tax rate at 12.4 percent; nevertheless real benefit is twice its 1984 amount. Under projection II-B, with less real wage growth, freezing the tax rate would bring a benefit in 2044, 155 percent of that in 1984.

ject to income tax would earn still less, but this liability also reduces their return under pay-as-you-go. At present the pretax real rate appears to be 4 to 5 percent, thus higher than the current 3 percent growth rate of real payrolls. Over a working career, this difference compounds to a 20 to 50 percent advantage in benefits.

An advantage of this kind is not, however, an opportunity available to OASI participants without a long transitional period of extra saving to do the funding, at the expense of the consumption of taxpayers and/or beneficiaries. Moreover, the differential in favor of funding may not last. In the past, real rates of interest in financial markets have often been lower than the growth of real payrolls.

I shall return shortly to the funding issue, but first I must consider some basic questions about OASI I mentioned at the beginning of this chapter: the compulsory nature of Social Security, and the relative roles of redistribution and insurance in the benefits provided.

Why is Social Security Compulsory?

What is the rationale for compulsory universal participation? If yuppies think they could do better on their own, why not let them opt out? Why not let workers and their families arrange and finance their own retirements? Why not leave it to parents and children to define the obligations of generations to each other? In the polls previously cited, 56 percent favored voluntary Social Security, although 75 percent said they would participate anyway.

The perception that market returns are today higher than those likely to be earned on Social Security contributions is evidently a source of the disillusionment reported in polls: 58 percent of respondents say they could do better "at the bank," and only 22 percent think they could not do better on their own.[18] Of course, many workers, including respondents who think they could provide better for their own retirement than by contributing to OASI, would not in fact succeed in doing so. Indeed, many would not in fact save the equivalent of their payroll taxes if they were free to choose.

There are several arguments for compulsion. The first is simple paternalism. It should not be lightly dismissed. Some citizens may not know what is good for them, or they may be too short-sighted or weak-willed to act. Young people find it difficult to save for that incredibly remote time of old age. When it does arrive, they will be grateful in retrospect if Uncle Sam has made them save. Many people like such discipline and prefer that money never pass through their hands.

[18] See note 7.

The second is a paternalistic argument with a different twist—society's interest in having individuals provide for their own old age. Society will not let the aged starve and die in the street (I hope that is still true in the United States). Instead, society will use public resources to help the destitute even if their own past improvidence might be the reason for their plight, a possibility very difficult to substantiate in any individual case. Consequently, it is argued, the state has the right to protect society, as well as the individual, against such improvidence.

Third, there are what economists call externalities in universal participation. The government can provide a better retirement plan for most people than they could obtain on their own, provided everyone participates. Some individuals could possibly do better personally if allowed to opt out, but if everyone were free to do so few would do better. The government plan itself would be impaired by adverse selection—the withdrawal of the better risks and their premiums. Moreover, a universal and uniform plan has economies of scale that would be lost if participation were voluntary.

Fourth, a universal plan underwritten by the taxing and monetary powers of the central government can offer some guarantees that a decentralized system of private pensions and voluntary saving cannot. These include protection against internal inflation. A big advantage of OASI over private plans is that OASI is portable and vested; rights and benefits once earned are not lost by changing jobs or residences or by leaving the work force. The founders of Social Security were very wise to establish it as a nationally uniform system, centrally governed and administered. Thanks to their foresight, we avoided the distortions a decentralized system would have introduced into workers' choices of jobs and residences and into employers' choices of locations. Such distortions occur because of differences among states and localities in unemployment compensation and welfare programs and because of the incomplete portability and vesting of most entitlements to private pensions. (Michael Graetz treats this latter issue in some detail in Chapter 4.)

Fifth, in a highly interdependent modern economy, the intergenerational social compact is not solely among blood relatives. We recognize a general social obligation for the welfare, education, and socialization of children, an obligation that extends to citizens who have no children and to parents with more than ample means to care for their own. Likewise, active workers have some responsibilities for the elders in society as a whole, whatever they may give to or receive from their own parents. Intergenerational transfers are legitimate agenda of democratic politics.

Some may find these defenses of compulsion unconvincing; others may not have seen compulsion as problematic in the first place. I think there is a strong case for a compulsory system, but I do wonder whether it justifies compulsory accumulation of ever higher benefits, far above absolute minimal requirements for subsistence. OASI enthusiasts point with pride to the fact that its benefits now replace about the same percentage of the earnings of active workers as when the program began, about 40 percent. They use that statistic to counter critics who claim present benefits are too generous. But this same replacement ratio provides now, and *a fortiori* in the next century, a much more comfortable retirement than it did half a century ago.

At some point the generations who will be working and retiring in the twenty-first century may wish to limit the growth of compulsory contributions and the benefits they buy, while inviting voluntary supplementary participation in OASI. Individuals, or employers and employees in concert, would be free to make additional voluntary contributions and obtain higher benefits. OASI could be an attractively simple channel for individuals' retirement saving and private retirement plans.

Insurance versus Redistribution

From its inception OASI was a carefully conceived compromise among several not wholly compatible objectives. Its overriding purpose, of course, was to enable older people to live decently and independently once they could no longer earn income from employment. OASI's reliance on contributions collected by taxing workers and their employers, and the absence of a means test for benefits, follow from the principle that participants earn benefits as a matter of right. The analogy to insurance benefits earned by premiums was deliberate; here the "risk" is living too long after wages stop, and the "premiums" buy "security" from destitution or dependence. But in fact the connection of benefits to contributions, within age cohorts and between them, has always been loose and uneven.

The variability of that connection comes from another objective. The system is intentionally redistributive among workers of any given birth date. (It is *unintentionally* redistributive across generations, as already noted.) High wage earners receive significantly lower pensions per dollar of payroll tax contributions than do their lower wage contemporaries. Consider, for example, three hypothetical workers retiring at the same age in 1982. One always worked at the minimum wage, one at the average wage, one at or above the wage at which payroll taxes are capped. Their Adjusted Indexed Monthly Earnings (AIMEs) fairly closely reflect their relative cumulative contributions. Their Primary Insurance Amounts (PIAs) reflect quite closely the relative sizes of their annuities. The PIAs as percent of AIMEs for these three workers are 57, 45, and 40

PIA/Average Wages (%)

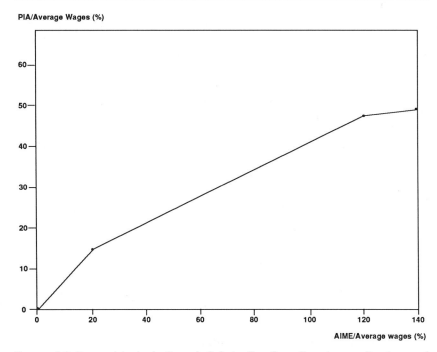

AIME/Average wages (%)

FIGURE 2.9. Progressivity in the Formula Relating Benefits to Preretirement Earnings, and Relation of Primary Insurance Amount to Adjusted Indexed Monthly Earnings.

Source: *Financing Social Security*, Congressional Budget Office, Nov. 1982, p. 20. Conversion to percentages of average wage was done by the author.

Note: AIME is an average of individual earnings subject to payroll tax prior to retirement; earnings for each year included in the average are indexed to a common preretirement age by a national wage index. PIA is the base from which all OASI benefits, for spouse as well as for earner, are calculated prior to indexation during retirement by the CPI. The figure shows both AIME and PIA are percentages of average wages. Their dollar amounts both rise proportionately from year to year, thus from cohort to cohort, as average wages rise. The two breakpoints are at (19 percent, 17.1 percent) and (115 percent, 36.8 percent). The three slopes are 0.90, 0.32, and 0.15.

respectively.[19] The differences among the three workers' ratios arise because the two numbers, AIME and PIA, are linked by a progressive formula, with three brackets, as illustrated in Figure 2.9.

The progressivity of the formula does not convey the full impact of the system on the distribution of income among contemporaneous participants. Some ancillary government policies enhance progressivity. At the low end of the income spectrum, Supplemental Security Income (SSI) is a federal means-tested assistance program for the elderly, financed not

[19] Congressional Budget Office, *Financing Social Security: Issues and Options for the Long Run* (Washington, D.C.: GPO, 1982), pp. 32–33.

from the OASI trust fund but from general revenues. It is a "safety net" for old people whose entitlements to Social Security do not meet minimal needs. At the affluent end of the income spectrum, the 1983 provision for partial income taxation of OASI benefits makes Social Security per se more progressive. However, AIMES are not perfect indicators of income and wealth; low cumulative contributions may have resulted from loose connection to covered employment rather than from low incomes during working years.

A more important point is that beneficiaries with higher AIMEs, thus with lower monthly benefits relative to lifetime contributions, tend to live longer and receive those benefits a longer time. On an actuarial basis, this longevity effect roughly, and serendipitously, offsets the progressivity of the AIME-to-PIA formula.[20] OASI pays virtually nothing except to living primary beneficiaries and their spouses. The risk against which OASI insures is that of living too long, and it makes no distinctions among its beneficiaries with respect to life expectancy. Private sellers of life annuities likewise make almost no distinctions of this kind. Individual OASI participants whose AIME-to-PIA conversions are the least favorable are unlikely to understand or appreciate the compensation they as a group receive by living and receiving benefits a longer time.

As is usually the case, equity and efficiency conflict. Use of the system's revenues to improve the lots of the poorer retirees and their families can create some perverse incentives. Participants can retire and begin receiving benefits as early as age 62. The weight of evidence is that the system has significantly reinforced the trend toward earlier retirement. Although a worker can gain higher monthly benefits by continuing to work, the gain has been actuarially inadequate, especially for postponing retirement age beyond the long standard age of 65. Under the 1983 amendments, this bias is being gradually eliminated. The legislation also schedules a gradual increase after 2000 in the normal retirement age in OASI calculus.[21] These changes seem quite appropriate. As the health and longevity of senior citizens improve gradually, it is a service to them, to their younger taxpaying contemporaries, and to the economy at large to employ their services.

[20] Michael D. Hurd and John B. Shoven, "The Distributional Impact of Social Security," in *Pensions, Labor, and Individual Choice*, ed. David Wise (Chicago: University of Chicago Press for National Bureau of Economic Research, 1985), chap. 7, especially Table 7.9.

Here and elsewhere *actuarial* calculations refer to values of streams of contributions and payments, allowing for probabilities of surviving and converting expected dollar amounts at past or future dates to a common date by compound interest.

[21] On these changes see U. S. Department of Health and Human Services, Social Security Administration, *Social Security Bulletin*, 47 (October 1984): 11–12. Calculations by my research assistant Daphne Butler convinced me that for couples, assuming reasonable interest rates, these changes will virtually remove the bias against deferring age of retirement.

In the past, a severe disincentive to work by the elderly has been the consequent total or partial loss of OASI benefits. Now, however, from age 70 on, OASI beneficiaries may work without losing any benefits. If they do work, however, they still pay Social Security taxes. This anomaly betrays an official attitude that those payments are just like other taxes, rather than contributions to earn retirement benefits. Working OASI beneficiaries should be excused from further contributions, especially now that earned income may make them liable for personal income taxes on their benefits as well as on the earnings themselves.

Serious disincentives prior to retirement are inherent in the size and growth of payroll tax rates noted above. Further increases—two to five percentage points—are likely in the twenty-first century, to handle the midcentury demographic crunch if benefit-earnings replacement ratios are maintained. Health insurance is also financed from payroll taxes. Total payroll tax rates, including health insurance, have risen from 8.8 percent in 1967 to 14.1 percent now and are scheduled to be 15.3 percent after 1989, probably even higher after the financing of Medicare is seriously reviewed over the next few years (see Figure 2.6). In the middle of the next century total payroll taxes will have to be 21 to 26 percent of taxable payrolls, according to middle-range official projections.[22]

Payroll taxes, to the extent they are regarded as ordinary taxes rather than as contributions which earn full value in future benefits, are disincentives to work by employees. For workers with annual earnings above the limit of the payroll tax, however, they are not a *marginal* disincentive discouraging extra work. Likewise, if employers regard their payroll taxes as additional costs rather than as substitutes for wages, they are a disincentive to employment. High tax rates invite evasion and encourage substitution of capital and other inputs for labor, especially for low-wage and unskilled labor, all of whose earnings are taxable. If workers perceive no clear and fair link of contributions to benefits, the work and employment disincentives will be strong. But the disincentive to voluntary saving will be weak because distrust of Social Security might lead participants to make other provisions for retirement.

Social Security and Income Redistribution

Twenty or thirty years ago, I recall, many economists looked on OASI as essentially a redistributive tax–transfer program disguised as social insurance.[23] They regarded the trust fund—the accounting designed to seg-

[22] Board of Trustees, *1985 Annual Report*, Table 1, p. 8; Table E3, p. 123.

[23] This was the spirit of an influential book. See Pechman, Aaron, and Taussig, *Social Security*. In their introduction the authors write:

regate OASI transactions from the general budget—as so much window dressing. They questioned the equity and efficiency of payroll taxes, especially with taxable wages capped, and wondered why more progressively levied general revenues should not be used instead. They wondered, too, about the equity and efficiency of paying benefits without conditions on need, at least about their exemption from personal income taxation. This type of criticism has waned over the years, possibly because of some disillusionment with the general tax system and the means testing of other benefits. Moreover, economists have joined other social scientists in greater appreciation of the political and social values of a universal system somewhat separate from the general budget.

An opposite viewpoint is that insurance and redistribution should be clearly and explicitly separated.[24] Ideally, in this view, retirement insurance should be actuarially fair to contributing participants, as far as administratively feasible. In such a system it would be easy to cap compulsory contributions, while allowing voluntary supplements, as discussed above. Redistribution would then be accomplished by extra assistance to those in need, paid from general federal revenues, like SSI. This approach would eliminate from OASI the actuarial anomalies and disincentives incident to redistribution within the system, on the assumption that the redistribution could be handled more efficiently through the general budget.

The issues of intergenerational redistribution and equity are even more difficult. As explained above, they are especially acute right now. Present beneficiaries and participants who will retire before the turn of the century are getting high returns on their past contributions because of the past unsustainable growth of the system and the indexation of benefits in 1973. Many of them are much better off than many young payroll taxpayers are now or ever will be. Should the present fortunate elderly be asked to give up some of their windfalls either to enable payroll taxes to be reduced or to start building up a larger fund for the benefit of future retirees? Note that these purposes are intergenerational transfers within the OASI system. To accomplish them, deficit reduction targets for the remainder of the federal budget should remain unchanged. In any case, the problem is that immediate or early reduction of benefits, particularly

---

The originators and many current proponents of social security have placed considerable reliance on the "insurance" aspects of the system. Although there are many differences between social security and private insurance, the idea of social security as a form of insurance has widespread acceptance and appeal. The differences are significant, however, and this volume argues that the present program is more appropriately viewed as a system of transfers which, like any other government program, must be financed by taxes. This approach provides the conceptual basis for the analysis and for devising methods to improve the major features of the program. (p. 4)

[24] See, for example, Boskin, *Too Many Promises*.

so soon after the 1983 compromise, seems like a breach of contract, further weakening the trust of all generations in Social Security. Although further cuts of benefits could be phased in slowly, the windfalls of the luckiest cohorts of retirees would be untouched.

A Possible Funded System

No radical change of OASI is likely in the near future. The Greenspan compromise has assured its "solvency" well into the next century. No crisis is likely to return OASI to the urgent agenda of politics for a couple of decades, although it may continue to be vulnerable to budget cutters who try to resolve general fiscal imbalances without raising taxes or cutting defense. The trust fund surpluses anticipated in the 1990s might tempt Congress to sweeten benefits or lower payroll taxes, although the deficits anticipated some decades later should be an inhibition. The Greenspan Commission left unresolved the financial crunch projected between 2030 and 2040. The generations involved have the time and opportunity to choose among various ways of averting it. As a contribution to that debate, let me spell out what a funded system recast along purer insurance lines would look like. I shall draw in part on the proposals of Professors Boskin, Kotlikoff, and Shoven for "personal security accounts."[25]

1. Every individual participant would have a funded account, which would vest him or her with rights to pensions and to ancillary insurance and benefits, from first covered job until actual retirement. The age of retirement (i.e., commencement of benefits) would be discretionary within a specified interval. Benefit claims would depend on the dates and amounts of contributions in the same way for all participants. The fund would grow during the participant's working career, not only by additional contributions but also by compound interest. The interest rate would vary with the government's borrowing rate, but it would never be less than the rate of inflation of a suitable consumer price index (purged of the price effects of uninsurable shocks and indirect taxes).

2. At the time of retirement, this fund—less amounts charged to it for disability insurance, death benefits, and other ancillary items—will be converted actuarially into an indexed annuity, either for the life of the participant alone or with continuing payments to a surviving spouse, at the choice of the participant.

3. Contributions of married workers will be divided equally between

[25] Michael J. Boskin, Laurence J. Kotlikoff, and John B. Shoven, "Personal Security Accounts: A Proposal for Fundamental Social Security Reform," Paper presented to the National Commission on Social Security Reform, August 1982. Revised version, September 1985.

the two spouses' accounts, as long as they are married. There will be no spousal benefits or benefits to a surviving spouse other than the optional survivor annuity mentioned above. But a married retired couple will receive all the benefits the two of them earned by working or by being married to a worker. Changes of this type are overdue. The present system does not do justice to working spouses or to divorcees.[26]

4. During periods of registered unemployment, a participant's compulsory payroll contributions to OASI in his previous job will be credited to his account without payments by the participant or his previous employer. The government could also credit extra contributions to participants who worked at low wages or were registered as unemployed for, say, at least forty weeks of a year. These extra contributions could be proportional to the shortfall of earnings from, say, half the earnings cap for the year. Thus could some progressivity be built into the system.

5. The system will be funded in aggregate. The trust fund will both receive the payroll contributions and credits and disburse the annuities and other benefits. The Treasury will pay the trust fund interest on its balance at the designated rates. Since the scheme is essentially a "defined contribution" plan, its solvency will not be a problem unless real interest rates are chronically so low as to bring into force the guarantees of purchasing power.

6. Transition to such a funded system could take place slowly, as follows. Following its adoption, only new participants below age 35 would play by the new rules. Their aggregate contributions and credits would built up a new trust fund, Trust Fund II. Everyone else would play out the game by the old rules, via existing Trust Fund I. That fund would be deprived of receipts from the Fund II participants. The Treasury would "borrow" those receipts from Fund II and pay them out as necessary to Fund I beneficiaries. At the end of some forty years of transition, Fund II would hold Treasury obligations equal in value to the accounts of its participants. From a macroeconomic standpoint, total receipts and payments throughout the transition would be virtually the same as if there were no new program. The difference would be simply that the government would now be acknowledging its liabilities to future beneficiaries, the Fund II participants. Present federal accounting does not reckon such liabilities as public debt, although they really are.

I do not want to be misunderstood. Accounting is not magic. It cannot produce the economic funding that Feldstein advocated unless the nation does some extra saving during the transition. This proposal does not assign that task to any particular generation, contributors or beneficiaries,

[26] On this complex subject see Richard Burkhauser and Karen Holden, eds., *A Challenge to Social Security* (New York: Academic Press, 1982).

but via the overall federal budget to the nation as a whole. Only if the gradual acknowledgment of the Treasury's debt to Fund II inspires presidents and congresses to lower their deficits on non-OASI transactions will the accounting reform have macroeconomic substance. At the end of the transition, OASI would be a funded system for its participants, but overall effects on national saving and capital formation would still depend on general fiscal and monetary policies.

This slow transition has the advantage of breaking the bad accounting news quite gradually. More important, it respects the legitimate expectations of everyone in the existing system. Faster transitions, under which many beneficiaries would receive benefits from both Funds I and II, would cause too many confusions, anomalies, and inequities.

The trade-off between workers' contribution rates and beneficiaries' earnings replacement rates is likely to be painful in the next century.[27] The generations concerned have time to work out a solution. The present system biases the result to maintaining the replacement rate and raising payroll taxes as necessary to pay the ever higher benefits. The proposed new system would be an opportunity to choose other options. One option is to freeze the payroll tax and to adjust future benefits accordingly; there are many options in between.

The new system would be much less vulnerable to economic and demographic shocks of the kind that spawned recent "crises." Blind adherence to pay-as-you-go seems to result in raising taxes to cover previously committed benefits whenever adverse events threaten to deplete the fund. Even when problems are foreseen, action is postponed so long that benefits cannot be touched without violating commitments to those retired or about to retire. At the same time, the new system would give participants a fair, clear, and continuously reported link between their individual contributions and their benefit rights. Although the system as outlined could accomplish some redistribution in favor of poorer participants, that burden is placed mainly on the general federal budget.

Proposals of this kind are worth considering in the next national debate about Social Security. The questions they raise are not in my view liberal versus conservative or Democrat versus Republican issues. They are issues of pragmatic management. Aging is a common human fate, irrespective of politics, ideologies, and generations. How people choose to trade consumption when they are young for consumption when they are old should not bring them to the barricades. It should bring them to face squarely economic and demographic realities. I hope the generations who will work out the structure of the system in the next century will do so in this spirit.

[27] See note 17.

In concluding I want to stress that Social Security is viable and afford-able in its present form. In suggesting possible changes for consideration, I am in no way departing from either my conviction that the Social Secu-rity Act was one of the greatest triumphs of political, social, and eco-nomic architecture in the history of the republic or my admiration for its original designers and builders and for those dedicated public servants, like Robert Ball, who have maintained, repaired, and improved the struc-ture these many years. Social Security deserves celebration of its golden anniversary.

3

Social Security and Constitutional Entitlement

ROBERT M. COVER

The contemporary debate on Social Security has ranged broadly over rich and varied economic and ideological territory. On the economic side, critics and defenders of the system have debated the effects of impending demographic developments that will radically alter the ratio of currently employed wage earners to retirees when the baby boom generation reaches retirement age during the second decade of the twenty-first century. They have debated the wisdom of continuing to employ a largely unfunded, pay-as-you-go system for providing benefits. They have differed on the magnitude of the effects of this system upon national savings. On the ideological level there has been considerable disagreement about combining "insurance" and "welfare" components in a single system. Critics of the system from the right frequently attack the involuntary character of payments into the system and extol the virtues of private pension alternatives that may employ subsidies (often regressive) to encourage though not compel participation. Critics of the system from the left have attacked some regressive features of the FICA tax and have sought greater redistribution in favor of low-income persons. These ideological battles are not without potential practical effects. There has been a strong push from the right to substitute a private pension option for all or part of the coverage now provided by Social Security.[1]

These broad-ranging disputes have paid little heed to the constitutional status of Social Security. One might suppose this to be a tribute to the wisdom of a firm constitutional settlement of the various questions which a Social Security system raises: the protection of future expectations

---

Bob Cover died unexpectedly on July 18, 1986. He had completed a final revision of his chapter shortly before his death. It appears here as he had prepared it for publication.

[1] See Chapter 5 by Paul Starr for an in-depth discussion of the move toward the privatization of Social Security.

through law; the differing treatment afforded different groups of similarly situated beneficiaries; the processes by which critical decisions are made.

In fact, the absence of public attention to the constitutional status of Social Security should surprise us, for the major economic and ideological issues before the public have substantial connections to the primary constitutional questions that have been raised or might be raised about the system. Moreover, although there has been an apparently clear decision by the Supreme Court to leave the broad outlines of Social Security to legislative discretion—that is, to avoid constitutionalizing it—that decision, upon reflection, raises more questions than it dispels. The primary decision of the Court in this area is now twenty-five years old; it was hotly contested when first rendered; and recent decisions of the Supreme Court on constitutional challenges to several technical details within Social Security betray a critical ambiguity in dealing with the concepts central to the settlement of a quarter century ago. I am not suggesting there is a current inclination on the part of the Supreme Court to discover a constitutional solution to any of the major policy issues in Social Security. I am, in fact, confident that there is no such inclination at all. Nonetheless, the pattern of decisions and their justifications do raise serious questions about the coherence of the prevailing view that avoids any major constitutional commitments arising out of this system.

This chapter will review the two major constitutional cases that located Social Security firmly within the domain of legislative discretion. It will also review the more recent cases that may be read to raise questions about that traditional status. It will be evident from the review of this case law that the constitutional issues potentially present in Social Security could have a significant effect on the contemporary policy and ideological debates. Social Security benefits are not now given the kind of constitutional protection that interests vested under private pension plans or annuity contracts would have. Every issue we now discuss in this field, from financing strategies to the psychology of public confidence, could change with a change in this basic rule. With this potential in mind we examine the constitutional history of the program.

The Constitutional Settlement of Social Security

In 1935 Social Security was born amid considerable doubt concerning its future prospects for success, indeed for its existence. Perhaps the most significant element in the doubt about that future arose from the looming presence of the Supreme Court of the United States and from the Constitution entrusted to that Court's gentle mercies. On May 27, 1935, the Court had invalidated important New Deal legislation—part of the Railroad Retirement and the National Recovery Act. Black Monday, then, as the Court's decision day was called, became a source of anger and anxiety within the New Deal administration.[2]

If anger was the principal note sounded by the administration, there was anxiety at the very least with respect to the Court's impact upon Social Security. The Court had already evinced a narrow reading of the commerce clause, failing to stretch that wording to support the New Deal legislation. But the justices did not offer an authoritative reading of the taxing and spending powers, those principally at issue with respect to Social Security, until their decision in *United States v. Butler* in 1936, a year after the enactment of the Social Security Act.[3]

The Agriculture Adjustment Act, at issue in *Butler*, was similar to Social Security in certain respects. It depended upon an integrated scheme of taxes and payments. In the Agriculture Adjustment Act, taxes were imposed upon the processors of agricultural products; the proceeds of the processing tax were then applied to a "spending" scheme through which payments were made to farmers who took acreage out of production according to administratively determined acreage reduction programs. The Supreme Court held first that the processors upon whom the tax was levied had standing to challenge the constitutionality of the purposes to which the payments were applied and, second, that those purposes were beyond the powers of the national government. The decision in *Butler*[4] was not in all respects ominous for Social Security. In writing the opinion, Justice Owen Roberts emphasized that the Court was adopting what he called the Hamilton view of the spending power of the national government. That position gives the national government an independent authority to spend for the general welfare beyond the power to spend for the pursuit of activities justified by other provisions of the Constitution.

Roberts's application of the general principle of hospitality to an independent spending power was very crimped indeed, but some commenta-

[2] *Railroad Retirement Board v. Alton Railroad Co.*, 295 U.S. 330 (1935). Decided three weeks before Black Monday, this decision invalidated the compulsory retirement and pension provisions of the Railroad Retirement Act of 1934. *Schechter Poultry Corp. v. United States*, 295 U.S. 495 (1935), invalidated, as an unconstitutional delegation of legislative powers, the industry codes of the NIRA; it also invalidated the codes as applied to intrastate activity, as beyond the commerce power of Congress. *Louisville Joint Stock Land Bank v. Radford*, 295 U.S. 555 (1935), invalidated provisions of the Frazier-Lemke Act with respect to farm mortgage relief. *Humphrey's Executor v. United States*, 295 U.S. 602 (1935), upheld limitations on the president's power to remove a member of the Federal Trade Commission; the case was seen by Roosevelt as a personal affront especially in light of *Myers v. United States*, 272 U.S. 52 (1926), in which a conservative court had struck down similar limitations on presidential removal powers during the administration of Calvin Coolidge.
[3] *United States v. Butler*, 297 U.S. 1 (1936), struck down the Agriculture Adjustment Act.
[4] 297 U.S. 1 (1936).

tors saw in the explicit adoption of the Hamiltonian position a sign that the Court might well accept the spending power basis for Social Security.[5] Unlike the Agriculture Adjustment Act, Social Security, at least with respect to the OASI provisions, had no essentially regulatory purposes.

In 1937 the Court did uphold the Social Security Act as constitutional.[6] Justice Benjamin Cardozo, for a majority of the Court, relied upon the language in *Butler*, with its Hamiltonian view of the spending power. He also accepted the income security objectives of the program as legitimate national general welfare spending goals. There can be no doubt that the Social Security Act cases—along with the decisions upholding the Wagner Act and holding state minimum wage legislation to be constitutional— constitute part of the massive turn of the Court in 1937–1938 from hostility toward economic legislation to eager receptivity. A distinct understanding had been achieved. The Court was emphatically out of the business of passing economic or moral judgment upon statutory and administrative programs of essentially economic import and impact. The Constitution had been removed as an impediment to policy-oriented legislation.[7]

The achievement of 1937 appeared to be a coherent one. The line between economic and other legislation seemed, though not without difficulty, real enough to contemporaries. Very little attention was given, however, to the distinctions among the various kinds of essentially economic legislation that the settlement of 1937 had lumped together. It made perfect sense to say that the essence of regulation was the supremacy of the political domain over markets. Therefore, it followed that a settlement which accepted regulation had to elevate the administrative and legislative judgments of politics above the principled application of the fundamental propositions of transactional liberty that constituted markets. Lurking beneath the surface of the settlement, however, was a

---

[5] For an important contemporaneous comment on *Butler*, which notes the promising adoption of the Hamilton view and which also notes the favorable implications for the Social Security Act, see Robert Jackson's comment to the New York Bar Association two weeks after *Butler*: "I find very real cause for hope in the future in the language of Justice Roberts upon the welfare clause." Quoted in C. Leonard, *A Search for a Judicial Philosophy: Mr. Justice Roberts and the Constitutional Revolution of 1937* (Port Washington, N.Y.: Kennikat Press, 1971), p. 56, n. 107.

[6] *Steward Machine Co. v. Davis*, 301 U.S. 548 (1937), upheld the unemployment compensation provisions of the Social Security Act. Title IX. *Helvering v. Davis*, 301 U.S. 619 (1937), upheld the old-age benefits provisions of the Social Security Act. See especially *Helvering*, 301 U.S. 619, at 640.

[7] The Court at the same time suggested that certain political liberties and equality provisions of the Constitution would operate as a meaningful set of limits to legislative and administrative action. See, for example, *United States v. Carolene Products Co.*, 304 U.S. 144 (1938), n. 4.

very different problem—the status of entitlements created out of government action. Here the question was not whether transactional liberty would trump the regulatory power of the polity but whether the state would create entitlements enjoying less security of interest than that afforded traditional property holders. That question was to be the constitutional agenda of another generation.[8]

By 1960 Social Security had celebrated its twenty-fifth birthday, and thoughtful Americans were well aware that they lived in a state in which interests created by and through governmental programs were an important, and an increasingly important, part of the economic lives of most people. The experience with McCarthyism in the early fifties and the lingering stigma attached to prior associations with communism had accentuated for many the peculiarly vulnerable nature of those dependent upon government either for their jobs or the receipt of important benefits. The bullying of this period had, after all, exploited those vulnerabilities. The second stage in the constitutional history of Social Security emerges out of the bullying and the responses to it.

In 1954 Congress passed §202(n) of the Social Security Act, which provided for the termination of old-age benefits otherwise payable to an alien who, after the effective date of the legislation, was deported from the United States for certain enumerated reasons. Among the reasons was that of having been a member of the Communist Party during specified periods. Nestor, a Bulgarian, had been in the United States forty-three years when, in 1956, he was deported for having been a Communist from 1933 to 1939. He challenged the termination of his old-age benefits and the constitutionality of §202(n).

Flemming v. Nestor[9] was only one of several cases the Supreme Court considered around 1960 that challenged adverse determinations concerning benefits and public employment on the basis of questions related to national security. In all these cases, an "interest" was threatened or taken away, and the Court gave a reason. First the Court had to analyze the interest to determine what kind of protection should be afforded by the Constitution, then it had to examine the reasons given to decide whether they were never, sometimes, or always sufficient to ground adverse consequences. For purposes of the constitutional history of Social Security I shall ignore what we might consider the first amendment freedom or political association issues of *Nestor*. The Court did not decide the case on the basis of such first amendment claims, and they are not germane to our story. *Flemming v. Nestor* did, however, mark a major watershed in the

[8] One must concede, in fairness, that Justice Roberts did see this problem in his *Butler* opinion and, indeed, that it constitutes the animating force behind the opinion. See, for example, 297 U.S. 1 (1936).

[9] *Flemming v. Nestor*, 363 U.S. 603 (1960).

task of defining the type of interest Social Security would be. In this respect there is a major conceptual cleavage in *Nestor* between the opinion of Justice John Harlan for the majority and the dissenting opinion of Justice Hugo Black. Justice Black, we should note, was President Roosevelt's first appointment to the Court. He had been a strong New Deal senator, and he was a vigorous proponent of the New Deal judicial settlement which had laid to rest interference by the Court in the economic and regulatory policy judgments made by Congress or the administration.

Justice Harlan's opinion first argued that a recipient's interest in Social Security is not "an accrued property right." The district court had held for Nestor on the ground that there was such a right. Harlan did concede that the recipient's interest in benefits is sufficient to trigger the usual requirement that government not act in an arbitrary or unreasonable way, but the test that legislation has to pass to be found neither arbitrary nor unreasonable is not very demanding. Harlan thus upheld the statute as applied to the alien claimant.

Justice Black's constitutional jurisprudence was such that he, too, was reluctant to second guess the legislature on the question of what was unreasonable or arbitrary. However, Black thought that Social Security benefits were protected under a far more rigorous standard of scrutiny than that afforded them by Harlan. Black argued that benefits were an accrued property right and therefore the action of the government "takes Nestor's insurance without just compensation and in violation of the Due Process Clause of the Fifth Amendment."[10]

Between Black and Harlan the lines were clearly drawn, and it is instructive to examine the respective bases for their positions. Black's is the more clear-cut of the two. He begins with a precedent and a very clear rule of law from that precedent. The precedent is *Lynch v. United States*.[11] In *Lynch*, Justice Louis Brandeis had held, for a unanimous court, that it was unconstitutional for the American government to use legislation to abrogate its obligations under renewable term life insurance policies issued to soldiers during World War I. He placed great emphasis upon the fact that the insurance policies were contracts, not gratuities, and that as contracts they were entitled to the protections of substantial government subsidy within them—that is, the cost of the insurance was subsidized to the extent that the government underwrote both the incremental risk of war and the administrative costs of the insurance. Brandeis concluded that subsidization in no way detracted from the status of the policies as contracts and therefore as property.[12]

---

[10] Ibid., at 622.
[11] *Lynch v. United States*, 292 U.S. 571 (1934).
[12] Ibid.

Black argued from *Lynch* that an earned property interest was entitled to 5th amendment protection from a "taking" by the government. Moreover, *Lynch* seemed to mean that the presence of redistributive elements within the insurance program was not sufficient to turn the program into a mere gratuity. In a particularly interesting argument about the nature of the program, Black states that Congress's purpose in passing the Social Security Act was explicitly to create a kind of interest that would be seen as an "earned right" rather than a gratuity so that a person would be willing and able to " 'receive his benefit in dignity and self-respect.' " In a peculiar sentence, Black writes: "It was then generally agreed, as it is today, that it is not desireable that aged people think of the government as giving them something for nothing."[13] There is a strange emphasis on the appearance of a gratuity or charity as opposed to the reality of one. But Black may be getting at a very fundamental point: the intention of Congress to have people earn their benefit by some payments not actuarially related to what they receive no more keeps them from being earned than did the subsidy in Lynch prevent the insurance policies from being characterized as contracts.

implies that it was payment — or an insurance program; but logic carries over to gratuities. We 'pay' with our taxes.

Finally, Black took on the argument that constitutionalization of the interest in Social Security would deny the government necessary flexibility. He argues that the interest in maintaining flexibility would not excuse the government from paying its just obligations. He read a statutory reservation of Congressional power to "alter, amend or repeal any provision" of the act as operative prospectively only.

It could repeal the act and cease to operate its old-age insurance activities for the future. This means that it could stop covering new people and even stop increasing its obligations to old contributors. But that is quite different from disappointing the just expectations of the contributors to the fund which the government has compelled them and their employers to pay its Treasury.[14]

Black agreed program could be cut; just that people ought to be reimb.

Harlan's majority opinion stresses an analytic distinction between the benefits received under Social Security and the taxes paid. Persons are taxed "to permit the payment of benefits to the retired and disabled and their dependents." Harlan is here seizing upon the pay-as-you-go character of Social Security financing to point out that, literally, the payments of taxes go to support the present beneficiary class. He concedes that there is an expectation that "many members of the present productive work force will in turn become beneficiaries." But, he argues, the benefits "are not dependent on the degree to which [the worker] was called upon to support the system by taxation." He concludes that the "noncontrac-

[13] *Flemming v. Nestor*, 363 U.S. 603, at 623.
[14] Ibid., at 624–25.

tual interest" of the worker "cannot be soundly analogized to that of the holder of an annuity, whose right to benefits is bottomed on his contractual premium payments."[15]

Because the Black–Harlan split on Social Security is so clear-cut, it can be used to explicate some of the as yet unexplored ramifications of their positions. In my view two characteristics of Social Security distinguish it from an annuity interest the government's taking of which would be unconstitutional under *Lynch*. First, Social Security is not voluntary. FICA taxes must be paid. Unquestionably the government relies upon its taxing power to justify that imposition. From a private law perspective the independent legal obligation to pay taxes regardless of return upon them renders the governmental quid pro quo a noncontractual one. Satisfaction of a preexisting and independent obligation is not good consideration. Second, the benefits received do not bear an individualized or group actuarial relation to the payments made. The program is redistributive both among recipients and over the generations.[16]

It is interesting to ask whether one or both these factors lead Harlan and the Court to their result. Black's dissent certainly emphasized the *Lynch* precedent, that case refused to treat the subsidy effects of the insurance plan as dispositive. It may be that the particular context of the subsidy in *Lynch*—the principal part of the subsidy was the coverage of risk from war imposed involuntarily on the soldier—has such a clear moral justification that it is not considered redistributive but rather compensatory and hence earned in another way. Nonetheless, however wise and morally just it may be for the government to subsidize soldiers' insurance in just this way, it is certainly not a constitutional obligation of the government. The power and authority to force people to go to war is there with or without insurance. In some sense the war risk element of the insurance is a distributive gratuity, albeit one fully earned in a moral sense.

As to the second distinction between Social Security and a true annuity contract right, it is useful to construct a hypothetical system. Suppose Social Security were changed so that each participant's contributions were separately accounted for and the benefits made to vary precisely as a private pension plan-death benefit would according to the amounts paid in and the time at which such payments were made. Each payment would be accounted for with appropriate rates of interest applied. Would Harlan and the Court have treated such an annuity as constitutional property if the payments in question were not voluntary but part of a compulsory social insurance system? If they were not to be voluntary, it would be

---

[15] Ibid., at 610.
[16] See Chapter 2 by James Tobin. For a simple explanation of some of the economic effects of intergenerational redistribution, see Aaron, *Economic Effects of Social Security*.

impossible to consider the interest acquired as contractual. Whether the Court would have reached the same result with an actuarially determined relation between payments and receipts I do not know. And whether it would have followed *Lynch* with a voluntary redistributive scheme I do not know. But what we do know is that from 1960 to this very day the characterization of Social Security payments as not "accrued property rights" has survived.

Flemming v. Nestor settled something for a generation: there is a constitutional distinction between the interest in Social Security and an interest in traditional property rights. The twenty-six years since *Nestor* have seen interesting constitutional developments in Social Security law, developments which do not rival in magnitude the primary legitimation of the system and the basic characterization of the payments-benefits relation. Still, the cases may be said to have both illuminated and deepened our understanding of *Nestor*, and in some ways they have challenged it. A sketch of these developments may therefore be useful.

Developing Ambiguities—Recent Case Law

In *United States v. Lee*,[17] an Old Order Amish employer of several Amish employees challenged the imposition of FICA taxes upon him on the ground that it abridged the free exercise of his religion. He alleged that the Amish believe that the Bible places responsibility for the old and disabled on the community and that assumption of such tasks by the State is sinful. Individual self-employed Amish are, in fact, permitted to opt out of the Social Security system by statutory exception, but not employers. In denying the constitutional claim of the Amish, Chief Justice Burger wrote:

> The obligation to pay the social security tax initially is not fundamentally different from the obligation to pay income taxes; the difference—in theory at least—is that the social security tax revenues are segregated for use only in furtherance of the statutory program. There is no principled way, however, for purposes of this case, to distinguish between general taxes and those imposed under the Social Security Act. . . . Because the broad public interest in maintaining a sound tax system is of such a high order, religious belief in conflict with the payment of taxes affords no basis for resisting the tax.[18]

I take the Chief Justice's position to be that FICA must be understood as a true and independently justified tax quite apart from its linkage to the benefit program. It is hard to imagine writing such a paragraph with re-

[17] *United States v. Lee*, 455 U.S. 242 (1982).
[18] Ibid.

spect to insurance premiums, even compulsory ones. Thus, *Lee* reinforces the Harlan view of the severable character of tax and benefits.

Another case that strongly reinforces a different element of the *Nestor* majority opinion is *Weinberger v. Salfi*.[19] In *Salfi* the court had before it a provision of the act that denies to surviving spouses benefits derivative from the deceased spouse if the marriage to the deceased took place within nine months before death. Justice William Rehnquist wrote a very strong majority opinion upholding the statute and applying a "minimal scrutiny" standard of review; that is, the Court refused to require of the act and its administration that there be a "tight fit" between the categories used and the objectives pursued. Specifically, the majority rejected application of an "irrebuttable presumption" analysis that has been justified by some commentators on the ground that it is a way (perhaps a fiction) to require the legislature to use classifications that are neither unduly over or under inclusive. Thus, *Salfi* reinforced the conclusion in *Nestor* that the benefit classifications in Social Security are required to meet only the general prohibitions against arbitrary government action.

Although *Lee* and *Salfi* have reinforced basic elements of the *Nestor* settlement, other cases, especially in the gender classification area, have created some tension about the meaning of *Nestor*. Several provisions of the Act resulted in the widows of covered male decedents receiving better treatment than did widowers of covered female decedents. Gender-based classifications, under current constitutional doctrine, require that the Court impose an intermediate level of scrutiny to determine whether or not there is an adequate justification for the different treatment. In general, a provision that favors women on a plausible theory of compensation for past discrimination is more likely to be upheld than a similar provision that favors the privileged group—men.[20] The provisions that favor widows as opposed to widowers could certainly be justified on such compensatory or affirmative action grounds. Women, especially elderly women, are more likely than men to have been dependent on their spouse's earnings and less likely to have had careers or vocational training. One would suppose, therefore, that the provisions favoring female surviving spouses would have been upheld, but in fact, a majority of the Court—a very precarious majority—has held such provisions unconstitutional. By linking the benefit side of the program to the taxation of the wage earner, the Court has viewed these provisions not as favoring women recipients but as disfavoring women insured employees. Still,

---

[19] *Weinberger v. Salfi*, 422 U.S. 749 (1975).

[20] On the degree of scrutiny afforded gender classifications see, for example, *Frontiero v. Richardson*, 420 U.S. 677 (1973), especially the plurality opinion of Brennan requiring strict scrutiny, and *Craig v. Boren*, 429 U.S. 190 (1976).

there is no explicit repudiation of *Nestor*. This is Justice William Brennan's careful, fence-sitting on the subject in *Weinberger v. Weisenfeld*:

> We held in *Flemming v. Nestor* that the interest of a covered employee is "noncontractual," because 'each worker's benefits, though flowing from the contribution he made to the national economy while actively employed, are not dependent upon the degree to which he was called upon to support the system by taxation.' Appellant apparently contends that since benefits derived from the social security program do not correlate necessarily with contributions made to the program, a covered employee has no right to be treated equally with other employees as regards the benefits which flow from his or her employment.[21]

Brennan goes on to point out that "the statutory right to benefits is directly related to years worked and amount earned by a covered employee" rather than the needs of the beneficiary. In other words, the structure of the program is one in which the proper focus, even when analyzing benefits, is the relation to the *payer*. The taxpayer is the "insured," and from or through the taxpayer any other beneficiary receives his or her benefit. It is, thus, in relation to the "insured" and his or her coverage under the Act that any beneficiaries' benefits or denials of benefits may be considered either reasonable or unreasonable.

In *Califano v. Goldfarb*[22] the Court had to consider a close cousin of the provision struck down in *Weisenfeld*. Section 402(f)(1)(D) of the Act provided widowers with survivors' benefits only if they had received more than one half of their support from the deceased, however, no comparable limitation was put on widows' receipt of survivors' benefits. Identical arguments were heard on both sides. In *Goldfarb*, however, Brennan was still more emphatic in rejecting the position that the cases should be analyzed from the perspective of the beneficiary. Again, he stressed that the only proper analysis is from the "insured's" perspective: "Mrs. Goldfarb worked and paid social security taxes for 25 years at the same rate as her male colleagues, but because of [the section requiring widowers to establish that they had received more than half of their support from the de-

---

[21] *Weinberger v. Weisenfeld*, 420 U.S. 636 (1975). In *Weisenfeld* the Court struck down 402(g) of the Social Security Act, which provided benefits to the "widow" of an employee who had been currently or fully insured when he died, but denied such benefits to widowers. Brennan was very explicit in his opinion in recognizing that there were *two* possible characterizations of the differential treatment mandated by 402(g)—as a provision favoring female beneficiaries and as a provision disfavoring female wage earners. He seems not to deny that the provision favors female beneficiaries. But he insists that it nonetheless disfavors and, thus, discriminates against female covered employees. This latter conclusion can, of course, be maintained only by insisting on a linkage between tax and benefit.

[22] *Califano v. Goldfarb*, 430 U.S. 199 (1977).

cedent] the insurance protection received by the males was broader than hers."[23] Brennan and the majority saw these cases as closely analogous to the situation in *Frontiero v. Richardson*[24] in which a woman member of the armed forces successfully challenged the provision of certain benefits to male spouses only if they were in fact dependent upon the female armed forces member, although female spouses of male soldiers automatically received the benefits. But in *Frontiero* clearly the benefits in question are earned compensation, but in the Social Security situation *Nestor* and *Lee* would have suggested precisely the opposite conclusion—that the tax imposed and the benefits received are in some sense independent of one another.

This much is clear: it is difficult to make much sense of the way in which Brennan has analyzed these gender cases without some belief that Social Security benefits are earned. It is nearly impossible to see these cases as presenting issues of discrimination against *women* unless the benefit is that which the woman wage earner/taxpayer has earned for her survivor. One might, at first glance, be inclined to belittle the significance of the resort to the rhetoric of insurance here. Perhaps, after all, the fact that a gender-based distinction is at issue would serve to invalidate the classifications in question, whether they be conceived as disfavoring either the woman "insured" or the male beneficiary. Brennan is, however, sniffing at the edge of a much more profound problem with Social Security: Could the array of benefits in Social Security as now constituted be constitutionally justified if it did not depend on the linkage to payment of the tax? Could we, in other words, hold constitutional the benefit distribution scheme of Social Security were we to imagine the program to have been funded out of general revenues without any wage tax imposed? The question almost resists comprehension, for the first and dominant classification in terms of benefits is the classification which singles out the "currently or fully insured" from those who do not have such status—that is, the distinction between those who have paid enough of the tax and those who have not.

Yet, I suppose we could imagine a complex statute that imposed no tax but defined categories of employees, much as the FICA statute now does and in effect conditions benefits upon the beneficiary (or his or her kin): for example, (a) having been employed in certain kinds of jobs for a specified length of time; (b) having earned at least so much for so many quarters; and so on. Thus, retired employees would receive or not receive retirement benefits depending on whether they had worked in government

23 Ibid.
24 *Frontiero v. Richardson*, 411 U.S. 677 (1973).

or private industry and whether they had worked a minimum number of "covered" quarters (now approximately eight years). The amount of benefits would vary with earnings history, generally giving greater retirement benefits to those who had received higher wages. All of this would happen, although none of the retirees would have "contributed" to the pension system and no special taxes would have been imposed in any way proportional to past earning or future benefits.

Such a system would be distinctly odd, especially if the pattern of exclusions and preferences were extended to aged widows and widowers and to surviving minor children of the employees. It is possible that a scheme of old-age pension benefits, survivor benefits, and disability benefits so structured would prove to be minimally rational to this Court. Nonetheless, I think one must admit it to be at least a very close question. In contrast, if such a system is linked to a history of wage proportional payments, the basic structure appears considerably less strange and much more likely to pass muster as "minimally rational," despite particular oddities or inequities in rates of return to particular groups.

Thus, the rationality and hence the constitutionality of the entire basis of the Social Security scheme is put at issue if one divorces completely the benefit part of the program from the payments. At the same time, there remains great force to the refusal to understand Social Security as an insurance scheme. Since, as currently administered and with appropriate discount rates applied to all sums, the Social Security system provides most if not all beneficiaries with more than they put in, one cannot escape the fact that the rhetoric of "payment for" or "earning of" benefits is inexact. The subsidy dimension of the program is in fact open to the constitutional question I have posed. Why are these "bonuses" distributed according to a scheme that is rational only when applied to "return" on payments made?

A somewhat different but related difficulty is also lurking behind these cases: Would it be possible for Congress in general to make the availability of important benefits depend on whether or not someone had been a general taxpayer? I am, of course, assuming that the scheme is not simply an enforcement device. But consider making eligibility for pensions or for public education depend on whether one had paid income tax for a certain minimum number of years, assuming always that both the payer and nonpayer of the income tax had fully, honestly, and in good faith complied with the tax laws. If such a statute would be unconstitutional—and I don't know that it would be—we must be at pains to distinguish the kind of tax involved in FICA/OASDI from the general revenue-raising tax. This is an unenviable position. Indeed, the system looks like the "vesting" provisions of many pensions systems.

A Challenge of Constitutional Entitlement?

We are now ready to address the central question. Should the settlement of the constitutional status of Social Security in the terms of *Flemming v. Nestor* be disturbed? The strongest argument against such a move combines the substance of Harlan's argument from prudence—that Congress and the administrators need a degree of flexibility in responding to changes in the economic and social scene that would be difficult to achieve under rigid constitutional entitlements—with the added prudential factor that for fifty years the system has more than held its own in the political arena without the aid of court articulated entitlements. A second argument against constitutionalization would be simply that there is no problem today to which that is a solution. Why upset the applecart?

INSTILLING A SENSE OF SECURITY

There are problems, indeed, to which constitutionalization of Social Security is part of the solution. There is today a radical failure of trust in the continuation of Social Security to the point of the retirement of the current generation of Yale students. I am constantly astonished by the number of my students who, when asked, assert with some positiveness that they will not get Social Security.[25] There seems to be no comparable skepticism about whether bonds and treasury notes will be repaid.

The psychology of entitlement and security is, of course, a very complicated matter. I have no idea whether constitutionalization would be a major boon in the creation of a sense of security, but it might work. Because of the character of Social Security politics, very minor budget adjustments in the program can generate intense hysteria, reinforced when critics of the program dare to suggest that the benefit scheme in one respect or another constitutes an "unearned" gratuity. Most Americans share the judgment of political economy made by the Court or implicit in *Nestor*: mere gratuities are not entitled to the same confidence of entitlement and repose as are earned property rights. Moreover, they are aware of and in some respects share the ideological hostility to such gratuities evinced by certain politicians. Thus, the political litany of fidelity to the sacred character of Social Security benefits is necessary precisely because there are such deep doubts about it. And any tampering with the program is particularly risky lest it mark the beginning of an attack on the whole sensitive structure.

The Court, however, is not a very good public relations organ. It is doubtful whether a technical decision reversing in some respects the rea-

[25] See discussions of public opinion about Social Security in the Introduction and in Chapter 2 of this volume.

soning of *Flemming v. Nestor* would shake the foundations of the world and become a major media event. Nonetheless, the fabric of our confidence in traditional property interests, especially long-term debt, is woven of many strands. Of course, we need to have confidence in the economic order so that interest rates may be presumed to bear some rough relation to the time value of money. Of course we must have sufficient confidence that the political order will be stable enough to protect our property from force and violence. But we must also have some confidence that the structure of legal entitlement will have a similarly broad stability over time—not an ironclad guarantee against any change, but a continuity of expectation shaped to divergent as well as convergent circumstance. That part of the fabric of confidence constitutional rules may provide. At some point someone might say of Social Security, as one might say of a treasury note, "I am not sure whether the return is quite adequate, but I know it is safe." That seems to me a desirable turn of affairs.

SOCIAL SECURITY AS INSURANCE

The instrumental reasons for constitutionalizing Social Security are not the only ones. The Constitution ought not be thought of as essentially a confidence booster lest it be manipulated like GPO pamphlets to every other use. Quite apart from confidence boosting, however, it seems quite right to consider the government's obligation to Social Security participants as greater than the responsibility entailed in almost all other programs. Through its statutory structure as well as through the political rhetoric of its officials, the government has carefully nurtured the insurance characterization of Social Security. If the entire structure of the program cannot be explained in insurance terms, neither can it coherently be explained without insurance terms. The program would be blatantly unreasonable—more so in the past than now—did we not have the metaphor of currently and fully insured individuals. The redistributive elements of the program are, of course, present, but redistribution is not entirely absent from any classification of pooled risks. For example, in conventional group life insurance in the private market, the factors chosen as salient premium or eligibility variables carry an implicit redistribution in favor of some individuals who would not have fared as well with the choice of other variables.

One must ask, finally, whether the coerced payment in Social Security simply makes it different. Does transactional liberty create a distinct kind of entitlement in the market that ought not to be extended to the government imposed pooling of risks? In such cases, the argument might run, the judgment concerning the risks to pool and choice of payment or taxing scheme imposed are politically determined. They are not the choice of Social Security participants except through their role as citizens. Thus, the appropriate expectations to protect are politically salient—that is, participation and nondiscrimination in the relevant political processes. If the Social Security program existed in a vacuum, this argument would have considerable force. However, the existence of Social Security in something like its present form is the premise for almost all market activity related to retirement and insurance planning of moderate and low income people in the United States. Many private pension plans are keyed to the existence and gross characteristics of Social Security.[26] With perhaps the exception of the most affluent, individuals generally consider it a part of their insurance portfolio. The system has been designed to have this effect. Congress, in a number of instances, has recognized this interrelation of Social Security and other retirement or insurance programs by providing for rather gradual phase-ins of changes—even constitutionally mandated changes—to permit adjustment to the system. In 1984, the Supreme Court approved a five-year phase-in that prolonged the operation of what the Court had held to be an unconstitutional gender discriminatory rule, on the ground that it was desirable for Congress to permit affected individuals to adjust their retirement plans to the change.[27]

The law frequently attaches contract-like consequences to noncontractual transactions because of the reliance interests justifiably created among second and third parties. In the case of Social Security the United States has not purported to embark on an experiment; it has not purported to meet an emergency; and it has not purported to create a transition from one kind of condition to another. But the United States has purported to create a massive social insurance scheme that would be a permanent part of the security framework of every working family. When such an objective is accomplished, as it has been, the usual property presumptions should attach, for this change has been analogous to that worked by copyright or patent laws. Once the system is in place, change should occur to the extent possible prospectively rather than retroactively. The basic interest should be treated as vested as to those who have been thoroughly committed within the system. Finally, I address the question of what it means to give the system these property characteristics.

PROPERTY CHARACTERISTICS FOR SOCIAL SECURITY

Some critics of constitutionalizing what Bruce Ackerman calls "social property interests" suggest that to do so would entail a system by which

[26] See discussions of the integration of Social Security with private pensions in both Chapters 4 and 5 of this volume.
[27] See *Heckler v. Mathews*, 465 U.S. 728 (1984).

every change in entitlement would create the difficulties of running a highway over my backyard. The fact is that the cases involving changes in systems with long-term future obligations, though terribly confused, evince little reason to fear that flexibility could not and would not be preserved. The Supreme Court has had before it important state and federal legislation affecting private pension systems and their funding apparatus. Quite recently, in *Pension Benefit Guarantee Corp. v. R. A. Gray & Co.*,[28] the Court upheld provisions of the Multiemployer Pension Plan Amendments to Employee Retirement Income Security Act (ERISA) that retroactively required, employers withdrawing from multiemployer funds to pay certain withdrawal payments to help fund the future obligations to their prorata share of covered employees. Such payments were not required under prior law or under the terms of the contracts between the employer and its unions employees or between the employer and the multiemployer plan. In 1978 the Court reached a different conclusion in *Allied Structural Steel v. Spannaus*,[29] which struck down a state statute imposing a "pension funding charge" on employers terminating a pension plan or closing a Minnesota facility. *Spannaus* is distinguished in *R. A. Gray & Co.* on the ground that it rests on the more stringent restrictions on state legislation imposed by the contracts clause of the Constitution. The decision in *Spannaus* may also have been motivated by suspicion that the Minnesota statute was unfairly directed at a single company.

There is a long tradition, most prominently exhibited in the Sinking Fund Cases in 1878, of permitting the imposition of important changes in long-term obligations through the device of requiring particular accounting or security provisions with respect to the obligations.[30] Insofar as such changes have an obvious and direct relation to the real value of the obligations themselves, they can hardly be understood today as distinct regulatory matters. Indeed, the best way to understand these cases is to bring them within a principle of permissable readjustment of long-term obligation structures.

Thus, the closest private analogy to Social Security is a defined contributions system of annuities and insurance benefits. There is, in such systems, no property right to a defined benefit—only to share appropriately in the return. That seems to me to provide the base line for a constitutional protection in Social Security as well. Classifications that alter and amend the ways in which individuals do share in the return on the contribution mass as a whole should be afforded a reasonable level of scrutiny. Cases like *Flemming v. Nestor* are absurd injustices, and there is no

---

[28] *Pension Benefit Guaranty Corp. v. R. A. Gray & Co.*, 467 U.S. 717 (1984).

[29] *Allied Structural Steel v. Spannans*, 438 U.S. 259 (1978).

[30] The Sinking Fund Cases, 99 U.S. 700 (1878).

strong reason for tolerating such obviously punitive and political deprivations of benefits. Classificatory differences relating to widows and widowers or to legitimate and illegitimate children do present problems of justice that should be decided not as technical matters of pension law but as part of a broad conception of the salience of gender and legitimacy; that is, they should be decided by courts, not by administrative law judges or the secretary's delegates. Such issues need not impose massive problems for the system provided the courts permit flexible transitions to compliance and provided the courts generally permit the achievement of required parities or equality through adjustment down as well as adjustment up. In *Heckler v. Mathews*, decided in 1984, the Court has evinced good sense on both these aspects.[31]

The shift to constitutional property recognition for Social Security benefits will not, therefore, create massive changes in current or future entitlement. It will provide a check, probably wholly unnecessary, against wholesale abrogation that would leave some or all current participants radically unprotected. That check, even if unnecessary, may instill further confidence in the young that they, too, once embarked on this program, will reap a modest share of its benefits. Constitutionalization would also provide a check against a transition out of Social Security that leaves certain groups cared for while others are relegated to a welfare status. Should the campaign of the political far right for a transition to IRA's succeed, it is absolutely necessary, if we are not to break faith with those who have trusted in the "earned pension" rhetoric and statutory structure of Social Security, that the less well off retain their share as a matter of constitutional right. The worst of all worlds would be an exit of the affluent into an IRA structure that would upgrade their protection into constitutional status while the less affluent would remain as gratuity recipients without the added political clout of a truly broad-based program.

It goes without saying that nothing I propose would impose limits on the taxation of Social Security benefits. The tax question is a direct analogy to traditional property interests. An extant tax preference is never a constitutional barrier to the removal of that preference.

The extension of constitutional entitlement status to programs such as Social Security is hardly a first priority for the current Supreme Court. Yet, it is appropriate to consider the merits and demerits of any such changes before the crises that may provoke demands for them. Social Security does differ from most transfer programs because it does generally condition the receipt of benefits upon a substantial record of payments over time—either by the beneficiary or by a close relative of the benefici-

---

[31] *Heckler v. Mathews*, 467 U.S. 717 (1984).

ary. The Constitution can be read to require, as Justice Black argued, that the government "keep faith" with the participants in the program. The required faith is not the same faith a private insurer would be pledged to keep, for the program has a design of its own. But neither abrogation nor arbitrariness can plausibly be said to be keeping faith with the millions who depend on the system. A modest constitutional entitlement might go a long way.

II

4

Retirement Security Policy:
Toward a More Unified View

MICHAEL J. GRAETZ

Complaints about the unfairness of the Social Security pension system have become common. There are many variations on this theme, but the core of the unfairness claim is the failure of Social Security pensions to replicate the payment and benefit distribution structure of an "actuarially fair" insurance scheme. Middle- and high-income individuals would do better in such a private system. In this chapter I will argue that there is, indeed, unfairness in the Social Security tax and payments scheme, but that it is very nearly the opposite of the problem identified by private insurance advocates. Viewed from the perspective of overall retirement security policy, particularly when one interprets into the Social Security debate how income tax expenditures now shape that policy, the real fairness problems with Social Security are the regressivity of its tax structure and its modest capacity to maintain the standard of living of low and moderate wage earners.

Commentators typically describe a tripartite system that enables and encourages provision of income security for individuals for the years following their retirement from the work force: Social Security, employer-provided pensions, and individual savings. After acknowledging the existence of these three components of our national retirement security program, however, analysts routinely focus exclusively on one or another aspect.

To a large extent, the compartmentalization of analysis of the retirement security issue reflects a compartmentalization of expertise; there are experts on federal taxes other than Social Security, experts on federal

The author would like to thank Loretta Lynch for valuable research assistance. For a more extensive treatment of the general views expressed here, see Michael J. Graetz, "The Troubled Marriage of Retirement Security and Tax Policies," *University of Pennsylvania Law Review* 135 (April 1987): 851–908.

spending other than Social Security, experts on Social Security, experts on private pensions, and so on, who rarely seem to communicate with one another and, indeed, seem often to be operating with independent and unrelated criteria for their evaluations and policy recommendations. In this chapter, I treat all three elements—Social Security, employer-provided pensions, and individual savings—as separate parts of an overall national retirement security policy.[1]

Both the Social Security tax provisions and the income tax provisions have been subject to significant recent revisions. The 1983 Social Security Amendments apparently have put that program on a sound financial footing for many years to come,[2] and the massive 1986 Tax Reform Act contains substantial revisions in the income tax rules governing both private employer-provided pensions and individual retirement savings intended to make these provisions more responsive to national retirement security concerns.[3] These recent reexaminations of Social Security financing and income tax policies toward retirement savings make this an auspicious time—one almost uniquely free from a crisis atmosphere—for reviewing federal tax policies designed to facilitate retirement income security for the populace.

An effort to analyze as a unified system the three aspects of retirement security policy is inherently complex. It is difficult to conceive of a wider spectrum of public policy mechanisms intended to implement a single goal. Social Security is a mandatory national public program financed by the federal government's power to tax, fulfilled by the government's power to spend, and explicitly redistributional in both purpose and effect—redistributional both across generations and within the same generation.[4] Reliance on individual savings as a source of retirement security

---

[1] In the discussion I treat retirement security public policy goals as distinct from other national policy concerns. For example, although antipoverty and health insurance programs might well be influenced by the inability of retirees to return to the labor force and are sometimes treated in other countries as an integral part of retirement security policy, I here regard the antipoverty and health insurance issues as separate national problems and do not discuss them.

[2] Board of Trustees, *1985 Annual Report*, pp. 25–34; C. Ballantyne, "Actuarial Status of the OASI and DI Trust Funds," *Social Security Bulletin*, 44 (June 1985): 27; Munnell, "The Current Status of Social Security Financing," pp. 8–12; and Ball, Chapter 1 of this volume.

[3] U.S. Congress, Tax Reform Act of 1986, Conf. Rep. 841, 99th Cong., 2nd sess., Title XI, 1: Secs. 1101–03 (limitations on IRA deductions); Secs. 1111–20 (tightened nondiscrimination rules); Secs. 1121–24 (taxation of distributions from qualified pension plans). September 18, 1986.

[4] The distribution of Social Security benefits was intended from the outset to provide a minimum level of retirement security for all workers. Richard A. Musgrave, "A Reappraisal of Social Security Financing," in *Social Security Financing*, ed. Felicity Skidmore (Cambridge: MIT Press, 1981), p. 110; "Social Security provides proportionately larger benefits to lower-paid workers than to higher-paid workers." Nancy Altman-Lupu, "Rethinking

at the opposite extreme is often regarded as unaffected by direct government action. The important role played by federal tax policy—sometimes encouraging and sometimes inhibiting such savings—is typically ignored. Employer-provided pensions bridge these public and private extremes through a voluntary private program heavily influenced by the government. Employer pension plans are encouraged through income tax reductions, regulated according to the requirements to qualify for tax benefits, and backed, at least in a limited way, by a national insurance system. Together, these three retirement security sources reflect a full spectrum of policy initiatives—a federal social program for all Americans, a pluralistic communitarian program involving both employers and employees, and an individualistic program dependent principally upon familial self-reliance.

The Goals Of Retirement Security Policy

At the outset, I want to describe the goals of retirement security policy by which its success or failure may be measured in order to assess the extent to which these public and private programs together coherently address the retirement security problem. Although there are no doubt disagreements at the margin, the income shortfall because of retirement is lost income from labor, and this creates the "insecurity" that retirement security policy must address. Replacement of some significant portion of preretirement wages must therefore be the fundamental goal of retirement security policy. (At the limit, replacement of 100 percent of final preretirement wages, adjusted for inflation, would by this definition provide retirement security.) Further refinement of the retirement policy goal—for example, by specifying an appropriate percentage of wages that should be replaced for various categories of earners upon retirement—may prove more controversial. Yet it seems clear that national retirement policy includes two elements: (1) the maintenance of an adequate retirement income that will protect the elderly from widespread poverty, and (2) an income supplement to help ensure against an abrupt decline in a retiree's lifestyle. From a public policy perspective, this implies that a

---

Retirement Income Policies: Nondiscrimination, Integration and the Quest for Worker Security," *Tax Law Review* 42 (Spring 1986): 54. The pay-as-you-go financing mechanism of Social Security creates a redistribution of income from workers currently paying Social Security payroll taxes to retired workers. This financing method, coupled with rapidly increasing payroll tax rules, is viewed by many current workers as a wealth transfer to an affluent older population. James Tobin, Chapter 2 of this volume; Munnell, "Social Security Financing." This essay does not address the intergenerational distributional concerns regarding Social Security because Social Security is only one component of the retirement equity problem.

higher percentage of preretirement wages must be replaced for low- and moderate-income workers to ensure that retirement not produce a less than adequate income and that some percentage of income—perhaps targeted to achieve a standard of retirement living adequate to meet basic needs—should be replaced for all workers. It would be indefensible to consciously construct a national retirement security program that replaces a greater percentage of wages for higher than for moderate and lower earners.

This statement of retirement security policy, providing a postretirement threshold income to all retirees and maintaining preretirement lifestyles, at least of low- and moderate-income workers, serves to clarify the proper spheres of public subsidies and private savings. Factors such as retirees' incapacity to respond to income losses by working harder, the special health and mortality uncertainties of retirement, the general inabilities of persons to assess adequately such risks during their young or middle years, and, perhaps, a special or increased risk aversion of elderly persons suggest that, although low- and moderate-income employees deserve the greatest public policy attention, some public role in encouraging retirement savings is warranted for all workers.[5] Risks of advanced age may eliminate confidence about the continuing adequacy of even a substantial income level. However, the appropriate public role should decline in importance, however, as an individual's wealth increases, and at some point, since wealthier retirees will own investment assets that will produce income available for retirement consumption, reliance on individual and familial savings should dominate.

The completely public part of our tripartite retirement security system, Social Security, should meet fully the basic income adequacy goal for poorer workers, contribute substantially toward ensuring an adequate threshold retirement income for moderate income workers, and somewhat assist postretirement maintenance of lifestyle for all workers. This vision of a public social security function would require at least that all individuals with enough earnings to satisfy current basic needs substitute future for current consumption, for example, by taxing current wages now in exchange for subsequent wage-replacement retirement benefits. In addition, such a view confirms as appropriate the redistributional aspects of Social Security and dismisses the contention that a public Social Security program should resemble an actuarially sound retirement insurance plan for all workers, even those at the highest income levels.

[5] Daniel I. Halperin, "Tax Policy and Retirement Income: A Rational Model for the 21st Century," in J. Vanderhei, ed., *Search for a National Retirement Security Policy* (Homewood, Ill.: R. D. Irwin, 1987), pp. 1–2; Lawrence H. Thompson, "The Social Security Reform Debate," *Journal of Economic Literature* 21 (1983): 1425–67.

The Role of Federal Tax Policy

Federal tax provisions and policies serve as the common mechanisms for implementing this nation's retirement security policy, and they influence all three means of financing retirement security. This means that both tax policy goals and retirement security goals are at stake. The obviously dominant role of the payroll tax for funding Social Security has been the subject of considerable expert and public attention.[6] The public, however, has paid far less attention to how the provision of other benefits to retirees is also dramatically affected by federal tax rules, most importantly through the income "tax expenditure" provisions for qualified employer-provided pension plans and for individual savings through "individual retirement accounts" but also through income tax advantages for savings in other forms, such as home ownership and life insurance policies.[7] Implementation of retirement security policy through the tax system has not only failed to satisfy these retirement security goals, but it has also introduced important questions of tax fairness from the tax policy perspective. Tax equity requires that tax burdens be correlated with people's ability to pay; thus, persons with equal ability to pay taxes should pay equal taxes and persons with greater ability should pay more taxes. An ability-to-pay criterion for evaluating tax fairness conflicts in no way with the goals of retirement security policy; indeed, the two should be complementary. The ability-to-pay criterion enjoys broad acceptance as a fundamental tenet of tax justice, even though the details of its implementation are controversial. One need not reach the controversial boundaries, however, to conclude that the tax provisions implementing our na-

[6] Halperin, *Tax Policy and Retirement Income*; Thompson, "Social Security Reform Debate." See Munnell, "Social Security Financing." "The growing importance of the payroll tax in the federal tax structure has been a major factor in reducing the progressivity of the system, especially over the lower end of the income scale and for the working age population." Musgrave, "Reappraisal." See also, U.S. Congress, House, Select Committee on Aging, *Taxes, Social Security and the Deficit: Hearings*, 99th Cong., 1st sess., April 15, 1985. The enormous growth of the payroll tax over recent decades has also resulted in a substantial increase in the relative share of taxes imposed on labor (as opposed to capital income).

[7] "Approximately $79 billion was excluded from annual income tax liability, in 1986, as a consequence of pension contributions to and earnings under employer-sponsored pension arrangements." Altman-Lupu, "Rethinking Retirement Income Policies," n. 4. "The Dept. of the Treasury estimates the federal revenue loss associated with the IRA tax deduction at $12.7 billion in 1985." Employee Benefit Research Institute (EBRI), Issue Brief No. 52, *Retirement Income and Individual Retirement Accounts* (March 1986), p. 1.

See U.S. Congress, Senate, Committee on the Budget, *Tax Expenditures: Relationships to Spending Programs and Background Material on Individual Provisions*, 99th Cong., 2nd sess., 1986, pp. 121, 155–63; Merrill, "Home Equity and the Elderly," in *Retirement and Economic Behavior*, ed. Henry J. Aaron and Gary Bartless (Washington, D.C.: Brookings, 1984), p. 197; U.S. Congress, Joint Committee on Taxation, *Estimates of Federal Tax Expenditures for Fiscal Years 1987–1991*, Table 3, March 1, 1986.

tional retirement security goals fail to satisfy an ability-to-pay criterion, in fact, they present a serious threat to this basic principle of tax justice.

The first step in the analysis is to ask whether the tax provisions implementing national retirement security policy, viewed as if they constitute a coherent whole, satisfy this fundamental principle of tax justice. If not, we must then ascertain whether the distribution of federal retirement security benefits sufficiently offsets failures revealed on the tax side.[8] Along the way, we must endeavor to integrate retirement security and tax policy goals. The payroll tax is the appropriate place to begin.

The Payroll Tax

The Social Security tax rate is a proportional one; however, the Social Security tax burden is regressive. The fundamental problems in the imposition of the payroll taxes to finance Social Security occur at the bottom and top ends of the tax schedule. At the bottom, the payroll tax provides no exemption level or floor of wages below which the tax is not imposed, but at the top it does contain a maximum level or ceiling of wages subject to tax.

BURDEN ON THE WORKING POOR

Historically, the most significant inequity in the Social Security tax has been its imposition of a substantial tax burden on the working poor.[9] Unlike most taxing systems, the first dollar of wages has been subject to Social Security tax. For a family of four at the poverty level in 1984, payroll taxes equalled $711, nearly double the income tax burden of $365.[10] Increasing numbers of poor individuals and families are receiving a larger

[8] The question whether the inequities produced by the tax laws implementing national retirement security policy are somehow compensated for elsewhere in the tax system so that the ability-to-pay criterion is satisfied generally as a matter of overall tax policy is beyond the scope of this essay. For a more comprehensive discussion, see Michael J. Graetz, "The Troubled Marriage of Retirement Security and Tax Policies," *University of Pennsylvania Law Review* 135 (Spring 1987): 851–908. The dramatic growth of payroll tax burdens on income from labor in recent decades, coupled with substantial reductions in the 1980s in the burdens of federal taxation on capital and capital income, make it extremely unlikely that overall federal tax policy can be shown to redress the failures internal to the retirement security provisions.

[9] U.S. Congress, House, Committee on Ways and Means, *Federal Tax Treatment of Low Income Persons: Hearing Before the Subcommittee on Oversight*, statement of Charles McLure, 98th Cong., 2nd sess., 1984, p. 11; U.S. Congress, House, Committee on Government Operations, *Work and Poverty: The Special Problems of the Working Poor: Hearings Before the Subcommittee on Employment and Housing*, 99th Cong., 1st sess., 1985, pp. 21–22, Table 5.

[10] Committee on Ways and Means, *Tax Treatment*, p. 11.

share of their income from earnings, the percentage of total income from earnings of families at the poverty level increased from 28 percent in 1974 to 40 percent in 1981.[11] It is now essential to reexamine carefully the impact of Social Security taxes on the working poor. In 1981, 42 percent of all households below the poverty level paid Social Security payroll taxes,[12] and during the 1980s, the burden of Social Security taxes became much greater than federal income taxes for those at the poverty level.[13] The 1986 removal of six million poverty-level families from the income tax rolls leaves the payroll tax as the only substantial federal tax imposed on the working poor.[14]

Beginning in 1975, Congress recognized the fundamental unfairness of subjecting poor working families to a significant Social Security tax burden and enacted an Earned Income Tax Credit (EITC) in the income tax to provide a refundable income tax credit to poor families with dependent children. The 1986 legislation increased the EITC maximum earnings level and introduced indexing of the credit for inflation. To the extent that the earned income credit exceeds the income tax liability of poor families, it effectively reduces the Social Security tax burden of those families. This indirect relief from the Social Security tax burden of the working poor, however, even after its latest expansion, remains inadequate as an equivalent of an exemption level from the Social Security tax burden. The earned income tax credit is available only to a limited portion of the working poor: families with dependent children.[15] Moreover, if experience with the prior mechanism to relieve income taxes as an offset to Social Security—the retirement income credit—is any guide, the earned income tax credit seems likely not to be claimed by a substantial number of families entitled to it.[16]

Economists generally agree that both the employers' and the employees' shares of Social Security taxes are borne by employees in the form of reduced wages.[17] Thus, the 1987 combined payroll tax rate of 14.1 per-

[11] Ibid., 35; Statement of J. Coder, Census Bureau, Income Statistics branch chief.

[12] Ibid., p. 13; Statement of C. McLure.

[13] In 1981, 42 percent of all families below the poverty level paid Social Security taxes.

[14] Tax Reform Act, 1: 2–9.

[15] Internal Revenue Code Sec. 32; Tax Reform Act, 1: 24; sec. 111(b) of the amending 26 U.S.C. Sec. 32(i).

[16] Erwin N. Griswold and Michael J. Graetz, Federal Income Taxation: Principles and Policies (Mineola, N.Y.: Foundation Press, 1976).

[17] Both shares "are actually born by the employee in the form of lower real wages." Thompson, "Social Security Reform Debate," p. 1453; George F. Break, "The Economic Effects of the OASDI Program," in Skidmore, Social Security Financing, p. 47 and studies cited therein. But see, Browning, "Tax Incidence, Indirect Taxes, and Transfers," National Tax Journal 37 (1986): 532. Social Security payroll tax cannot fall exclusively on labor income.

cent is a substantial burden on low-income workers. In recent years, for example, the combined marginal income and payroll tax rate on a family of four earning $12,000 a year has been greater than the tax rate paid by wealthy investors on profits from capital gains.[18] The 1986 income tax legislation may well reverse this particular relationship, but it fails to address directly the basic problem of the significant tax burden of payroll taxes on the working poor.

This burden of Social Security taxes on the working poor is exacerbated by the income tax treatment of the Social Security tax. For those low- and moderate-income workers subject to the income tax, the inclusion of the Social Security tax in current wages and the corresponding subjection of that tax to current income taxation, although equivalent in present value terms (as long as tax rates remain constant) to the treatment of private pensions, requires an additional reduction of current consumption.[19]

The tax burden on the working poor is not the only source of regressivity. In addition, significant fringe benefits are exempted, and these accrue disproportionately to higher wage earners. The regressivity of the Social Security tax also occurs because of the declining effective rate of the tax that results from the ceiling on wages subject to the payroll tax. In 1987, all wages over $43,800 were exempt from payroll taxes (see also Table 4.1). Each of these problems demands revision.

FRINGE BENEFITS

Nontaxable fringe benefits as a percentage of employee compensation were estimated to have amounted to about 8 percent in 1960 and 16 percent in 1984. The Social Security Trustees' Report estimates that by the year 2060 fringe benefits will amount to more than one third of total compensation.[20] Although this estimation is merely an extrapolation from the past and thus may be unreliable, it does not seem unreasonable. In fact, the percentage of excluded fringe benefits is lower with respect to Social Security than for wages generally (estimated by the national Chamber of Commerce to be 37 percent of total wages) because of the interac-

[18] Committee on Ways and Means, *Tax Treatment*, p. 56; Statement of R. Greenstein, director, Center on Budget and Policy Priorities.

[19] Halperin, "Interest in Disguise: Taxing the 'Time Value of Money,'" *Yale Law Journal* 95 (1986): 506, demonstrates this equivalence.

[20] U.S. Congress, House Committee on Ways and Means, *Distribution and Economics of Employer Provided Fringe Benefits: Hearings Before the Subcommittee on Social Security and on Select Revenue Measures*, 99th Cong., 1st sess., 1985, p. 51; Statement of C. Ballantyne, chief actuary, Social Security Administration. See also Tobin, Chapter 2 of this volume.

TABLE 4.1   Social Security Tax Rates, Maximum Taxable Payroll, Taxable Payroll as Percentage of Total Payroll, and the Percentage of Workers with Earnings below the Taxable Maximum, Selected Years, 1960–1983

Year	Tax Rate (%)	Maximum Taxable Wages and Salaries ($)	Reported Taxable Wages and Salaries as Percentage of Total Wages and Salaries	Percentage of Workers with Earnings below Social Security Taxable Maximum
1960	3.0	4,800	79.9	72.6
1965	3.6	4,800	74.1	64.9
1970	4.8	7,800	80.4	74.9
1975	5.8	14,100	86.6	85.8
1976	5.8	15,300	86.4	85.8
1977	5.8	16,500	86.1	85.9
1978	6.1	17,700	85.6	85.9
1979	6.1	22,900	89.2	90.5
1980	6.1	25,900	90.0	91.5
1981	6.6	29,700	90.4	93.0
1982	6.7	32,400	90.7	93.5
1983	6.7	35,700	91.2	94.5[a]

SOURCE: U.S. Senate. Committee on Finance. *Tax Reform Proposals*, Section XVII, "Employee Benefits." Hearing, 99th Congress, lst sess., table IV.2 (replicating chapter 4 of a study by Dr. Chollet of EBRI).

[a] *Revising Federal Tax Preferences for Health Insurance.*

tion of the fringe benefit exclusion and the wage ceiling. The shift from cash compensation to fringe benefits narrows the Social Security wage base and requires a higher tax rate to produce identical revenues. A significant gain in tax equity would be accomplished by including in the Social Security wage base fringe benefits currently excluded. An equity gain would occur even if fringe benefits, as a percentage of total compensation, were relatively equally distributed throughout income classes; greater gains would occur if (as is probably true for pension benefits, for example) higher-income taxpayers had greater opportunity to avoid payroll taxes by obtaining compensation in the form of excluded fringe benefits. Obviously, the inclusion of fringe benefits in the payroll tax base would be of much greater importance if the wage ceiling were also repealed.

Implementing such a proposal would not be difficult technically. The rules under §401(k) of the Internal Revenue Code with respect to certain employee benefit plans provide a guide for including fringe benefit items in the Social Security wage tax base, even if those items are excluded from the income tax base. Under present law, including fringe benefits in the income tax base would automatically include such benefits in the Social Security tax base.[21]

PAYROLL TAX WAGE CEILING

Equity would also be significantly improved by eliminating the wage ceiling on payroll taxes. As Table 4.1 shows, currently only about 5 percent of workers covered by Social Security earn more than the maximum taxable earnings base. As the earnings of these individuals rise, the effective Social Security tax rate lessens as a percentage of total wages. Elimination of the wage ceiling would permit a revenue neutral reduction of about 2 percent in payroll tax rate,[22] or, alternatively, could finance significant tax relief for the working poor. Moreover, elimination of the wage ceiling, if accompanied either by a rate reduction or an exemption for the working poor, would not increase the overall burden of the payroll tax on labor and, therefore, would not further shift the tax burden from capital to labor. The massive cut in the top income tax rate—from 70 percent in 1941 to 28 percent in 1988—and the attendant virtual elimination of a progressive income tax rate structure make even more compelling the case for eliminating the regressivity caused by the payroll tax wage ceiling.

Thus, the first part of the tripartite retirement security system has three sources of inequity in its mandatory payroll tax contributions: (1) the imposition of a substantial tax burden on the working poor; (2) the exemption of significant fringe benefits which accrue disproportionately to higher wage earners; and (3) the payroll tax wage ceiling which leaves the highest earners with a lower effective tax rate than the rest of the earnings distribution.

Two major arguments are typically advanced against payroll tax reforms of the kind I have just suggested. First, the benefit structure is redistributive, and such redistribution justifies the regressivity of the tax contributions. Second, the objective of wage displacement makes the current system "unfair," precisely because it does not amount to an actuarially sound insurance scheme; under this view, lifting the payroll tax limit

[21] The Internal Revenue Code defines income subject to Social Security tax to include, but not limited to, all income subject to the income tax. Generally, the Code allows inclusion of some benefits for Social Security (FICA) tax purposes which are not counted as income for income tax purposes. See, e.g. Internal Revenue Code, sec. 409.

[22] House Select Committee on Aging, *Taxes Hearing*; Statement of Rep. Roybal, p. 4.

would exacerbate the lack of fairness. The first is the more straightforward argument.

PAYROLL TAX LINKAGE WITH BENEFITS

Opponents of changes at the top and bottom of the payroll tax system typically rely on the distribution of Social Security benefits as a complete justification for the inequities of the payroll tax. To be sure, when the benefits of Social Security are taken into account, Social Security has, for its first fifty years at least, been a very successful redistributive program. Social Security wealth (that is, the contribution of Social Security to household wealth) is distributed among different households far more equally than privately accumulated wealth, and Social Security has reduced the concentration of total household wealth. As noted in Chapter 2, Social Security benefits now replace about 41 percent of the earnings of active workers, about the same percentage as when the program began, but benefits today extend far more broadly over the labor force; about 96 percent of persons aged 65 or over receive benefits, as compared to 16 percent in 1950.

This redistribution does not go so far as to replace fully the income of low earners, in spite of the widespread belief that it does. This myth persists because, as Alicia Munnell has pointed out, benefits calculations are routinely based upon hypothetical workers with both a history of low earnings and a nonworking spouse, for whom Social Security will replace nearly 100 percent of preretirement earnings. Actual replacement rates for couples in the lowest earning quintile were 56 percent of preretirement wages.[23] Thus, Social Security benefits are inadequate to prevent widespread declines in living standards upon retirement, even of low and moderate wage earners.

The role of Social Security benefits in combating the prospects of widespread poverty among the elderly nevertheless accounts for a significant element of the redistributive quality of Social Security. To the extent that the United States is a nation committed to a national antipoverty "safety net" for all its people, apart from retirement security concerns, some portion of Social Security benefits might properly be regarded as attributable to our overall system of government transfers to the poor.[24] Surely this is

[23] Alicia Munnell, *The Economics of Private Pensions* (Washington, D.C.: Brookings, 1982), p. 20, Table 2–3.

[24] In FY 1984, approximately $8.1 billion of federally financed Supplemental Security Income payments were made. $5.8 billion, or 71 percent went to the disabled poor; $2.2 billion, or 27 percent, to the elderly poor; and $183 million, or 2 percent, to the blind. Staff of House Ways and Means Committee, 99th Cong., 2nd sess., *Background Material and Data on Programs within the Jurisdiction of the Committee on Ways and Means* (Washing-

the case, for example, whenever total government transfers to the elderly exceed 100 percent of inflation-adjusted final preretirement wages. It is not at all clear that the general antipoverty component of Social Security, as opposed to the wage-replacement retirement security component, should be financed by wage taxes rather than from more progressive sources of general revenues.[25]

In any event, within the context of the Social Security program taken by itself, the inequity of the contributions is redressed, at least in part, by the redistributive nature of the benefits.[26] But, critics assert, if that is the case, the argument for eliminating the payroll tax ceiling fails. They contend that elimination of the ceiling must be accompanied by a massive increase in the maximum Social Security benefits—up to as much as a hundred and fifty thousand dollars a year. For example, the basic contention is that subjecting the full amount of Lee Iacocca's wages to taxes must be accompanied by a dramatic increase in Lee Iacocca's Social Security retirement benefit in order to be actuarially fair.

The notion that eliminating the wage ceiling requires a massive increase in maximum benefits reflects a fundamental misunderstanding of the public function of the Social Security program as part of a more comprehensive national retirement system. Regarding the Social Security system as if it were a self-contained system necessarily linked to actuarially fair private insurance is simply inconsistent with decisions taken elsewhere within the public policies governing the overall national package of retirement security benefits. Looking solely to Social Security benefits as the test of fairness for high earners, including fairness of the payroll tax wage ceiling, skews analysis—to the great disadvantage of low- and moderate-income workers. This is where the other parts of the retirement system become relevant. Again, Lee Iacocca's retirement benefits are enhanced by a variety of tax advantages, both to plans sponsored by his employer and to his individual retirement savings.[27] As the next sections of this

ton, D.C.: Government Printing Office, 1985), p. 88. See p. 446: "Social security had the greatest impact upon reducing poverty other than earnings. . . . Social security income lifted approximately 9.7 million older persons out of poverty. Social security reduced the poverty rate among the aged from 51 percent to 14.1 percent—a reduction of 72.3 percent." Eligibility for ssi payments is detailed at 42 U.S.C. secs. 401 and following.

[25] For a discussion of the tax-transfer perspective on Social Security benefits see, Thompson, "Social Security Reform Debate," pp. 1436–37.

[26] But see Chapter 2 where James Tobin argues that differences in life expectancy as related to income act to offset the redistributive nature of Social Security.

[27] The tax advantages enjoyed by highly paid employees are not limited to retirement incentives. Favorable income tax treatment of capital gains and incentive stock options accrue to the benefit of employees in a position to exercise incentive stock options. Tax Reform Act, 1: 107, sec. 321 (Sept. 18, 1986). While a discussion of the cumulative effects of all tax advantages enjoyed by highly paid individuals is beyond the scope of this essay, the

chapter detail, a more comprehensive assessment of the distribution of retirement security benefits justifies wage payroll tax reform to reduce its regressiveness.

Employer-Provided Pensions

The public component of employer-provided pensions, both in subsidization and regulation, makes the common label "private pensions" quite misleading. Under the income tax laws, employer-provided pensions may qualify for special tax treatment in two ways. First, employers' payments into a pension plan are immediately deductible by employers, but they are not currently included in employees' income; in addition, the earnings of pension funds are not taxed as earned but accumulate free of income tax. This income tax treatment is clearly more favorable than for cash compensation, not only because pension funds accumulate earnings tax-free in contrast to the normal current income taxation of investment income but also because the deferral of taxation of compensation until retirement may permit taxation at lower rates.[28]

According to recent estimates of tax expenditures (that is, the revenue losses attributable to special federal income tax provisions), the largest tax expenditure for individuals by far is the net exclusion for employer-sponsored pension contributions and earnings. In 1985, for example, tax expenditures for employer-provided pensions were estimated to cost the Treasury nearly $53 billion, more than double the next largest tax expenditure item, the $25.5 billion lost because of the home mortgage interest deduction.[29] In fiscal 1987 before the effects of the 1986 Tax Reform Act are considered, the revenue loss attributable to employer pensions was estimated to total $77.45 billion.[30] Even if these estimates somewhat overstate the size of the government subsidy,[31] the tax incen-

tax advantages attached to retirement benefits are analyzed in subsequent sections in this chapter.

[28] The Tax Reform Act of 1986 may reduce opportunities for advantages of lowering an employee's marginal tax rate during retirement through revisions narrowing the income tax rates. If such rate revision is permanent, the 1986 Act may eliminate or decrease the shifting of income to a lower post retirement rate. See Senate Committee on the Budget, *Tax Expenditures* (Washington, D.C.: Government Printing Office), 1986, pp. 313–14. For the argument that a critical element regarding retirement savings is shifting the rate of tax see, Halperin, "Interest in Disguise," p. 520.

[29] For FY 1986–1991 projections, see, "Joint Tax Committee Releases Estimates of Federal Tax Expenditures," *Tax Notes* 762 (19 November 1985). Senate Committee on the Budget, *Tax Expenditures*, 1986, pp. 155, 159, 313.

[30] Senate Committee on the Budget, *Tax Expenditures*, 1986, pp. 313, 317. Halperin, *Tax Policy and Retirement Income*, p. 40, n. 117.

[31] The tax expenditure may be overstated for two reasons. First, they are on a cash flow,

tive to employer-provided pensions undoubtedly constitutes an extremely significant aspect of this nation's retirement security program.

Although there are nontax reasons for employers to establish pension plans and some employer plans predate the income tax, tax incentives to employer-provided pensions, at a minimum, have produced a substantial shift away from other savings toward pensions.[32] Private pension assets total more than one trillion dollars and now account for about one-half of all available U.S. investment capital.[33] It is therefore essential to evaluate the distribution of the benefits and burdens of this major element of government retirement security policy.

The distribution of government benefits to employer-provided pensions contrasts significantly with the targeting of Social Security benefits to low- and moderate-income workers. The revenue loss attributable to private pensions has been estimated to benefit disproportionately higher-income workers and the distribution of benefits from private pension plans is skewed in the same direction. Only 56 percent of nonagricultural workers are covered by employer-sponsored pension plans, and those most likely to be covered are employees with high earnings. In 1983, only 54 percent of employees with earnings below $25,000 were covered, compared to 82 percent with earnings of $25,000 or more.[34] Only the top quintile of the income distribution receives as much private pension income as Social Security. The recent expansion of pension fund assets notwithstanding, half the married couples and two-thirds of the unmarried persons who had recently retired received no more than $100 a month in 1982, and many of these received no private pensions. Historically, 66 percent of the tax benefit from employer plans went to the 16 percent of employees with incomes of over $20,000.[35]

---

not a present value basis, Munnell, *Economics of Private Pensions*. Second, they include more than the exemption of investment income. See Halperin, "Interest in Disguise."

[32] U.S. Congress, House Committee on Ways and Means, *Retirement Income Security in the United States: Hearings*, 99th Cong., 1st sess., 1985, Serial 50. For a discussion of the debate regarding whether retirement savings replace or increase savings, see Aaron, *Economic Effects of Social Security*; Skidmore, *Social Security Financing*. The savings is transferred to all types of tax-favored retirement vehicles. "Between 1980 and 1983, one percent of national savings was shifted to the IRA and KEOGH plan forms, while national savings fell." "Age Conference Explores Adequacy of Private Pension System," *Tax Notes* 335 (April 28, 1986) (statement of D. Salisbury, Pres., EBRI).

[33] "Ways & Means Subcommittees Consider Retirement Income Security," *Tax Notes*, 391 (July 22, 1985). See generally, Eugene Steuerle, *Taxes Loans and Inflation* (Washington, D.C.: Brookings Institution, 1985), pp. 15–18.

[34] EBRI, Issue Brief No. 51, *Pension Vesting Standards*; U.S. Congress, Senate, Special Committee on Aging, *The Employee Retirement Security Act of 1974: The First Decade*, 98th Cong., 2nd sess., Comm. Print 1984; Snyder, "Pension Status of Recently Retired Workers on their Longest Job: Findings from the New Beneficiary Study," *Social Security Bulletin* 49 (August 1986), pp. 9–11.

[35] Inadequate or less-than-expected benefits levels combine with the fact that pension cov-

In an effort better to correlate the conditions for pension eligibility for favored tax treatment with retirement security goals, the Tax Reform Act of 1986 contains a major revision of private pension rules. However, considerable uncertainties about that legislation's effectiveness remain. Critics are already complaining that the 1986 legislation is inadequate from a retirement security perspective;[36] this criticism may ultimately reflect inherent difficulties with relying heavily on voluntary employer-sponsored pensions as a significant source of retirement income for rank-and-file workers. The reasons for this difficulty are not hard to identify. There is a natural bias in a voluntary system that relies on tax incentives. High-wage workers are much more likely than low-wage workers, whose wages have already been reduced by more than 14 percent by the payroll tax, to make a trade-off between current cash compensation and deferred compensation in exchange for a tax reduction.

This natural distribution of private pension benefits toward higher wage earners has been further skewed by the existence of progressive rates under the income tax; the exclusion of wages from income is worth more to a higher-bracket than to a lower-bracket taxpayer. The 1986 lowering of tax rates and flattening of the tax-rate schedule will mitigate this factor somewhat, but there will remain a substantially greater incentive for a higher income taxpayer, subject to a marginal rate as high as 33 percent under the 1986 legislation, to reduce taxes than for a lower-income taxpayer with a 15 percent marginal rate. Moreover, the ability to borrow—either from pension plans or to finance pension savings—has the potential to undermine the effectiveness of the tax expenditure for retirement savings, and this disproportionately favors higher earners.

Public policy has attempted to redress the bias of private pension plans toward higher income earners by developing rules intended to ensure more adequate distribution of benefits to moderate-income workers. Most important are requirements about length of work before vesting, nondiscrimination, and integration with Social Security.

Vesting

A vested pension is one that carries nonforfeitable rights to benefits. A worker is entitled to full minimum Social Security benefits immediately

---

erage increases as earnings increase to result in little coverage or pension benefits paid to the lowest income workers who presumably need it most. Only 23 percent of men and 15 percent of women earning less than $5,000 per year had pension coverage, disregarding whether these employees were "integrated out" of any real benefits. More than 86 percent of men and 78 percent of women earning more than $20,000 per year were covered. "Pension Status of Recently Retired Workers," p. 9.

[36] See, Halperin, *Tax Policy and Retirement Income*; Altman-Lupu, "Rethinking Retirement."

after paying Social Security taxes for a minimum number of earning quarters.[37] Employer-provided pensions, in contrast, do not vest until the employee has worked for the same employer for a specified period of time during which the employer has made pension contribution on that employee's behalf. Although the Treasury had long attacked what it regarded as excessive delays in vesting, Congress did not require a minimum vesting schedule until it enacted the Employee Retirement Income Security Act of 1974 (ERISA).[38]

Length-of-service requirements attached to the receipt of pension benefits discriminate against marginal or unconventional workers. For example, part-time workers (those working 500 to 1,000 hours per year) can be entirely excluded under current pension participation standards.[39] As the work force becomes more mobile, increasing numbers of workers may forfeit pension contributions made on their behalf because of insufficient periods of employment with the same employer. Vesting requirements tend adversely to affect low-income workers and particularly to disadvantage minorities and women because of the demographics of their career patterns. Minorities have particular difficulties accumulating pension benefits because of their mobility, high rates of unemployment, and employment in jobs not covered by plans.[40] Similarly, the average woman stays at a job only 3.3 years, while the average man stays at a job 5.1 years.[41]

In practice, stringent vesting requirements have deprived important numbers of low- and moderate-income employees of any employer-provided pension benefits. They have also effectively redistributed pension contributions from lower-paid employees to higher-paid employees with more years of service. Stringent vesting requirements create a high rate of forfeited contributions which may be distributed among remaining plan participants; this both keeps employer costs down and further concen-

---

[37] The number of quarters has changed over time so that different standards apply to different age groups. See 42 U.S.C., 413 (1982 and 1985).

[38] ERISA contained three alternative minimum vesting schedules; full vesting of benefits was required either (1) upon the completion of ten years of job service with the same employer (ten-year cliff vesting); or (2) 25 percent vesting beginning after the completion of five years of service and increasing to 100 percent vesting after fifteen years of service; or (3) partial vesting of 50 percent was required after ten years of service with an additional 10 percent of the benefit vesting each year until 100 percent vesting occurs after 15 years of service. (The latter option was limited to plans which factor in age as well as service years). Beginning in 1982, so-called "top heavy plans" were required to meet three-year cliff vesting or six-year gradual vesting requirements. See generally, EBRI, *Vesting Standards.*

[39] Internal Revenue Code, sec. 416(b).

[40] U.S. Congress, House, Select Committee on Aging, *The Black Elderly in Poverty: Hearing,* 99th Cong., 1st sess., September 27, 1985.

[41] EBRI, *Pension Vesting.*

trates the tax advantages received by high-income employees. Thus, pension vesting requirements may actually reverse some progressive redistributive effects of Social Security benefits by allowing employers to shift forfeitures by lower-income shorter-service employees into the pension benefits of higher-income longer-service employees.

The Tax Reform Act of 1986 replaces the previous vesting standards with two new minimum requirements. Under the new rules, an employer must either fully vest pension benefits in workers after five years of service or vest 20 percent of benefits each year beginning at the end of three years of service so that such employees will be fully vested at the end of seven years of service.[42] These new minimum vesting requirements of the 1986 legislation improve substantially on the ERISA standards. If a five-year standard had been applicable in 1985, almost 2 million additional workers would have been entitled to vested benefits—a 7 percent increase in the number of men and a 10 percent increase for women. A three-year vesting requirement would have enabled 6.3 million more women to be eligible to receive pension benefits than under prior law.[43] It remains to be seen, however, whether the 1986 vesting compromise, which retains for employers some ability to use pension plan benefits as a means of promoting stability of their work force and avoids the additional administrative costs of an immediate vesting standard, will approach either the retirement security or tax justice advantages of an immediate vesting rule.

NONDISCRIMINATION

Nondiscrimination requirements specify that a minimum level of coverage must be met for a plan to qualify for favorable tax treatment. Nondiscrimination coverage requirements historically could be met by satisfying any of three alternative mechanical tests. The 1986 tax legislation strengthened the previous nondiscrimination requirement by stipulating that the percentage of employees covered under the plan who do not earn high wages be (1) at least 70 percent of highly compensated employees covered under the plan and (2) the lesser of 50 employees or 40 percent of all employees covered by the plan.[44]

The 1986 act, however, does not eliminate the ability of employer-provided plans to qualify for favorable tax treatment even though they cover a lower percentage of middle-income workers than of higher-income workers. A number of important exceptions to the nondiscrimination re-

[42] Tax Reform Act, 1: sec. 1113.

[43] President's Commission on Pension Policy, "Dimensions of the Retirement Income Problem," in *Coming of Age: Toward a National Retirement Income Policy* (Washington, D.C.: Government Printing Office, 1981), pp. 26–30.

[44] Tax Reform Act, 2: 412–18; 435–40.

quirements remain, for example, part-time employees and employees covered by collective bargaining agreements are excluded. And coverage of lower- and moderate-income employees remains restricted by the ability of employers to integrate their pension plans with Social Security benefits. The tightening of the nondiscrimination rules by the 1986 legislation provides little assurance that tax advantages for employer pension plans will be confined to those plans that meet national retirement security goals.

INTEGRATION

Prior to the Tax Reform Act of 1986, rules permitting integration of employer-provided plans with Social Security benefits allowed employers to limit pension benefits to employees whose earnings exceeded the Social Security wage ceiling. The 1986 legislation simplifies the extraordinarily complex rules of prior law, attempts to increase employer contributions and benefits on behalf of lower wage earners, and eliminates the ability of employers to provide no benefits for low wage earners and still qualify for favorable tax treatment.[45] The new integration rules, however, continue the prior practice of allowing employer plans to take into account the disproportionately larger benefits of Social Security for lower- and moderate-income workers. Such plans may thereby provide disproportionately greater benefits to higher wage earners, as long as proportionate benefits are achieved by the combination of Social Security and the employer plan throughout the wage scale.[46]

The basic concept of allowing integration of employer plans and Social Security is consistent with a unified view of retirement security policy, namely that Social Security and employer-provided plans should be considered together in structuring national retirement security policy. But such a policy allows benefits under employer plans to reverse the progressive distribution of Social Security benefits and, even after the improvements of the 1986 legislation, fails to ensure a coherent structure of retirement benefits in terms of a sliding scale percentage wage replacement

[45] Tax Reform Act, 1: 377, 379, sec. 1112.

[46] Tax Reform Act, 1: 371–377, secs. 1111, 1112(b)(3). Many plans meet the Code's nondiscrimination standards only if the Social Security benefits/payments by an employer are taken into account as if they were pension benefits provided under a pension plan. Although the Tax Reform Act reduces the percentage disparity allowed, employees earning more than $42,000 can still contribute a higher percentage of their annual income to a tax-advantaged pension plan. For example, under a defined contribution plan, the employer can still contribute at a rate of 10 percent, for compensation in excess of $42,000, while contributing only 5 percent for compensation below $42,000; and the plan will be considered as not discriminating in favor of highly paid individuals. See also, Altman-Lupu, "Rethinking Retirement," pp. 61–69.

goal that would provide greater than proportional wage replacement for lower- and moderate-income workers.

Individual Savings for Retirement

The third element of America's retirement income security program is individual savings. Necessarily, such savings will prove an effective source of retirement income only for those individuals who are able to save during their working lives or who have acquired investment assets from another source; the ability to save adequate private retirement assets therefore will tend to be concentrated in the higher-income classes.

Again, tax policy plays an important role. Because of the current taxation of investment income, an income tax has a natural tendency to favor current consumption as opposed to deferred consumption. In other words, an income tax is inherently less favorable toward savings than would be a consumption or wage tax.[47] Therefore, the heavy reliance of the federal government on the individual income tax as a source of revenues makes individual savings more costly than would be true if such revenues were raised through, for example, consumption taxation. As a result, a variety of income tax preferences have been enacted over the years in an effort both to stimulate savings generally and to encourage savings through particular kinds of investments or for specified purposes.

INCOME TAX INCENTIVES

The closest analogue to employer-sponsored pension plans are so-called Keogh Plans for self-employed persons. Benefits analogous to those available to employees under qualified pension plans were made available to the self-employed in 1962 but maximum benefits and the maximum annual contributions were much more limited until the Tax Equity and Fiscal Responsibility Act of 1982 generally created parity between Keogh plans and qualified pension plans. The tax revenue lost due to Keogh plans was estimated at $2 billion in 1986.[48]

In recent years, however, the most important tax incentive for individual retirement savings has been the Individual Retirement Account (IRA).[49] When the tax preference for IRAs was originally enacted in 1974, it provided an opportunity for tax-advantaged savings limited in amount and available only to eligible participants. Persons could not qualify for

---

[47] See Joseph Pechman, ed., *What Should Be Taxed: Income or Expenditure?* (Washington, D.C.: Brookings Institution, 1980).

[48] See EBRI, *Tax Expenditures.*

[49] In Chapter 5, Paul Starr expands on the discussion of the role of IRA in America's retirement security system.

the tax reduction if they were covered under an employer-sponsored pension plan. The 1981 tax legislation dramatically expanded opportunities for IRAs by allowing all individuals an identical tax savings. Up to $2,000 of annual earnings was permitted to be excluded from the income tax base through an immediate deduction; in addition, investment earnings on IRAs could be accumulated free of current income tax with payments from the account during retirement includable in the recipient's income.

This 1981 extension of IRA eligibility produced a revenue loss more than six times greater than that originally estimated.[50] Although the bulk of this revenue loss has been concentrated among higher-earning employees, the mass marketing of IRAs by savings institutions apparently also induced large numbers of middle-income taxpayers to shift away from general savings accounts (ineligible for tax savings) to tax-preferred retirement savings. At the end of 1982, people with less than $20,000 of taxable income accounted for 14.6 percent of the total IRA deductions claimed on income tax returns, compared to 28.4 percent for people with over $50,000 in taxable income. Despite this shift, only 15.3 percent of people making between $15,000 and $20,000 in 1982 had an IRA, compared to 59.7 percent of those earning $50,000 or more.[51] The revenue loss from the IRA provisions was estimated to be $14 billion in 1986.

The 1986 Tax Reform Act once again restricted the ability to enjoy the full benefits of IRAs to individuals not covered by employer plans. Under the 1986 legislation, single persons with more than $25,000 of income and married couples with more than $40,000 of income who are covered by employer plans are no longer eligible to deduct IRA contributions, but they may continue to receive tax free accumulations of investment income both on their pre-1986 contributions to IRAs and from additional annual IRA contributions of not more than $2,000 a year.[52] With this change, it is estimated that, of the 24.4 million individuals who had established IRAs prior to the 1986 Tax Reform Act, 15 percent (or 3.7 million) would have lost the IRA deduction completely, 12 percent (or 2.9 million) would have been eligible for a partial deduction, and 73 percent (or 19.8 million) would have been eligible for a full deduction had the Tax Reform Act been in effect.[53] The Joint Committee on Taxation estimated that eliminating the IRA deduction for people covered by pension plans would raise $25 billion of revenue over the fiscal years 1986–1991 and thereby contribute significantly to Congress's ability to lower income tax rates. Given the inaccuracy of prior estimates of people's behavior in response to IRA

[50] See, EBRI, *Tax Expenditures*, p. 317, for estimates of projected revenue losses from IRAs through 1991.

[51] EBRI, *Retirement Income*, pp. 7–8, Table 2.

[52] Internal Revenue Code, Sec. 219, 408.

[53] EBRI, Issue Brief No. 54, *Tax Reform and Employee Benefits* (1986), p. 19.

tax incentives, however, it is difficult to predict how many people will continue to establish or add to IRA accounts to take advantage of this more limited tax incentive or, alternatively, to begin or expand alternative tax-preferred retirement savings plans, such as cash or deferred arrangements (CODAS) to retain the IRA advantages of prior law.

Almost by accident,[54] the IRA provisions are now structured quite nicely to serve retirement security goals. Tax benefits comparable to those available to employer-provided pensions are available only to employees and other workers not covered by employer pension plans; in fact, for these workers, the $2,000 annual ceiling seems quite low compared to potential pension or Keogh benefits. Other individuals covered by employer plans are allowed to earn tax free investment income with respect to limited amounts of earnings annually put aside for retirement, but they do not enjoy the benefit of excluding these amounts from current income.

Alternative forms of tax-preferred savings, however, may undermine the efficacy of the 1986 limitations. In addition to IRAS, some provisions allow employees to make their own contributions to retirement savings plans in lieu of receiving cash salary and, by so doing, to achieve tax savings comparable to those available for employer contributions to employer-sponsored pension plans. The most important of these "salary reduction plans" are so-called § 401(k) plans, commonly known as CODAS.

[54] Congress did not adopt the 1986 restrictions on IRAs in response to concerns about their potential impact on employer-provided pension plans; on the contrary, retirement security concerns were dwarfed by other fiscal policies. Political momentum for a major tax reform required a reduction in the top income tax rates that could be accomplished without massive and unacceptable revenue losses only by slashing a wide variety of tax incentives, including those targeted to retirement savings. Congress's primary concern was that the long-term potential revenue loss from this increasingly popular retirement savings incentive would require significantly higher income tax rates than would be possible with the more limited incentive. The direct linkage of tax rates and tax expenditures for retirement savings occasioned by the requirement of revenue neutrality in the 1986 legislation has made unmistakable the contention of tax expenditure critics that income tax reductions such as these must ultimately be paid for by higher taxes on those who do not benefit. The potential distributional consequences, therefore, of income tax incentives for retirement savings utilized predominantly by higher-income taxpayers call into question not only the fairness of such incentives themselves but also the routine practice of ignoring the existence of such incentives when assessing the overall fairness of our public retirement security policies.

Congress was also aware of the sparse evidence that the IRA provisions had been effective in stimulating overall national savings; widely available IRAs had instead simply induced a massive shift of general savings to IRAs. From the perspective of retirement security policy, such a shift of savings may be desirable, even without any substantial increase in aggregate national savings. The 1986 restrictions on income tax incentives for IRAs, however, demonstrate an important political difficulty in relying heavily upon income tax incentives as a principal mechanism for implementing national retirement security policy: retirement security concerns may often be overridden by Congress's perceptions of more pressing fiscal policy needs.

From the perspective of national retirement security policy, the critical issue with respect to CODAs is whether, on balance, these tax preferences stimulate additional net increases to retirement savings by encouraging savings for retirement that would not otherwise occur or whether these plans primarily are substitutes for employer contributions to pension plans that would discriminate less in favor of high earners.[55]

The 1986 legislation both tightens nondiscrimination requirements for CODAs and limits the maximum annual elective deferral of compensation under such plans to $7,000, including any amounts added to an IRA. Tax-deferred annuity plans offered by charitable organizations, public schools, colleges, or universities are also brought more closely into conformity with qualified employer-provided pension plans with respect to coverage, nondiscrimination, withdrawal, and distribution provisions; a special annual $9,500 contribution limit is also included.[56] These new limits are substantially lower than the new maximum annual deductions available under qualified employer-provided pension plans; for example, under defined contribution plans the 1986 act permits a maximum annual contribution of $30,000, to be adjusted in subsequent years for inflation. (The defined benefit limitation is not readily comparable.) The 1986 Tax Reform Act changes with respect to these types of salary reduction plans WERE intended better to rationalize the relationship between IRAs, salary reduction plans, and employer-provided pension plans and to inhibit further trends in the direction of substituting salary reduction plans for pension coverage.

The Tax Reform Act of 1986 reflects a major effort to rationalize the rules governing employer-provided pension plans, IRAs, and salary reduction plans by independently assessing these programs in terms of either tax policy or retirement security policy. In addition, by limiting availability of IRAs and maximum deductible employee contributions to salary reduction plans, the 1986 legislation should strengthen the relationships among these alternative arrangements for tax-preferred retirement savings from the perspective of a unified retirement security policy. The efficacy of these retirement savings incentives, however, both as an independent stimulus to retirement savings and as a complement to Social Security

[55] See, Halperin, *Tax Policy and Retirement Income*, for a discussion of the operation of 401(k) plans. These savings plans, which do not meet the minimum participation and nondiscrimination requirements to qualify for the additional tax advantages of qualified pension plans, are named 401(k) plans after the Internal Revenue Code section which provides guidelines for their use.

[56] Internal Revenue Code, sec. 457, allows governmental organizations to gain some tax advantages through the use of unfunded deferred compensation plans. Internal Revenue Code, sec. 501(c)(18), allows nongovernmental tax-exempt organizations to establish pension plans which qualify for some tax advantages without requiring such plans to meet strict nondiscrimination standards.

and employer-provided pensions, may depend on whether other less restrictive tax-favored means of savings could constrict the desirability of
either IRAs or salary reduction plans for moderate- and high-income
workers.

INCENTIVES FOR NONRETIREMENT SAVINGS

The existence of tax-preferred savings opportunities not explicitly directed toward retirement may serve to enhance the total amount of individual savings that occurs during an individual's working years; thus, it
may make a greater amount of savings available for spending during retirement than otherwise would have been the case. However, the existence of opportunities for tax-preferred savings not directed toward retirement, by allowing taxpayers equivalent tax reductions through less
restrictive alternatives, may inhibit the ability of Congress to fashion restrictions on tax-preferred retirement savings that would better serve national retirement security policy. Thus, the nature and extent of tax-preferred savings opportunities other than explicitly for retirement savings
may have a very significant impact on both the efficacy and fairness of
tax provisions directed toward retirement savings. The potential deflec-
tion of savings because of such seemingly unrelated provisions may affect
employer-sponsored plans as well as individual retirement savings. Income tax preferences for home ownership and life insurance illustrate this
tension.

My purposes here do not require a detailed look at the tax preferences
for savings through either home ownership or life insurance. Suffice it to
say, both enjoy significant tax advantages. All of the real and imputed
income from owner-occupied housing (the returns to equity and the annual rental value) is, in effect, tax exempt, and deductions for interest and
property taxes may produce a negative tax on income from owner-occupied housing.[57] The exemption from current taxation of investment income earned by individuals in connection with reserves on savings
through life insurance products offers a widely available means of unlimited tax-free savings.

Options to save through investments in home ownership or life insurance may therefore offer individuals significant opportunities to achieve
tax reductions generally comparable to those available from tax-preferred retirement savings without subjecting them to the retirement sav-

[57] Although this is not the only tax advantage to owner-occupied housing involved, some
sense of the magnitude of this aspect can be garnered from the fact that the estimated revenue loss from the deductibility of mortgage interest on owner-occupied homes was $27.1
billion in 1986, and it is projected to rise from $33 billion in 1987 to $51.5 billion in 1991.
Senate, *Tax Expenditures*, 155.

ings restrictions. There are no maximum limitations on the annual investments eligible for such benefits, no nondiscrimination requirements that demand substantially equal treatment for other individuals, no restrictions on the time at which funds may be withdrawn from such savings, no delays in vesting of such benefits, and no loss of benefits when one changes employers. The ability to save through home ownership and life insurance free from the burdens of income taxation should serve to enhance the amounts of overall individual savings of higher-income individuals who have discretionary income available for such savings during their working years. It is unclear, however, from the point of view of national retirement security policy, whether this advantage outweighs the potential effects of these less restrictive tax-preferred alternative savings opportunities in reducing pressures from higher-income employees on employers to establish and maintain pension plans and in moving IRAs and salary reduction plans lower on higher-earning employees' lists of savings priorities.

Although restrictions on both these forms of savings were considered in connection with the 1986 legislation, none were adopted, and the continued vitality of such nonretirement savings incentives in the income tax seems assured. This should ease concerns about the need to provide new tax preferences to assure that higher-income individuals have tax-preferred opportunities to save as a means of maintaining lifestyle during their retirement. But it should also limit significantly the potential efficacy of severely restricting opportunities for high-income individuals to enjoy tax-preferred savings for retirement.

Moreover, the continued existence of tax preferences for nonretirement savings emphasizes the importance of directing regulations on incentives for creating and maintaining retirement pension plans at employers rather than relying principally on exhortations from moderate- and higher-income employees as a stimulus to such plans. Such nonretirement income tax savings incentives also make apparent the risks inherent in relying predominantly on income tax incentives as a means of implementing national retirement security policy, risks that become even greater when the possibility of borrowing is taken into account.

THE EFFECTS OF BORROWING

In recent years tax analysts have identified a phenomenon labeled "tax arbitrage." One version of this phenomenon is borrowing and making tax-deductible interest payments to purchase or carry assets that produce tax-preferred income; for example, a person borrows money to purchase or carry tax-exempt state and local bonds. A second type of tax arbitrage—labeled by Eugene Steuerle as "pure tax arbitrage"—occurs when taxpayers are able to borrow to purchase or carry tax-preferred assets whose pretax rate of return has not been reduced as a result of their tax advantage; for example, the retirement security tax preferences offer important opportunities for pure tax arbitrage. Such opportunities may both defeat the retirement security goals of the income tax expenditures for retirement savings and, in addition, undermine distributional goals of both tax and retirement policy. The following example demonstrates this point.

Assume that an individual borrows money from a bank and deposits the money in an IRA either with the same bank or another bank. For simplicity, assume that the interest paid on borrowing is identical to that earned by the IRA, say 8 percent. The taxpayer will achieve an overall tax reduction by deducting the interest payment on the borrowing, while excluding or deferring from taxation the IRA receipts. Note that in this case there has been no increase in savings either by the individual or in the aggregate; liabilities and assets have increased by an equal amount both in the economy and for the individual. A taxpayer in the 28 percent bracket who could engage in $10,000 of borrowing and asset transactions would save $224 in tax even though nothing was added to net savings. This is an identical tax saving to that which would occur from investing $10,000 of the taxpayer's own assets and excluding the $800 investment income from tax. Thus, the full tax expenditure is available to taxpayers who can borrow, even though no additional net savings has been made available either to the economy or to the individual for spending during retirement.

Borrowing to purchase pension assets, salary reduction, IRAs, and life insurance all offer opportunities for pure tax arbitrage of the sort described in the preceding example. These tax and savings effects will occur whether the individual borrows directly from the tax-preferred assets or whether the taxpayer borrows from an unrelated lender. Limitations on borrowing from IRAs, salary reduction plans, or pension funds will therefore be effective in precluding "pure tax arbitrage" only for those taxpayers who do not have other borrowing sources on which the interest is deductible. Limiting the maximum amounts that can be placed in the tax-preferred account will likewise limit the amount of tax arbitrage possible, and denying deductions for interest paid will also restrict such arbitrage.

The Tax Reform Act of 1986 reduces the maximum amount of annual tax-preferred retirement savings, constricts taxpayers' abilities to borrow from retirement savings assets, and limits the deductibility of interest in connection with borrowing to purchase or carry tax-preferred retirement security assets. In combination, these restrictions should inhibit the aggregate ability of taxpayers to undermine retirement security policies by engaging in borrowing transactions. They do not, however, eliminate all opportunities for pure tax arbitrage. Such opportunities will remain available, for example, to those individuals who can borrow on home equity loans and retain the advantage of interest deductibility.

The constraints on tax arbitrage included in the 1986 act should be most effective with regard to taxpayers whose ability to borrow is similarly constrained. Thus, low- and moderate-income individuals, unable to borrow additional amounts in a manner that produces deductible interest payments, will be eligible for the income tax expenditures directed to retirement savings only if they actually increase net savings for retirement. But high-income taxpayers may continue to have arbitrage opportunities that will enable them to take full advantage of the retirement security income tax preferences without adding at all to their retirement savings. This state of affairs not only raises additional questions about both the fairness and the efficacy of relying on income tax preferences for retirement savings as a major element of our national security policy, but it also further skews the distribution of the income tax advantages in the direction of high earners.

Viewing Social Security and income tax preferences for employer-provided pension plans and individual retirement savings as a comprehensive retirement security package calls into question much common wisdom regarding our national retirement security program. The income tax benefits skewed in the direction of higher-income individuals render indefensible the dramatic regressivity of the payroll tax to finance Social Security. A floor to exempt low-income workers from Social Security tax burdens, at least once a minimum number of quarters to assure benefits has been accumulated, would be a significant improvement in the fairness of the payroll tax; the earned income tax credit remains inadequate to this task even after its 1986 expansion. When the distribution of income tax benefits for private retirement savings is taken into account, the payroll tax ceiling that reduces the burden of the wage tax for the less than 5 percent of employees with wages in excess of $43,000 also becomes indefensible. Income tax-favored benefits are sufficiently great that those who argue that elimination of the payroll tax ceiling requires an extraordinary increase in the maximum Social Security benefit need not be taken seriously.

The income tax contains massive tax benefits intended to stimulate voluntary employer-provided pension plans and discretionary individual savings for retirement.[58] The only justification for these subsidies is that Social Security provides an inadequate level of wage replacement for workers in all income classes. The analysis of this chapter, however, dem-

---

[58] For more detailed discussion of the scope and distribution of such benefits, see Graetz, "Troubled Marriage."

onstrates that reliance on tax expenditures for voluntary employer and individual retirement savings plans is highly questionable as a means of furthering national retirement security policy; the tax expenditure mechanism is naturally skewed in favor of higher earners. And it is not at all clear that even substantial tightening of the conditions necessary to obtain such tax benefits, as contained in both the 1974 and 1986 legislation, will be sufficient to guarantee a distribution of benefits that is fair to the low- and moderate-income workers who should have first claim on public subsidies to retirement savings. The ability to ensure a fair distribution of benefits is constrained by the voluntariness of the system, by the necessary prospect that the details of retirement security income tax expenditures will be held hostage to overriding fiscal or tax policy concerns, and by the ability of tax planning—particularly borrowing in this instance—to undermine public policy goals.

The analysis in this chapter raises a significant question: Is there any alternative to extension of mandatory retirement security provisions as a means of ensuring both a fair distribution of public benefits and adequate retirement income for retirees at all income classes? The massive reexaminations of the income tax expenditures for employer-sponsored pension plans and individual retirement accounts in 1974 and again in 1986 imply that, although Congress is willing to go quite far in an effort to ensure some distribution of benefits to low- and moderate-wage earners, tax expenditures to continue the private pension system seem to have become politically untouchable. Even the prospect of a 20 percent or greater reduction in tax rate overall from repealing these tax expenditures does not seem sufficient to generate their demise. The restructuring of the IRA provisions in order to cap the top income tax rate at a percentage lower than 30 percent seems as far as Congress is currently willing to go. At the same time, current political attitudes are moving the economy in the direction of less rather than more regulation and a requirement of mandatory employer-provided pension plans does not seem politically realistic. Thus, as a practical matter, the pressing question is whether a better compromise can be achieved.

Without a basic change, the present structure offers little hope for providing a retirement income security for middle-income employees. Great improvement seems possible by imposing an income tax flat rate—say of 10 to 15 percent—on the investment income of pension funds or, alternatively, imposing an excise tax similar to that now imposed on assets of private foundations—equal to about 2 to 4 percent of total assets contained in pension funds Keoghs, salary reduction accounts, and IRAs— and adding the proceeds of such a tax to the trust fund for Social Security. In combination with the elimination of the payroll tax wage ceiling recommended above, these revenues could be used to provide current payroll tax relief to the working poor and to provide funds that would move significantly in the direction of 100 percent wage replacement for low- and moderate-income retirees. These monies might also forestall future increases in the payroll tax burden on the middle class. Such a tax would not inhibit the opportunities for higher-income individuals to save through both employer-sponsored plans and tax-favored discretionary savings.

If a substantial change of this sort is not made, further attention must then be given to tightening opportunities for tax savings in the absence of any significant retirement savings. In particular, the problems that arise from coupling tax-preferred retirement savings with borrowing must be considered in greater detail in an effort to limit tax preferences for retirement savings to those instances where net addition to retirement savings actually occurs.

5

Social Security and the American Public Household

PAUL STARR

Few other programs illustrate the achievements and limits of the American public household better than Social Security. By public household I mean the collectively recognized sphere of common needs and obligations.[1] Beginning in 1935, Social Security brought into that sphere a series of major obligations for income support, most especially insurance against income loss in old age. The program that has unfolded since then represents the largest and to all appearances the most durable commitment of our public household. Its erosion, replacement, or collapse would be an unmistakable watershed in American history.

For the elderly, the achievements of Social Security have been at once material and political. Primarily as a result of its benefits, the median per capita income of the aged is today as high as that of younger people, although the unmarried elderly—mainly women—continue to be worse off, receiving only three-fifths the income of single adults under age 65.[2] The rate of poverty among the aged has dropped to approximately the same level as the population as a whole.[3] Moreover, these gains in income security seem to have significantly improved the lives of the elderly. Indicators of social well-being and distress, such as rates of suicide and mental illness and overall measures of health, suggest that the elderly are better off today than twenty years earlier, particularly when compared to the young, whose condition has worsened during the same period.[4]

For the elderly, the political achievement of Social Security lies in

---

[1] On the concept of the public household, see Daniel Bell, *The Cultural Contradictions of Capitalism* (New York: Basic Books, 1976), pp. 220–27.

[2] Susan Grad, "Incomes of the Aged and Nonaged, 1950–82," *Social Security Bulletin* 47 (June 1984): 3.

[3] *Ibid.*, p. 7

[4] Samuel H. Preston, "Children and the Elderly in the U.S.," *Scientific American* 251 (December 1984), 44–49.

largely overcoming the risks and uncertainties that might be expected to follow from depending on the public budget. No doubt the voting power of the elderly discourages any tampering with Social Security. But more than that, the structure of the old-age insurance program, its earmarked financing, and the rhetoric used to explain it have also given the obligations to beneficiaries an exceptional moral and political force. For decades that force shielded the program from direct assault, promoted its expansion, and even now, amid severe budgetary pressure, helps preserve it against retrenchment. The exemption of Social Security from the Gramm-Rudman balanced-budget legislation exemplifies its special position.

However, it would be shortsighted to say that public opinion today produces this protected position in the budgetary process, since contemporary opinion is in part the result of the special position given Social Security from its inception. Because Social Security is financed by its own tax, it can be segregated from the rest of the budget. Because the tax payments are represented and understood as contributions toward one's own retirement, benefits are "earned." And because they are earned, it is unthinkable to deny them or terminate the program. The social contract established by Social Security, together with the indexing of benefits in 1972, moved income determination for the aged into the public household but largely out of partisan politics and the budgetary process. And this, in a sense, is another kind of security: the political security that protects Social Security, which in turn protects the economic security of the elderly.

Yet Social Security also testifies to the limited reach of the American public household. When all its programs are considered together, Social Security seems less generous than its Western European counterparts. To this day it fails to provide health insurance to all citizens or even to a majority of the poor, and it has no provision for short-term sickness benefits.[5] Social Security financing is regressive, and the insurance analogy used to explain its retirement benefits suggests individuals pay entirely for themselves and hence encourages Social Security recipients to distinguish their claims as morally superior to those of people on "welfare." These widely shared moral sentiments narrow the boundaries of the public household, but they anchor Social Security in it. In effect, the New Deal sacrificed broader income redistribution for the sake of politically entrenching old-age pensions. President Roosevelt knew exactly what he was doing when he personally insisted on financing Social Security en-

[5] For more on the origins and limitations of America's system of government-provided health insurance, see Paul Starr, *The Social Transformation of American Medicine* (New York: Basic Books, 1982) and Chapter 7 of this volume.

tirely out of the payroll tax. Responding to a complaint by an academic that the payroll tax was regressive, F.D.R. declared that the reasons for the tax were "political all the way through. We put those payroll contributions there so as to give the contributors a legal, moral, and political right to collect their pensions. . . . With those taxes in there, no damn politician can ever scrap my social security program."[6] And ever since Alf Landon went down to thunderous defeat, no serious national candidate has tried.

But Social Security may not remain impregnable, as it has so long appeared.[7] I am not suggesting that the program is likely to be "scrapped," but it may well lose its dominant role in providing retirement income. For decades, however much they resented Social Security as a symbol of the New Deal and resisted its expansion, conservatives were obliged to accept the framework it established. But in the last decade, they have worked out a more subtle and attractive alternative: privatization. Rather than abolish the program, as conservatives like Milton Friedman have long advocated, they want to substitute tax-subsidized instruments of private retirement provision. The leading proposal would pay off current beneficiaries while allowing taxpayers to opt out of Social Security by switching an increasing portion of their taxes into enlarged individual retirement accounts (IRAS).[8]

Of course, proposals for privatization made no headway whatsoever during what might seem at first glance to have been a golden opportunity in the early 1980s: the most conservative national administration of the last fifty years and Social Security's most serious fiscal crisis. But although the crisis shook public confidence in the program, it aroused the anxieties of beneficiaries and left little room for structural change. A more serious opportunity for conservative reform may develop in the 1990s, when, contrary to public expectations, Social Security should start accumulating the large reserves meant to be drawn down between 2020 and 2060 to pay for the retired baby-boomers. The prospect of those growing reserves may open up room for shifting the public/private balance in the direction of the private sector without an immediate threat to current beneficiaries.

For four additional reasons it would be a mistake to dismiss the long-

[6] Martha Derthick, *Policymaking for Social Security* (Washington, D.C.: Brookings Institution, 1979), p. 230; Arthur J. Schlesinger, *The Age of Roosevelt*, vol. 2, *The Coming of the New Deal* (Boston: Houghton Mifflin, 1959), pp. 308–9.

[7] For the rest of this chapter, "Social Security" is primarily used, as it is commonly understood, to refer to old-age pensions alone, not to other social insurance programs, such as survivors, disability, health, and unemployment insurance.

[8] The plan is the work of Peter Ferrara and has been sponsored by such organizations as the Heritage Foundation and U.S. Chambers of Commerce. For the most extensive treatment, see Ferrara, *Social Security: The Inherent Contradiction*.

run prospects of privatization. First, Social Security has lost legitimacy in the eyes of economists and other professional analysts of public policy. The program now stands accused of grave crimes against capital accumulation and economic growth; that these accusations may well be groundless is not necessarily decisive. Social Security is no longer above suspicion. In the mass media and journals of opinion the program is regularly subject to severe criticism for its effects on equity among generations. Precisely because the program has succeeded, the elderly are no longer seen as necessarily needing transfers from the young.[9]

Second, the last decade, with its repeated crises in Social Security finance, has gravely weakened the popular mandate the system long enjoyed. Public opinion studies in the early 1980s indicated that the majority of young workers doubted Social Security would ever pay them back. Moreover, workers, old and young alike, as well as retirees, believed they would get less for their money from Social Security than from private pension plans.[10] When asked how much money out of $100 in Social Security taxes goes for administration, the median response in a 1981 opinion survey was $52.10. The real figure that year was just $1.30, but only 2 percent of the sample thought that it might be nine dollars or less.[11] These perceptions of future benefits, the rate of return, and administrative costs reflect a pervasive disbelief that government can do anything efficiently. Even if unfounded, this distrust may provide a source of political support for privatization. Had Social Security been voluntary, the last decade might well have seen a run on the system. When taken as interest groups, Americans seem strongly in support of the program, but their commitment would appear weaker if as individuals they were allowed to vote with their feet—and this is the opportunity many conservatives would like to give them.

Third, just as Social Security was a slow-starting program whose full implications were not evident for decades, so, too, may a more recent,

---

[9] For some examples, see Paul Taylor, "The Coming Conflict as We Soak the Young to Enrich the Old," *Washington Post*, January 5, 1986; Thomas E. Ricks, "People's Perception of the Elderly as Being Poor is Starting to Fade," *Wall Street Journal*, December 19, 1985; and Phillip Longman, "Justice Between Generations," *The Atlantic Monthly* (June 1985): 73–81.

[10] Louis J. Harris & Associates, Inc., *Retirement and Income: A National Research Report of Behavior and Opinion Concerning Retirement, Pensions, and Social Security* (New York: Garland Publishing, 1984), pp. 38–42; comparing Social Security, private employer pensions, government pensions, and union pension, Harris found that current and retired employees as well as business leaders gave Social Security the lowest rating. See also "Social Security Insecurity," *Public Opinion* (August–September 1981): 35; Leonard Goodwin and Joseph Tu, "The Social Psychological Basis for Public Acceptance of the Social Security System," *American Psychologist* (September 1975): 875–83; and Introduction, n. 6, and Chapter 2, n. 6.

[11] "Social Security Insecurity," *Public Opinion*, p. 35.

slow-starting group of federally subsidized retirement programs have major impact in the future. I am referring to the IRAs, Keogh plans, and
401(k) and 403(b) salary reduction plans. These individualized retirement plans lost ground in the 1986 tax reforms, but the IRAs, in particular, remain an important and popular prototype for the alternative envisioned by advocates of privatization. In the long run they may be more
seductive as an alternative to Social Security than employer-run pensions.
Unlike most pensions, they are immediately vested and fully portable;
and unlike both pensions and Social Security, they permit individual control and represent cashable and bequeathable assets.

Finally, the Social Security system is maturing. Over the next several
decades, the implicit real return on Social Security, although still positive,
will be falling, compared to the high returns provided to earlier beneficiaries. The program initially conferred a "lifetime bonus" on the earliest
cohorts, who paid taxes into the system for only part of their working
lives. Similarly, whenever benefits have been raised, as in the 1970s, current beneficiaries have received a windfall. Because of its progressive benefit structure, Social Security has always offered a smaller return to upper
income workers than to lower income workers of equal longevity; yet
even for the rich the return has exceeded that of any private annuity. But
as the system matures and the value of the lifetime bonus declines, upper
income groups especially will have more of an objective basis for the dissatisfaction they already feel.

I am not suggesting that exit from the system would be smart, even for
the affluent. Because Social Security benefits are indexed, they offer protection against inflation that cannot now be duplicated in the private sector. Even those with private pension benefits might be well advised to
retain Social Security coverage as part of a balanced portfolio of retirement assets. But like many other aspects of public/private comparisons,
this difference in risk protection may not be understood widely enough
or valued highly enough to assure Social Security the political security it
has enjoyed in the past.

So the case for privatizing Social Security—wholly or partially—needs
to be examined from the standpoint of its merits, potential appeal, and
political practicality. I begin by reviewing the system of public/private
relations in the provision of retirement income; then I turn to a critical
review of the proposals and claims for privatization; and, finally, I look
at the forces likely to shape the future of the public/private controversy.

The Mixed Structure of
Retirement Income Provision

Public/private relations in a system of retirement provision may be
understood at several levels of complexity. There is, most obviously, the

manifest composition of the mix: how much income comes from public sources (social insurance and other government programs) and how much from private sources (pensions, savings, family support, and so on). But this gives us only a first approximation, for a major portion of private provision is often subsidized through tax expenditures and other, low-visibility public subsidies. Taking into account these means of public support gives us a more complete view of the public role in retirement provision. In addition, the various parts of a retirement income system—public and private in varying degrees—function on different principles. These principles must be understood to grasp how privatization would change not only the composition and distribution of retirement income but also the workings of the system as a whole.

THE CHANGING COMPOSITION OF THE MIX

The common metaphors for describing the relation of public and private sources of retirement income are "layers" or "tiers" of protection. In the United States we think of welfare programs at the bottom, then Social Security benefits, employment-based pensions, and at the top individual savings, now including IRAs. The chief basis of support in old age, at least in legend, used to be the family, but expectations of support by children have almost disappeared. In public opinion polls, the proportion of Americans saying children should be financially responsible for their parents has dropped from 50 to 10 percent between the mid-fifties and mid-seventies.[12] The earnings of the elderly have also diminished, as the proportion of men over age 65 in the labor force has dropped sharply during the twentieth century. The income of the aged today comes primarily from collective or collectively subsidized sources, of which Social Security is the single largest. In 1982 the median yearly Social Security payment to newly retiring couples was $7,600, out of a median yearly income of about $18,000. In 1983 the retirement income system, as the Employee Benefit Research Institute calls it, paid out $306 billion to the retired or on their behalf. Of this total, $149 billion came from Social Security, another $51 billion from Medicare, $91 billion in employer-sponsored pensions, and $16 billion in Medicaid, Supplemental Security Income, and food stamps.[13]

Collective provision of retirement income to groups other than the poor is comparatively recent in the history of the United States. It was

[12] Stephen Crystal, *America's Old Age Crisis* (New York: Basic Books, 1982), pp. 56–57; see also Daniel Yankelovich, *New Rules: Searching for Self-Fulfillment in a World Turned Upside Down* (New York: Random House, 1981), p. 104.

[13] Emily S. Andrews, *The Changing Profile of Pensions in America* (Washington, D.C.: Employee Benefit Research Institute, 1985), p. 4.

only in the early 1950s that Social Security payments surpassed old-age assistance (welfare payments), and the rate of receipt of employment-based pensions has increased sharply just in the last two decades. In 1962 only 16 percent of married couples with heads of household 65 years of age and older received private pensions; by 1982 the proportion had risen to 33 percent. In the same population, former public employees receiving pensions increased from 8 to 13 percent in the decade after 1971.[14] By 1982, 56 percent of newly retired married couples were receiving some pension income, with a median amount of $6,000 a year.[15]

It may seem puzzling that pensions have grown during the same period as Social Security benefits have risen, since state expenditure is often viewed as inevitably driving out private provision. But this cannot be said of the historical relation between Social Security and private pensions. They have developed side by side. While expanding Social Security, the federal government also provided growing tax incentives for private pensions. Moreover, far from displacing private pensions, the advent of Social Security may have helped institutionalize retirement and clarify the need for retirement income, which it incompletely met, particularly for high-income employees. However, since that time, increases in Social Security benefits may well have retarded growth in private pensions.[16]

The distributive patterns of Social Security and employment-based pensions vary in exactly the direction one would expect. The lowest in income rely most heavily on Social Security. For example, among newly retiring couples in 1982, the bottom 10 percent received 77 percent of their average household income from Social Security. Social Security represented more than half of total income up through the 45th percentile of the income distribution for couples and the 55th percentile for the unmarried.[17]

Pensions still contribute remarkably little to the income of a majority of the retired. Among all those newly retiring, half the couples and two-thirds of the unmarried were receiving either nothing or no more than $100 a month in pension income in 1982—and this among the newly retiring, who receive pension income at a higher rate than the aged as a whole, and after decades of pension growth.[18] Although the total assets of pension plans reached $1.4 trillion in 1986,[19] they still provided less

[14] *Ibid.*, 123–24.

[15] Linda Drazga Maxfield and Virginia P. Reno, "Distribution of Income Sources of Recent Retirees: Findings from the New Beneficiary Survey," *Social Security Bulletin*, 48 (January 1985): 11.

[16] For the argument that they are almost perfect substitutes, see Munnell, *Economics of Private Pensions*, pp. 7–29.

[17] Maxfield and Reno, "Distribution of Income Sources," p. 12.

[18] *Ibid.*

[19] William S. Cohen, "Gambling with the Future," *New York Times*, August 12, 1982.

retirement income than Social Security to all but the top quintile in the income distribution.

The relatively small contribution of pensions to retirement income stems from several factors: the still limited coverage of the labor force, limited portability, widely used methods for integrating pension benefits with Social Security, and inadequate inflation adjustments. The rate of pension coverage for all workers in May 1983, the most recent period for which data are available, was 52 percent, down from 56 percent in May 1979—a decline attributed primarily to shifts in employment from high- to low-coverage industries and the decline in unionization of the labor force.[20] Since these industrial trends are unlikely to be reversed soon, pension coverage cannot be expected to grow in the foreseeable future. At bottom, the limits of pension coverage stem from the structure of jobs in the economy. Firms use pensions to increase employee loyalty and reduce turnover, but management in many enterprises does not view such investments in long-term employment as likely to be profitable.

Even the 52 percent rate of pension coverage may overstate the proportion accumulating benefits. Workers are classified as covered if their employer contributes to a pension plan. Many of those nominally covered by pensions will never receive any pension benefits from their current employers because of job changes. Only 24 percent of all workers in 1983 reported themselves "entitled to benefits," although this percentage rises as workers approach retirement age.[21]

Workers who ultimately receive pensions often get less than their length of employment might suggest they had earned. Under federal regulations for "defined-benefit" plans, employers may take Social Security into account in determining benefit levels. Since Social Security replaces a higher proportion of income for lower-income employees, private pensions are often skewed in favor of upper-income employees to enable them to achieve the same level of income replacement from both sources combined.[22] Private pension recipients have also been disappointed in the long-term real value of their benefits, which are typically frozen at retirement. Later adjustments are generally ad hoc and have historically made up only part of what inflation has taken away.[23]

In recent years many corporations, particularly those involved in merg-

[20] Andrews, *Changing Profile*, pp. 12–16, 93–113.

[21] *Ibid.*, p. 13.

[22] See Donald Bell and Diane Hill, "How Social Security Payments Affect Private Pensions," *Monthly Labor Review* (May 1984): 15–20; James H. Schulz and Thomas D. Leavitt, *Pension Integration: Concepts, Issues and Proposals* (Washington, D.C.: Employee Benefit Research Institute, 1983); and Michael Graetz, Chapter 4 of this volume.

[23] Robert L. Clark et al., *Inflation and the Economic Well-Being of the Elderly* (Baltimore: Johns Hopkins University Press, 1984), p. 75.

ers or attempting to thwart takeovers, have terminated their pension plans, purchased fixed annuities from insurance companies, and reappropriated millions of dollars in excess pension accumulations. In some cases, the insurance firms providing the annuities have been able to give employers a bargain price only because the insurers have invested heavily in "junk" bonds. These investments expose retired employees to considerable risk. For if the bonds have a high default rate, or if they are refunded prior to maturity as interest rates fall, the insurers may be unable to meet their obligations.[24]

Other employers have simply reduced their contributions to pension plans because the plans have had higher than expected returns from the stock and bond markets and lower than expected benefit obligations, in part due to the high mobility of workers and the closing of domestic plants. But as Joan and Merton Bernstein point out, if the firms do not use the high returns from the proverbial "seven fat years" to tide them over the "seven lean years" that sooner or later are likely to occur, the pension plans may run into trouble.[25] Employees depending upon them will be inadequately protected by the Pension Guarantee Benefit Corporation, unless its assets are dramatically increased.[26]

The use of pension funds in corporate strategy has raised serious questions about the ethics and future of the private pension system. Rather than being managed in the interests of their beneficiaries, pension assets are now frequently being deployed and raided in takeover maneuvers for the benefit of management. Today's pension asset "raids," as a congressional committee has called them, also make a mockery of Peter Drucker's announcement a decade ago that "pension fund socialism" had arrived in an "unseen revolution" in America.[27] If pension funds had really turned workers into the principal stockholders in the economy, the workers could not be so easily dispossessed of capital gains.

These facts help put the accomplishment of Social Security into perspective. Retirement security is not an area where the private sector has shown its natural superiority. By any reasonable standard, its performance has been abysmal. Rather than fearing default in the public sector,

[24] Louis Lowenstein, "Three New Reasons to Fear Junk Bonds," *New York Times*, August 24, 1986.

[25] Merton C. Bernstein and Joan Brodshaug Bernstein, *Social Security: The System that Works* (New York: Basic Books, 1987).

[26] "Tremors in the Pension System Finally Wake Congress Up," *Business Week*, November 18, 1985.

[27] Peter F. Drucker, *The Unseen Revolution: How Pension Fund Socialism Came to America* (New York: Harper and Row, 1976); U.S. Congress, House, Select Committee on Aging, *Pension Asset Raids*, Hearing, 98th Cong., 1st sess., Sept. 28, 1983, Comm. Pub. 98–438. See also Winston Williams, "Raking in Billions from the Company Pension Plan," *New York Times*, November 3, 1985.

workers and taxpayers today have far more reason to fear pension plan bankruptcies—the major costs of which will likely fall on government. Neither now nor in the future are private pensions likely to provide a functional alternative to Social Security. In 1986 Congress sought to extend pension coverage by requiring employers to vest pensions after five years and by disallowing tax exemptions for plans sharply skewed in favor of high-income employees. But, as Michael Graetz explains in Chapter 4, these reforms have serious limitations. Under present and foreseeable circumstances, the pension system promises only to be a supplement, not the foundation of retirement provision. Nor do private employers and pension plan directors want any larger role. Indeed, because of the methods of pension integration, they have much to lose from cutbacks in Social Security. The enthusiasts of privatization come from another quarter, and they look to another device as their preferred instrument: the individually controlled retirement account

Individual retirement plans were originally devised to extend the boundaries of pension coverage. Keogh plans were introduced in 1962 and IRAs in 1974 to enable the self-employed and workers in firms lacking pension plans to shelter funds for retirement. Neither succeeded in accomplishing its original purpose. Keogh plans spread only among a small minority of the self-employed (nearly two-thirds of Keoghs belong to just three groups—doctors, dentists, and lawyers), and by 1978 only 4.4 percent of workers uncovered by pension plans had IRAs.[28] But though the IRA failed in its original mission of tax equity, it soon found a new rationale as an incentive to savings. In 1981 Congress opened IRAs to covered workers in the hope that the measure would stimulate capital formation. The legislation even made it possible, at least for some people, to pyramid as many as four tax-sheltered retirement plans—an employer pension, a Keogh plan, an IRA, and 401(k) salary reduction plan.

It is doubtful whether IRAs and these other tax shelters have significantly stimulated savings. Much of the money deposited in IRAs probably would have been saved anyway. A controversial study by Steven Venti and David Wise estimates that about half of IRA deposits in 1982 did represent new savings (that is, money that would have otherwise gone to consumption).[29] But even if that is true, discretionary individual savings

[28] Andrews, *Changing Profile*, pp. 78, 88.

[29] Steven F. Venti and David A. Wise, "IRAs and Saving," Working Paper No. 1879, National Bureau of Economic Research, Cambridge, Mass., April 1986. For a summary of the arguments in favor of IRAs, see Lawrence H. Summers, "I.R.A.'s Really Do Spark New Savings," *New York Times*, May 25, 1986. See also Harvey Galper and Eugene Steuerle, "Tax Incentives for Saving," *The Brookings Review* (Winter 1983): 16–23; Robin C. DeMagistris and Carl J. Palash, "Impact of IRAs on Saving," *Federal Reserve Bank of New York Quarterly Review* (Winter 1982–83): 24–30.

are a small proportion of net savings overall, and the household savings rate, as measured by government statistics, has actually fallen in the years since IRAS were introduced.[30]

Although IRAS failed both to improve tax equity and increase savings, they grew to large proportions and did trickle down—a bit. Between 1982 and 1984 IRA deposits grew from $4 billion to $29 billion.[31] A series of Gallup studies over that three-year period shows the proportion of nonretired adults owning IRAS almost doubling from 12 to 23 percent. Gallup also found that the more recently an account was opened, the lower was the household income. The majority of new IRA accounts in 1984 were started by people earning less than $30,000 a year. However, high-income adults had much higher rates of IRA ownership: in 1984, 59 percent of those with household income over $50,000 a year, compared to 13 percent of those with annual incomes under $30,000, owned IRAS.[32] IRA assets and the tax benefits of IRA ownership have been overwhelmingly concentrated among upper-income households—at least until the 1986 tax changes limiting the deductibility of IRA contributions for households that have both employer-provided pensions and incomes over $40,000 (in the case of couples) or $25,000 (in the case of individuals).

As I indicated earlier, the public/private mix is complicated by the public role in private savings. Private instruments of retirement provision benefit from indirect public expenditures by virtue of special tax treatment ("tax expenditures"). From a life-cycle perspective, the tax advantage of sheltered retirement plans has three separate elements. First, pre-tax dollars are invested; second, the earnings from those investments grow untaxed; and third, benefits are paid out during years when people generally face lower tax rates.[33] The federal government, however, usually computes expenditures on an annual basis. To make them comparable to direct government appropriations, the Office of Management and Budget expresses them in outlay equivalents—that is, the amount the government would have to spend to provide benefits that after taxes would equal tax preferences in value. For 1986, the outlay equivalents amounted

[30] According to a more useful measure of personal savings than the standard figures produced by the Bureau of Economic Analysis, households contributed less than 3 percent of nonhousehold gross capital formation between 1947 and 1983. See Richard Ruggles and Nancy Ruggles, "The Integration of Macro and Micro Data for the Household Sector," Working Paper No. 1031, Institution for Social and Policy Studies, Yale University, October 1985, pp. 29–31.

[31] DeMagistris and Palash, "Impact of IRAS," p. 63.

[32] Gallup Organization, *The 1984 Gallup Study of Eligible Non-Owners of Individual Retirement Accounts*, vol. I: *Summary of Findings* (Princeton, N.J.: Gallup Organization, October 1984).

[33] Munnell, *Economics of Private Pensions*, pp. 35–37.

to $81 billion for employer pensions and $23.5 billion for IRA and Keogh plans.[34]

These estimates are controversial. That in itself is part of the story. Even to experts the measurement of the public share of private retirement benefits is less clear than the measurement of direct expenditures.[35] To the general public, the tax expenditures for pensions and IRAs are still more obscure; they are never compared to the cost of Social Security. Nor is the distribution of tax expenditures well understood. Yet for pensions and sheltered retirement accounts, the benefits have accrued chiefly to the affluent, offsetting the progressive structure of Social Security benefits. Critics of Social Security say that if Americans fully understood it as a system of income transfers, they would never approve. The case can be made more persuasively about the distribution of tax expenditures for pensions and IRAs. Were these tax expenditures turned into programs for which the affluent had to establish eligibility at welfare offices, they might be sufficiently shamed never to stand in line to collect their checks.

The 1986 tax reforms represented a significant reduction in these benefits for higher-income groups. In addition to limiting IRAs, Congress curtailed the allowable contributions to 401(k) plans. Moreover, the new lower marginal tax rates reduce the value of all tax expenditures, including those for pensions. The structural deficit and the regular accounting for tax expenditures by the Office of Management and Budget and the Congressional Budget Office made tax expenditures more salient than ever before in the budgetary process.[36] But, as Graetz argues in Chapter 4, the 1986 reforms by no means eliminated all the tax expenditures for retirement income that go disproportionately to the affluent.

In the United States, tax expenditures have long been a major avenue of retirement support, fully deserving coequal status with Social Security in public policy debates about provision for old age. Virtually all primary retirement assets benefit from tax expenditures: not just pensions and other sheltered retirement accounts but also life insurance and savings accumulated through home ownership receive large tax preferences. The proposals to privatize Social Security by expanding IRAs would mean even greater use of tax expenditures than ever before. Here they run into an unexpected obstacle; although these proposals reflect one policy trend

[34] U.S. Office of Management and Budget, *Special Analysis of the Budget of the U.S. Government 1986* (Washington, D.C.: Government Printing Office, 1985), Special Analysis G.

[35] Munnell, *Economics of Private Pensions*, pp. 40–50; Sophie M. Korczyk, *Retirement Security and Tax Policy* (Washington, D.C.: Employee Benefit Research Institute, 1984), pp. 51–64.

[36] Herman B. Leonard, *Checks Unbalanced: The Quiet Side of Public Spending* (New York: Basic Books, 1986), pp. 107–29.

of the 1980s, they conflict with another. Turning from Social Security to
IRAS is consistent with the preference for relying on private markets, but
it clashes with the effort to lower marginal tax rates. Furthermore, privatization through the use of expanded tax preferences would not make
governmental decision making any less important in retirement provision. It would merely substitute indirect for direct expenditures as a preferred instrument of policy. In the process it would alter the distribution
of retirement income and decrease the visibility of public subsidies.

The Framework of Retirement Provision

In every domain of welfare policy where the state provides benefits, it
establishes the framework for private provision as well. It regulates private transactions and institutions, spreads risks, and sometimes assumes
them.

The public framework of retirement provision consists in part of the
rules that govern each of the various instruments of policy. Alan Blinder
suggests we imagine not only IRAS but also pensions and Social Security
to be special kinds of bank accounts.[37] Compare the rules governing deposits and withdrawals. First, consider deposits: Individual workers have
little, if any discretion over the amounts deposited in both Social Security
and pensions, whereas they may choose whether and how much to de-
posit in IRAS and 401(k) plans, within prescribed ceilings. Similarly, individuals have no choice among alternative investments in Social Security
and most pension accounts, whereas in IRAS they have considerable discretion, including the freedom to make imprudent choices.

Second, consider withdrawals: In both Social Security and employer-
provided pensions, workers cannot begin withdrawing funds before
reaching a given age, whereas from IRAS they can withdraw funds early,
albeit with a penalty, and from 401(k) plans they can make unpenalized
withdrawals at times of special hardship. To withdraw funds from the
pension account, they have to leave their firms; to make withdrawals
from the Social Security account, they generally have to reduce sharply
their hours of work. IRAS have no work-reduction requirement. If workers leave their firms too early, they may lose the entire balance in the
pension account; and if they fail to work in covered employment for ten
years, their Social Security benefits are not vested. No such risk attaches
to IRAS. Most pension withdrawals and all Social Security withdrawals
must take the form of annuity payments rather than lump sums. IRAS
again allow more discretion, though withdrawals must meet a minimum

[37] Alan S. Blinder, "Private Pensions and Public Pensions: Theory and Fact," Working
Paper No. 902, National Bureau of Economic Research, Cambridge, Mass., June 1982.

schedule. Finally, the balance in the IRAs, unlike that in pension accounts, may be withdrawn at death and left to heirs, while Social Security provides survivors' benefits and hence a form of life insurance.

The similarities between Social Security and employment-based pensions, especially when compared to IRAs, are striking. Yet in five fundamental respects Social Security differs from pensions: the greater portability of Social Security benefits; Social Security's provision of survivors' benefits; its progressive benefit structure; its organization on a pay-as-you-go basis; and its automatic indexing. The last two features figure prominently in the debate over the merits of public versus private retirement provision. Like IRAs, the private pensions that qualify for tax exemptions are at least partly advance-funded; on the other hand, neither IRA nor pension income is protected against inflation. These characteristics, of course, are not intrinsically necessary. Public systems of retirement benefits may be funded, and in some countries such as Sweden they are. Were the U.S. government to issue indexed bonds, they might be bought for IRAs and private pension funds, which could then provide indexed benefits. Thus, not only the mix but also the nature of the contrast between public and private alternatives depends on choices of public policy.

The framework of retirement provision consists also of the underlying principles of operation in the different sectors. Two principles compete with each other in retirement provision. One emphasizes earnings-related contributions and benefits and is modeled after insurance; basically, what the retired receive in benefits depends on what they put in. Americans call this principle "equity"; Europeans call it "equivalence." The second principle stresses universality of coverage and progressivity in benefits and seeks to achieve a more equal distribution of income or at least a decent floor of income protection. In America this principle is called "adequacy," while in Europe it is called "solidarity," not so subtly reflecting ideological differences in the traditions that have guided social insurance.[38]

The tension between equity and adequacy, or equivalence and solidarity, is closely related to the development of the balance between public and private provision. For while the principle of adequacy or solidarity can be achieved only through the state, earnings-related pension plans may be provided in either the public or the private sectors. Thus, in the organization of retirement provision, a key set of questions concerns whether any earnings-related benefits will be public (leaving aside those for state employees) and, if so, what relation they will have to private provision. Of the countless choices available, three general models of

[38] Herman van Gunsteren and Martin Rein, "The Dialectic of Public and Private Pensions," *Journal of Social Policy* 14 (1985): 129–49.

public/private relations stand out as particularly important for under-standing the contemporary debate about privatization.

First, the state may attempt to combine the principles of equity and adequacy in a single public program while providing for an additional welfare safety net and allowing or encouraging private supplementation. This is the American pattern of Social Security and private pensions.

Second, the state may provide two systems of retirement benefits: one program to meet concerns of adequacy or solidarity (a welfare program or a guaranteed minimum pension) and a social insurance system to pro-vide benefits in relation to earnings. Like the first combined structure, this model involves the state in providing earnings-related pensions. How-ever, by keeping the earnings-related portion separate, it opens up the possibility of partial private substitution. For example, the state may al-low employer-sponsored pensions to serve as an alternative to the public earnings-related plan. This is the current approach in Great Britain; the state provides a flat-rate pension to all retired workers, a separate earn-ings-related program, and an option for employers to drop out of the latter if they provide pension benefits at least as generous.[39] This splitting of old-age benefits into two components and the provision for "opting out" figure in some American work supporting the privatization of Social Security.

A third alternative calls for a clear separation between the functions and principles of the public and private sectors. In this model, the state provides welfare benefits to meet the demands of adequacy, leaving earn-ings-related pensions entirely to the private sphere. This is the structure of public/private relations recommended as an ideal in the more radical proposals for the total privatization of Social Security. Chile is the only nation thus far to have adopted this model.

Privatization Proposals

The proposals to privatize Social Security are not simply a throwback to the position of its original opponents. The advocates of privatization generally acknowledge that the state has a legitimate interest in requiring savings for retirement, but paternalism is not the rationale they accept.

[39] For contrasting treatments of the British system, see John C. Goodman, "Private Alter-natives to Social Security: The Experience of Other Countries," in *Social Security: Prospects for Real Reform*, ed. Peter J. Ferrara (Washington, D.C.: Cato Institute, 1985), pp. 103–12; and Michael O'Higgins, "Public-Private Interaction and Pension Provision," in *The Public-Private Interplay in Social Protection*, ed. Lee Rainwater and Martin Rein (Armonk, N.Y.: M.E. Sharpe, 1986). O'Higgins points out that employers who opt out of the public pro-gram are still guaranteed that the government will pay for postretirement inflation adjust-ments to the earnings-related pensions.

Rather, they are reluctant to let people who fail to provide for their old age take a "free ride" on society's welfare cushion, which they accept as necessary to prevent the neediest from starving. As in other arenas of public policy, the privatizers argue that even where some intervention is needed, government does not necessarily have to meet the need itself, since there may be better private alternatives than a wholly government-produced service. In the case of retirement provision, they maintain that the government has an interest in maintaining a floor of protection, but providing anything above that floor should be left to private choice. Here moderate and radical market-oriented reformers divide. In the view of radical privatizers, who hold to the third model of public/private relations I have just sketched, the role of the state in providing welfare to the minority who are poor ought not to become the basis for providing *any* earnings-related benefits to the majority. In the view of moderate privatizers, who hold to the second model, the legitimate role of the state in providing welfare to the poor and guaranteeing minimal earnings-related benefits to all ought not become the basis for providing *all* or *most* earnings-related benefits in old age.

The proponents of privatization generally do not expect to change the system of retirement provision overnight. They plan to guarantee all benefits currently being received by Social Security beneficiaries. Private alternatives could then be introduced gradually in various ways.[40]

The most extensively developed, radical case for privatization comes in the work of Peter Ferrara, variously sponsored by the Cato Institute, the Heritage Foundation, and the U.S. Chambers of Commerce. Ferrara would divide Social Security into its welfare (transfer payment) and insurance (annuity) components. The welfare component—that is, the portion above and beyond an actuarially fair return—would be turned over to a means-tested program such as Supplemental Security Income (SSI). Individuals could then opt out of the insurance program by making larger contributions to a "super IRA." At the start, they could take a credit against their income taxes for contributions equal to as much as 20 percent of their Social Security taxes; their future claims against Social Security would be reduced proportionately. Ultimately, they could take credits for IRA contributions up to 100 percent of payroll taxes (including the employer's share), and with the funds in their IRAs they would purchase private substitutes for Social Security protection. Insofar as people took this option, Social Security's old-age insurance, survivors' benefits, disability benefits, and Medicare would wither away.[41]

More mainstream economists, although opposed to total privatization,

[40] Peter J. Ferrara, "Social Security and the Super IRA," in Ferrara, ed., *Social Security: Prospects for Real Reform.*

[41] Peter J. Ferrara, "Rebuilding Social Security: Part 2, Toward Lasting Reform," *Backgrounder*, No. 346 (Washington, D.C.: Heritage Foundation, April 1984).

have suggested reforms that would, in effect, partially privatize the program. Michael Boskin has developed one such proposal. Like Ferrara, Boskin would divide Social Security's old-age insurance into its welfare and insurance components. Social Security would then become a two-tier program. As in the Ferrara scheme, all the welfare benefits would be means-tested. The insurance portion would provide actuarially fair annuities; all elements of the progressive benefit structure would be eliminated. Unlike Ferrara, however, Boskin does not envision a transfer of the entire insurance function into the private sector, but he does favor limiting the scale of public provision to encourage partial privatization.[42]

These two approaches are quite different. Ferrara and Boskin have criticized each other—quite successfully—but they do make many of the same claims about the effects of Social Security and the desirability of market-oriented reform. However, in the following discussion I shall have Ferrara's outlook chiefly in mind, as his work calls unambiguously for privatization as a total solution to Social Security's problems. I shall come back to partial privatization later.

THE CLAIMS FOR PRIVATIZATION

Privatization is a theme of conservative campaigns to change a broad array of government programs. The general case for privatization, as Michael O'Higgins has pointed out, characteristically includes three different claims. On the macroeconomic level, privatizers claim that reduced public expenditure will result in more productive private investment and thereby stimulate economic growth. On the microeconomic level, they claim privatization will yield both greater efficiency in the production of any given service and a greater range of choice for consumers because of the diversity possible in the market.[43] Conservative advocates of a privatized Social Security system make precisely these claims to increase economic growth, efficiency, and individual choice, but the arguments proceed in a distinctive way.

The usual macroeconomic claim by conservatives is that high public expenditure impedes growth because of the effects of public debt and taxes: debt crowds out private investment, and taxes reduce incentives for work. Although the effects of payroll taxes on labor supply are cited

[42] Boskin, *Too Many Promises*. See p. 102; Boskin's position on privatization is tentative: "Replacement of public provision by compulsory private coverage should be considered. Short of *complete* privatization, a variety of intervening levels and forms of private provision of old-age insurance also deserves serious attention. . . . I am somewhat in sympathy with those who would like to privatize *part* of *some* of the components of Social Security beyond minimally adequate coverage."

[43] Michael O'Higgins, "Privatisation and Social Security," *Political Quarterly* 55 (April 1984): 129.

in criticisms of Social Security, the chief objection is that it depresses the overall rate of savings in the economy. According to this argument, Social Security taxes reduce earnings that might be saved, and entitlements to Social Security permit individuals to avoid saving money for retirement. Since the system runs on an unfunded, pay-as-you-go basis, it fails to replace the savings individuals would have otherwise accumulated.

The usual microeconomic claim by conservatives is that private firms are more efficient than government in producing any given commodity because of the discipline of the market. In this instance, the microeconomic claim emphasizes the fact that Social Security performs both welfare and insurance functions, the combination of which allegedly produces two kinds of inefficiency. First, because the system has no means test, the welfare portion of Social Security benefits goes to many people who do not genuinely need any additional income. In other words, as a welfare program, Social Security is target inefficient. Second, if the welfare function were removed elsewhere, the insurance services might then be turned over in whole or part to private firms, which (so the proponents of total privatization claim) could produce a higher rate of return for beneficiaries. Furthermore, the combined effect of terminating unjustified welfare payments and excess public insurance services would be to relieve Social Security's alleged long-run financial problems. Hence privatization is a path not just to greater efficiency but to the continued solvency of government.

Regarding the claim of greater individual choice, advocates of privatization argue that Social Security is a straitjacket. If people were free to hold their own individual retirement accounts, they could select investments according to their own tastes or buy annuities from competitive private plans. Such diversity, the privatizers argue, would particularly benefit minorities.

And so, thanks to the tonic of privatization, the savings rate would increase, welfare benefits would be distributed more fairly, employees would receive more retirement benefits for their money, the nation would avoid the coming collapse of Social Security, and individuals would enjoy greater freedom of choice. According to Ferrara, the benefits of privatization would be so great that the changeover could take place without any cost to those now or prospectively relying upon Social Security. Not all proponents of change take this rosy view. That the transition has low or no costs is the final claim we need to examine, but since it turns, above all, on the macroeconomic issue, let us begin there.

THE MACROECONOMIC CASE FOR PRIVATIZATION

The thesis that Social Security reduces savings originated with Martin Feldstein a decade ago. Feldstein has recently commented that this and other adverse consequences of Social Security have been so "carefully documented" by economists in statistical studies that the findings now represent the "center of gravity" in informed, professional circles.[44] An altogether different impression emerges from reading the now abundant professional literature on the subject. Many prominent economists believe that Feldstein's findings on the impact of Social Security on savings have been discredited.[45] Even those who hold to his view say that the issue remains undecided but that the enormous effects he originally claimed to find were probably overestimated.

The difficulties arise from numerous directions. First, as Alicia Munnell and Feldstein himself originally pointed out, the theory on which the empirical work rests—the hypothesis that people rationally plan savings and investment over the life cycle—is ambiguous in its implications for Social Security. Although it predicts reduced savings because of the substitution of Social Security benefits, it predicts higher savings from induced retirement (that is, by shortening years of work). Moreover, the life-cycle theory was never demonstrated; it was simply assumed, even though much empirical evidence contradicts it. For example, the theory predicts the elderly "dissave" during retirement, although some empirical research indicates that they do not.[46] Still more distressing, researchers at the Social Security Administration discovered that as a result of a programming error Feldstein's initial work grossly overestimated the effect on savings. Using the same model, Lesnoy and Leimer could demonstrate no impact.[47] Since then the results of a series of investigations, using cross-sectional as well as time-series data, have proved extremely sensitive to assumptions. Henry Aaron concludes in a review that, depending on equally plausible assumptions, Social Security may be said to have reduced, increased, or had no effect at all on savings.[48]

But even if, for the sake of prudence, we assume that Social Security reduces savings, it follows neither that Social Security should be the vehicle to build up savings nor that Social Security ought to be privatized. If we must generate more savings, there may be better means than the use of the payroll tax and the Social Security system. For example, we could reduce the budget deficit. To say we need more savings is not to prove we

[44] Martin Feldstein, "The Social Security Explosion," *Public Interest*, 81 (Fall 1985): 95.

[45] Aaron, *Economic Effects of Social Security*; Sheldon Danziger, Robert Havemann, and Robert Plotnick, "How Income Transfer Programs Affect Work, Savings and the Income Distribution: A Critical Review," *Journal of Economic Literature* 19 (September 1981); Blinder, "Private Pensions"; and Selig D. Lesnoy and Dean R. Leimer, "Social Security and Private Savings: Theory and Historical Evidence," *Social Security Bulletin* 48 (January 1985): 14–30.

[46] Danziger, Havemann, and Plotnick, "Income Transfer Programs."

[47] Dean R. Leimer and Selig D. Lesnoy, "Social Security and Private Saving: New Time-Series Evidence," *Journal of Political Economy* (June 1982): 606–29.

[48] Aaron, *Economic Effects of Social Security*, pp. 40–52.

need more personal savings; government and business savings will also suffice.

And even if, for the sake of argument, it proved a good idea to build up savings through retirement provision, that would still not necessarily dictate that we privatize Social Security. The same result could be achieved in a public system. For if Social Security were to build up its reserves, it would presumably buy government securities; and if the government were to hold more of its own debt, private funds available for private investment would increase.

There is an historical irony about this entire debate. Social Security began as a funded system; the shift to pay-as-you-go was initiated by a conservative in the late 1930s. Republican Senator Arthur Vandenberg was particularly anxious about the prospect of trust fund accumulations. He thought that if the Social Security system were to buy government securities, it would legitimize deficits, and if it were to buy private securities, it would lead to government control of private firms. The danger was Keynesianism on the one hand and socialism on the other. Vandenberg set in motion the 1939 amendments that reduced the growing reserves by speeding up the first Social Security payments and adding extra benefits for dependents.[49] These amendments represented a shift from an insurance model built primarily around the principal of equity to a transfer program with a stronger commitment to adequacy. In other words, they helped create what conservatives now see as the contradiction between insurance and welfare responsible for the program's inefficiencies at the microeconomic level.

THE MICROECONOMIC CASE: TARGET EFFICIENCY AND HIGHER RETURNS

The commitment of Social Security to providing minimally adequate incomes to the aged is reflected in several different elements of the system, such as the progressive benefit structure, the additional payments to beneficiaries with dependents, and the high returns provided the Depression-damaged generation. The latter represents a transfer to a particular cohort; the others represent transfers within cohorts. All such extra transfers violate the principle of equity as understood in insurance. Though meant to serve as indicators of need, these provisions result in some benefits going to people who are not needy, such as the affluent members of early cohorts.

Improved target efficiency, however, has a social cost. To split Social

[49] Edward D. Berkowitz, "The First Social Security Crisis," *Prologue* 15 (Fall 1983): 133–48.

Security into its welfare and insur

millions of the aged into means-te

the moment, their political respoı   ... ıo be sure, some
savings might be achieved by denying benefits to the undeserving affluent,
but identifying them would raise costs and reduce privacy. The administration of means testing generally runs about 10 to 12 percent of program
costs—no minor increase in a program as large as Social Security.[50]
Means-tested programs also have perverse incentives, which conservatives themselves frequently emphasize. Rather than seeing their savings
eaten away gradually until they qualify for such a program, some of the
aged would divest themselves of their assets, transferring them to their
children. In so doing, they would lose not only their property but also
control of their own lives, subjecting themselves to the scrutiny of the
administrators who enforce the means test—this, in a reform that claims
to advance liberty.

Ferrara calls the combination of insurance and welfare functions Social
Security's "inherent contradiction." But many government programs, like
many private organizations, serve more than one purpose and must compromise among them. The federal income tax mixes welfare with efficiency considerations and incentives for growth. It is characteristic of
zealots that they regard compromise as contradiction, but it is rare for
any social institution to be organized on a single principle. Social insurance systems throughout the capitalist world show a mix of equity and
adequacy concerns. In a review of the experience of a wide range of countries, Herman van Gunsteren and Martin Rein argue that over time the
systems tend toward compromise of pure principles. Social insurance systems with equal, low pensions premised on ideals of solidarity or adequacy have been forced to develop stronger earnings-related benefits; the
systems most strongly committed to the principle of equity have incor-
porated a greater concern for adequacy.[51] If the mixing of equity and
adequacy is a contradiction, it appears more durable than the segregation
of welfare benefits in a public-sector slum. Contrary to Ferrara, policy
stability may not lie at the extreme where pure principles govern, but in
the messy center where bargains are struck.

Although the benefit structure of Social Security may well need reform,
particularly in view of changes in both the family and the role of women,
I fail to see why we ought to purge Social Security of transfers. Conservatives fume that the deceptive insurance language of Social Security ob-
scures its character as a transfer program. But it is hardly a secret that

[50] The estimate of the cost of means testing comes from Henry Aaron, personal communication.

[51] Van Gunsteren and Rein, "Dialectic of Public and Private Pensions."

Social Security was intended, from the beginning, to prevent poverty and dependency among the aged. In fact, the "transfer" to the poor just makes up for their lower life expectancies—it is the least we should do.[52] Nor have the extra benefits for dependents been hidden from taxpayers and beneficiaries who are single. The benefit structure is a collective judgment about reconciling adequacy with equity, tempering the strict logic of insurance with other norms of justice.

The second half of the efficiency argument is that, as an insurance program, Social Security provides lower returns than individuals might secure from alternative private investments of their tax money. Ferrara suggests a 12 percent real rate of return is available to private investments before (all) taxes; Boskin dismisses this figure as unrealistic. It vastly exceeds historical experience.[53] There is no question, however, that after reaching a peak in the 1970s, the real return from Social Security is headed down; for the first time in the history of the program, private investment alternatives may well yield a higher on average return. However, as I suggested earlier, the indexing of Social Security makes the entitlement to its benefits an asset that cannot now be reproduced in the private sector. According to one study, a portfolio of private securities, structured so that it would have kept pace with previous rates of inflation, would have yielded a zero return.[54] And no private financial institution could guarantee that its investments would keep up with future inflation. Furthermore, although over some historical intervals the return from private investments has been higher than Social Security, these returns have been highly unstable. In the wake of a downturn in the stock and bond markets, someone of retirement age seeking to convert IRA holdings into an annuity would be forced to accept a sharply reduced income. Privatizers cannot expect to abolish the business cycle. If *security* is what people want in retirement provision, a public system financed out of long-term economic growth may meet their objectives far better than more volatile and individually variable investment portfolios.

As a means of ensuring adequate retirement income, the super IRA has some obvious additional disadvantages. Early withdrawal may undermine retirement savings. Economies of scale and professional manage-

---

[52] See James Tobin's discussion of life expectancy and income in Chapter 2.

[53] Peter J. Ferrara, *Social Security: Averting the Crisis* (Washington, D.C.: Cato Institute, 1982), pp. 38–50; Boskin, *Too Many Promises*, pp. 100–101. On this point and other weaknesses of the privatization strategy, I have benefited from reading Selig D. Lesnoy, "Private Alternatives to Social Security," Paper presented at Commissioner's Briefing, Social Security Administration, June 18, 1984.

[54] Zvi Bodie, "Investment Strategy in an Inflationary Environment," Working Paper No. 701, National Bureau of Economic Research, Cambridge, Mass., June 1981; cited in Aaron, *Economic Effects of Social Security*, p. 76.

ment may be lost. The credit against federal taxes for IRA contributions may also be an insufficient incentive for low-income people, whose tax liabilities are limited and who may discount future retirement benefits so heavily as to underfund their own accounts and be forced onto the welfare rolls.

Advocates of privatization often cite the difficulties faced by Social Security in meeting the costs created by growing longevity and the retirement of the baby-boom generation in the next century. These costs are not to be lightly dismissed. However, the changes in the age structure present equally serious problems for private retirement provision. Longer survival in retirement will mean higher demands for pension income, which many plans will be unable to meet. Growing longevity will create a heavier burden for IRAs, too. If retirees begin drawing down their IRAs at age 59, they will have long depleted their assets by the time they are 85. If, on the other hand, they convert the IRAs into annuities, the annual income available will fall because of longer life expectancy. Furthermore, the real value of annuity payments is likely to be savaged over more than twenty-five years. Only if the government issued index bonds for purchase with IRA assets could the risk of steadily declining real income be avoided. In other words, the government would have to assume the risks of inflation, exactly what it does with Social Security.

INDIVIDUAL CHOICE AND THE INTERESTS OF MINORITIES

The original public/private controversy over Social Security, Martha Derthick tells us, had three elements: whether there would be a Social Security program at all; whether it would be voluntary, in the sense that people might opt out for private plans; and whether the government might sell supplemental annuities above and beyond the standard benefits. Only on the last of these issues did conservatives win. Thereafter, the public/private question turned on the size of the taxable wage base. Had the ceiling been left low, virtually all workers' wages would have risen above it. As a result, their expected benefits would have been relatively low and flat, leaving more of the gap between Social Security and income expectations for retirement to be met by the private sector.[55]

Instead, Congress raised the taxable wage base, and Social Security and Medicare met an increasing proportion of retirement needs. In the conservative critics' view, this expansion has denied Americans the opportunity to provide for their retirement according to their own individual tastes and circumstances. On the other hand, if the scale of public provision were reduced, private choice and a greater variety of plans would

[55] Derthick, *Policymaking for Social Security*, pp. 280–83.

flourish. The critics say that privatization would benefit low- and high-income groups alike; they often claim it would particularly help blacks. Because of their lower life expectancy, blacks collect retirement benefits for fewer years than do whites and hence allegedly suffer net losses in income transfers. A private market, the privatizers say, would advance the interests of disadvantaged minorities.

This argument neglects some serious problems of insurance markets. Private firms offering annuities and other retirement benefits need to protect themselves against the risks of adverse selection. To do so, they must charge more than an actuarially fair insurance premium. A social insurance system overcomes the problem of adverse selection by its mandatory and uniform character, which also reduces the marketing and administrative costs of private insurance. In rejecting total privatization, Boskin recognizes these problems of private insurance; he wants government to provide the actuarially fair policies the private market is unable to generate on its own.[56]

The privatizers' argument about blacks and other minorities with low median incomes also overlooks some crucial facts. It would be unconstitutional for private firms to use racial classifications in pricing annuities; they cannot charge blacks less than whites for annuities, just as they cannot charge blacks more for life or health insurance. The only means for blacks to achieve savings in retirement annuities would be to buy less coverage—in other words, to expose themselves to greater risk of impoverishment when they retire. Furthermore, although blacks on average collect retirement benefits for fewer years, the progressive benefit structure of Social Security enables them to collect more during those years than they would from private policies. The privatization of Social Security would reduce the income of the black elderly and make many more of them dependent on means-tested welfare benefits. In addition, blacks and other disadvantaged minorities depend especially on the other components of Social Security, such as disability, health insurance, and survivors benefits. Because of their higher costs in these areas, many of them would find it difficult, if possible at all, to purchase privately the full package of Social Security benefits. When taken as a whole, Social Security is an extraordinary bargain for low-income groups. Recall that among newly retiring couples, the lowest decile in the income distribution receive more than three-quarters of their income from Social Security. It is simply disingenuous of the privatizers to claim the poor would benefit from a reform that eliminates the progressive benefit structure and lets them fend for themselves in a private market shy of serving precisely those groups likely to have higher disability and health insurance claims.

[56] Boskin, *Too Many Promises*, p. 101.

The Future of the Public / Private Controversy

The preceding objections to privatizing Social Security would have been raised had the proposal ever received serious attention from the Reagan administration. But the idea was never entertained for one reason above all: the "double payment problem." If workers now began providing for their own retirement by shifting their payroll taxes into enlarged IRAs, how would we pay the benefits of current Social Security recipients? Alternatively, if payroll taxes continued to be paid but employees took a credit against their income taxes for super-IRA contributions, how would we make up the huge shortfall in general revenues? Ferrara has argued that Social Security would need an injection of general revenues only in the short run; soon the economic growth stimulated by a higher savings rate would pay for the changeover.[57] But this hope of a painless transition is not likely to soothe doubts in Congress or on Wall Street in the face of a massive structural deficit in the federal budget, particularly since the 1981 tax cuts failed to produce the cornucopia of increased revenue supply-siders promised.

The double payment comes from the pay-as-you-go method of financing, which conservatives often compare to a chain letter. However, unlike a private party, a national government can make the chain of responsibility work as long as each generation to assume the costs is more numerous and more productive than its predecessor whose benefits it must pay. But conservatives can justly complain that the pay-as-we-go system makes Social Security hard to undo. The tax on one generation creates an obligation for the next. It is not simply an intergenerational contract; it is a rolling intergenerational contract, and it is hard to stop rolling. Since people at work are paying for the retired, to ask them to fund their own retirement is to double their burden. The system is locked in, except for the periods when it is accumulating surpluses and taxpayers are paying partly for their own retirement. Then the political option exists for them to pay less, cut their later benefits, and rely more on private alternatives.

As I suggested at the outset, rather than dreaming about the bankruptcy of Social Security in the middle of the next century, the advocates of privatization ought to look forward to the projected surpluses before then. In the 1990s we are shifting from pay-as-you-go toward a partly funded Social Security system. The surpluses will then start to accumulate, reaching $10 trillion by 2010 and peaking at $20 trillion in the 2040s before being drawn down.[58] Even if this forecast proves too opti-

---

[57] Ferrara, "Social Security Reform: Some Theoretical Considerations," in Ferrara, ed., *Social Security: Prospects for Real Reform*, pp. 173–78.

[58] David Koitz, Congressional Research Service, *The Projected Social Security Surplus*, HD 7094 (Washington, D.C.: Library of Congress), 16 May 1984.

mistic, there still is little question that a major period of demographic relief will begin in the 1990s when the retiring cohorts drop in size because of the dip in birth rates during the Depression and World War II. That is privatization's demographic opportunity.

Herman Leonard points out that Social Security can run into two serious problems: it can bring in too little revenue, and it can bring in too much.[59] Too little revenue produced the kind of crisis we had in the 1970s and early eighties; too much revenue—that is, a growing surplus—may be a source of policy instability beginning in the 1990s and growing after the year 2000. Excess revenue can destabilize policy by raising difficult questions about whether to accumulate or dispose of the surplus; and if to dispose of it, whether to expand benefits or cut taxes. Moreover, since the accumulations are destined to pay for the taxpayers' own retirement income, they may vote to keep them in their own pockets, or IRAs, in exchange for lower public benefits later on.

Seesawing between too little revenue in one decade and too much in the next may be particularly destabilizing. Reform of Social Security would never have been considered had it not been for the succession of fiscal crises the program experienced over the last decade. The crises reopened the Social Security contract to renegotiation. Although the series of amendments passed by Congress in 1983 to rescue the program made only minor changes, the tenor of opinion about Social Security has changed radically. Americans are not entirely sure it will be around when it is their turn to collect benefits. These doubts are not the product of wild imaginations. As is well known, the ratio of working to retired Americans is expected to fall sharply in the twenty-first century because of longer life expectancy and the retirement of the postwar baby-boom cohort. The ratio has already shifted as Americans retire earlier and live longer. Although Social Security forecasts show the program to be solvent under all but the most pessimistic scenarios, critics point out that even the pessimistic projections may prove too optimistic since both mortality and fertility rates may decline more than expected. However, because of the approaching years of demographic relief, the difficulties anticipated under unfavorable conditions will not come until after the turn of the century and probably not until after 2015.

For potential problems that distant, ample time and various alternatives are available. Advocates of privatization have tried to sell their program as a solution to the fiscal problems they see ahead, but it is unclear whether so drastic a remedy is necessary. If a boost in Social Security revenues or reduction in costs is necessary, incremental change may again

[59] Leonard, *Checks Unbalanced*, p. 58.

be sufficient, as James Tobin suggests in Chapter 2.[60] Furthermore, it is not clear that privatization, even if it could be accomplished, would entirely eliminate the future stress in retirement provision. The enthusiasts of privatization seem to regard the changing ratio of workers to retirees as if it only affected a public pay-as-you-go system. But it would also pose problems if we had entirely private, funded retirement plans. We would have a large population drawing down its assets, that is, converting assets into income. Dissaving of such enormous proportions could not fail to have serious repercussions for an economy dependent on growing capital investment. It is not intuitively obvious that we would be better off in the middle of the next century if, instead of a potential revenue shortfall in a public system, we have a dwindling supply of capital caused by the drawing down of private retirement plans. If we had raised savings and investment in the interim, the economy would be larger, but it would then have to contract. Moreover, with labor in relatively short supply, capital will probably not be as productive, and the returns in super IRAs could well prove disappointing.

An aging population is a problem for the whole economy and the entire system of retirement provision. To maintain the solvency of that system, we may need to keep down the ratio of retirees to workers by reversing recent trends toward early retirement. The Social Security legislation of 1983 gradually extends the expected retirement age from 65 to 67 early in the next century. Another step would be to index the retirement age to life expectancy. For example, for every increase of a year in life expectancy, we could raise the retirement age by six months, thereby allocating half of every extra year of life to work. Such adjustments might take place once a decade and apply to those retiring ten or more years later.

Although the privatization of Social Security is not a necessary solution—and probably no solution at all—to the long-run problems of retirement provision, its political appeal may nonetheless grow in the 1990s. In earlier periods, conservative opposition to Social Security had a purely negative character, but now an alternative private instrument of retirement provision has taken shape. There is no denying that the IRA

[60] Many critics argue that the potential insolvency of Social Security in the twenty-first century requires action now. I am puzzled that people who consider five-year economic plans an absurdity take seriously the seventy-five year forecast of Social Security revenues and costs. The seventy-five year fiscal horizon required by Congress for Social Security has no parallel elsewhere in our government. Pity the Social Security actuary. Before indexing, the actuary could assume no increase in benefits, but now the costs of the program depend on more complex factors. The actuary must project unemployment and inflation rates far into the next century even though we have no idea what they will be in a year. The projections are hypothetical; except at the extremes, they are useless as a guide to current policy choices. Nevertheless, the numbers have contributed to the political destabilization of the Social Security system.

offers more individual discretion than do Social Security and pensions about how much to put aside for retirement, where to invest, and when and how much to withdraw. Moreover, because the IRA is individually controlled rather than corporate- or government-run, it is the perfect vehicle for conservative populism. It appeals to the individualism that runs deep in our culture and politics. At the same time, it is a vessel into which inconvenient corporate and government liabilities may be dumped.

Public opinion about Social Security will also be increasingly colored by the decline in the real rate of return stemming from the maturity of the system. The early cohorts enjoyed such spectacular returns from the system that it made no rational sense for them to oppose it. As returns fall, opposition for the first time becomes rational in a narrow, individualistic sense: some people, notably the affluent, could do better in the marketplace. However, whether the objective comparisons matter is hard to tell. It is a rare individual indeed who keeps track of what Social Security or private pension plans have cumulatively cost or what they will ultimately produce in benefits. Most people have no way to calculate the return on either "investment."

Thus, much depends on perceptions and sentiments. Public choice economists often argue that fiscal illusions cause government growth. In the standard theory, people see public-sector benefits as larger than their costs; rather, those on whom benefits are concentrated agitate more successfully for their interests than do the larger number over whom taxes are diffused. Conservatives argue that Americans underestimate the costs of Social Security: first, they do not see the employers' contribution or understand that it ultimately falls on the employee; and second, the whole language of contribution and insurance falsely suggests that the program gives a fair return.[61]

However, as I indicated earlier, surveys suggest that the public actually believes private pensions are a better deal. The explanation may be that there are even greater illusions about pensions than about Social Security. Many workers see no payroll deduction for their pensions, whereas they know they pay at least their half for Social Security. They certainly do not take into account the tax expenditures for private pensions. Fiscal illusions make private alternatives seem cheaper to the individual than they are to the society. So fiscal illusions will likely work in favor of privatization, not against it.

Nonetheless, even as the double payment problem begins to ease in the nineties, other political impediments will block the total privatization of Social Security. While guaranteeing benefits to current retirees, the Fer-

---

[61] William C. Mitchell, *The Popularity of Social Security: A Paradox in Public Choice* (Washington, D.C.: American Enterprise Institute for Policy Research, 1976).

rara approach, like Boskin's, would eliminate the progressive benefit structure for those now working and approaching retirement—a change that would threaten large numbers of low- and middle-income Americans with steep losses of retirement income. No other issue is so likely to mobilize them to vote liberal, and conservative politicians will not dare risk that reaction.

The more likely form of privatization might be called "privatization of the surplus"—a diversion into IRAs of some portion of the surplus Social Security would otherwise begin accumulating in the 1990s to pay benefits for the baby-boom generation.[62] Conservatives may propose in a populist vein that Americans be allowed the option of keeping a share of those national savings under their own individual control. In the process, the surplus now planned for the baby-boom generation could become permanently institutionalized but allowed to accumulate in individual accounts. In Chapter 2, Professor Tobin suggests that individual accounts of a similar kind could be set up as a part of Social Security through a long transitional period. This proposal for the individualization of the program might, in practice, be a step toward privatization. Once accounts were individually constituted and reported, it would be a short step to giving the beneficiaries the option of choosing among investment alternatives. My own view is that rather than a total shift, we are more likely to use individual accounts as a partial alternative to Social Security—or as a second tier within it. (Whether they are inside or outside the program may not really matter.) Under such an arrangement, taxpayers could be allowed a partial credit against payroll taxes for enlarged IRA contributions in exchange for reduced claims against the basic Social Security system in the future. By allowing only a partial credit, they could be charged an "opting out" tax that would help bolster the system in the short run while also reducing its long-run liabilities.[63]

Providing the option of a partial, taxed "exit" would not destroy the integrity of Social Security. In effect, it means changing the system from a defined-benefit plan to one with a defined benefit at its base and a defined-contribution plan as a limited option. To be sure, such a shift might mean a reduction in the governmentally guaranteed income replacement rate for those who used the defined-contribution provision. But with the growth of other retirement assets, some reduction might be in order for middle- and upper-income retirees, although that could also be accom-

[62] I am not the first to raise this possibility. See Stuart J. Sweet, "A Looming Federal Surplus," *Wall Street Journal*, March 28, 1984.

[63] On the "opting out" tax, see Goodman, "Private Alternatives to Social Security," pp. 111–12; Stuart Butler and Peter Germanis, "Achieving a Political Strategy for Reform," in Ferrara, ed., *Social Security: Prospects for Real Reform*, p. 168.

plished by taxing both the income of pension funds and a higher proportion of Social Security benefits.[64]

The chief risk of partial privatization, even in a reduced form, is that it
might eventually lead toward the more radical plan to strip Social Security of all progressive features. The market-oriented reformers all share
an antipathy toward mixing welfare and insurance and ultimately to welfare provision itself. They want to extract and purify the two and put the
welfare payments into a means-tested program, where the benefits could
be stringently regulated.

There is, however, a logic to building transfers into the structure of
Social Security. The purpose is not only to disguise welfare in a garb that
preserves self-respect. Social Security is, among other things, a setting
where we collectively set out our practical rules for distributive justice.
To put benefits for the aged poor into Social Security is to get different
distributive comparisons made than if they were lumped together with
the poor in general under other welfare programs. This is, of course,
highly favorable to the poor who are old, and that is how I think Americans intend it. We are not worried, after all, about undermining their
work incentives or encouraging a life of dissipation. The elderly are one
group who cannot be ruined by welfare.[65] Nor are they a special interest
in the same sense as the textile industry; after all, we all hope to join them.
At least, most of us do not like the alternative. Some critics marching
under the banner of "generational equity" now argue that the elderly are
getting too much from the rest of us. But "we" will be "them," and their
share will be ours. At least, we have the option of thinking that way and
acting as if we are members of a common national household.

[64] Under current legislation, half of Social Security benefits are taxable to the extent that
a beneficiary's annual income exceeds $25,000. In the interests of fiscal solvency and a more
progressive method of finance, some have suggested making Social Security benefits fully
taxable. However, half of Social Security contributions are taxed in the first place, whereas
no employer pension contributions are taxed. Hence, if both pension and Social Security
benefits were fully taxed, the Social Security system would bear a greater fiscal burden. It
would be odd for the federal government to tax the flow of money through Social Security
both coming in and going out while taxing pensions only going out. If more Social Security
benefits are to be taxed, it would only be fair to tax some or all of the income of pension
plans, thereby reducing the highly regressive tax expenditures for employer pensions.

[65] Irving Kristol, "Skepticism, Meliorism, and *The Public Interest*," *Public Interest*, 81
(Fall 1985): 39.

III

6

Disability Insurance in an Age of Retrenchment: The Politics of Implementing Rights

JERRY L. MASHAW

During the decade from 1975 to 1985 Social Security policy has been of more general political interest than at any time since the 1930s. On the fiftieth anniversary of the Social Security Act, in 1985, the body politic seemed to be searching for a new consensus concerning the basic philosophy of social insurance that the Social Security Act embodies. Social welfare programs generated by the depression of the 1930s and legitimated by decades of almost trouble-free operation were rendered problematic by the stagflation of the 1970s.

To look at the politics of Social Security in this way is to equate Social Security policy, or at least to align it, with macroeconomic policy generally. As Keynsian pump-priming supported the development of Social Security in the 1930s and economic expansion funded program growth in the 1950s and 1960s, so supply-side worries have called it into question in the late 1970s and 1980s. Yet, however true, that characterization reveals little of the distinctive character of political action surrounding issues of Social Security policy. Indeed, Martha Derthick, our leading political historian of Social Security policy making, argues that the truly interesting story of Social Security politics lies in observing the activities of a few "insiders" who over a remarkably long period of time have shaped the agenda and outcomes of public choice about Social Security.[1] Moreover, Derthick's study of the period 1935 to 1975 correctly predicted that fiscal strain was likely to shift the politics of pensions from the low visibility insiders game she so artfully describes to a more visible set of issues of general public interest. Derthick believed the general public

---

[1] Martha Derthick, *Policymaking for Social Security*. Much of the following discussion of the legislative politics in the 1956–1970 period is based on Derthick's account.

was likely to be unhappy with the size and scope of a Social Security program that had incrementally but steadily expanded for forty years.

Yet, if Derthick's predictions of renewed general interest in Social Security policy have turned out to be generally accurate, her predictions concerning the effects of "democratizing" Social Security politics now seem wide of the mark. If presidential electoral politics are a meaningful indication of the national will, then the lesson of the election of 1984 was that Social Security pensions, and perhaps other aspects of the program, are politically untouchable. In perhaps the only successful bit of issue-shaping in the whole of his campaign, Walter Mondale managed to make Ronald Reagan's commitment to Social Security the litmus test of his (and the Republican party's) compassion for the aged and the unfortunate. Having no wish to became the Alf Landon of the 1980s, Ronald Reagan has become an apparently intransigent defender of Social Security pension benefits. Thus, while the politics of Social Security pensions in the context of fiscal strain caused Social Security policy to have salience even at the level of presidential electoral politics, the results seem merely to reconfirm the anticipatory reactions of insiders from the thirties to the present; the consensus view of the American electorate is that Social Security is a very good thing. Indeed, one might have imagined that insiders could manipulate the agenda of choice to feature protective or expansionist alternatives over a considerable number of years only because their machinations reflected public sentiments.

Strangely, then, it would appear that insider politics may be coextensive with ideological politics, at least where there is a broad-based commitment to an ideology. The insiders—in Derthick's story the major leaders of the Social Security Administration (SSA)—were effective precisely because they embodied an ideological commitment widely shared by the general public. To be sure, this general commitment needs testing from time to time under varying conditions. And if the public's commitment has changed or is found wanting, then presumably insider politics could not be played in the same way. Nevertheless, it seems clear that an insider's game need not be viewed as some form of conspiracy to defraud. Instead, it may represent the technical elaboration of political ideology, subject to recurrent testing by political entrepreneurs who will survive or disappear depending upon the accuracy of their predictions of public tastes.

In this chapter I want to argue that the politics of Social Security disability insurance is, as Derthick's study also recognizes, somewhat different from the politics of Social Security pensions. It is in one sense a politics of interest groups whose number and level of participation have accelerated over the past decade. But to understand disability policy making in this way is also to miss much of crucial importance. A focus on interest group activity, like a focus on insider activity, may conceal as much as it illuminates. Political commitment to social insurance ideals and their programmatic elaboration as a set of individual rights or entitlements are also important starting points for understanding the disability insurance scheme. Moreover, because shifts in the generosity of the disability program are accomplished primarily through changes in administrative procedures, disability politics is also a highly technical game in which insiders play crucial roles.

More particularly still, the story of disability politics in the decade from 1975 to 1985 reveals that the ideology of entitlements or rights, implied by social insurance, gives a crucial political role to two sets of institutional actors—administrative law judges and the federal judiciary. For in the process of enforcing individual legal rights these institutions constrain attempts to tilt disability administration toward cost containment, serve as focal points for public and congressional interest in the program, and provide avenues for interest group formation, mobilization, and action, which spill over into the broader policy process. There are few better illustrations of the permeability of the social and institutional membranes separating law and politics than the history of Social Security disability policy making. The implementation of the disability insurance program is thus a curious and distinctive game in which rights may be the trump card politically as well as legally.

Ideology and Institutions in
the Politics of Disability Insurance

Social Security disability insurance is part of the state's basic commitment to safeguard its citizens against interruption of income from productive employment because of events beyond their control. In the words of President Roosevelt's Committee on Economic Security,

> The one almost all-embracing measure of security is an assured income. A program of economic security, as we envision it, must have as its primary aim the assurance of an adequate income to each human being in childhood, youth, middle age, or old age—in sickness or in health. It must provide safeguards against all the hazards leading to destitution and dependency.
>
> A piecemeal approach is dictated by practical considerations, but the broad objectives should never be forgotten. Whatever measures are deemed immediately expedient should be so designed that they can be embodied in the complete program which we must have ere long.[2]

[2] *Report of the Committee on Economic Security,* in *The Report of the Committee on*

Although the committee recommended and the 1935 Congress subsequently enacted only an unemployment compensation and pension
scheme, the failure to recommend immediate progress on national health
insurance and disability insurance was strategic. Both visionary and politically astute, the committee was unwilling to see consensual elements
of the system delayed while political compromise was achieved on health
care and disability.

Immediately upon signing the l935 Social Security Act, President Roosevelt appointed a committee to study the provision of both disability
insurance and medical insurance. That body, the Inter-departmental
Committee to Coordinate Health and Welfare Activities, proposed the
enactment of disability insurance as early as 1938. This proposal was
adopted by the Social Security Board, and the board repeatedly recommended it throughout the 1940s and early 1950s. The argument for going
forward was always essentially the same: disability insurance and medical
insurance were needed to complete the system of social insurance against
the major hazards to interruption of income.

The underlying commitment of program professionals and other proponents to a reasonably comprehensive scheme of social insurance never
wavered, but proposals for inclusion of disability insurance in the Social
Security system failed to generate much legislative enthusiasm. In part,
these proposals failed because the insurance industry and the American
Medical Association (AMA) opposed them, but that is an incomplete explanation at best. Both groups were lukewarm in their opposition, and at
one point the AMA actually endorsed disability insurance. More important, another deeply held ideological commitment—the commitment to
maintaining work incentives in a market economy—stood in the way.

Everyone concerned recognized that the development of a disability insurance program that provided both reasonable levels of protection and
safeguards against workers simply dropping out of the work force was a
difficult business. The private insurance industry was, in general, not interested in providing such coverage except for isolated groups. Many had
suffered dreadful experiences with their private disability insurance
schemes when the economy went bad in the late 1920s and early 1930s
and the judiciary reinterpreted their policies to radically expand their coverage. The insurance industry widely believed and constantly reported to
Congress and to the planning bodies of the Social Security Board that in
times of economic stress a disability system would fall prey to massive
overutilization. Thus, although the Social Security Board and some others

*Economic Security of 1935 and Other Basic Documents Relating to the Development of
the Social Security Act*, ed. Alan Pifer and Forrest Chisman (Washington, D.C.: National
Conference on Social Welfare, 1985), pp. 15–50.

were prepared to risk dramatically increased expenditures during times of unemployment to complete the general scheme of protection under Social Security, the relevant congressional leadership remained cautious well into the 1950s.

The ideological stand-off between disability insurance and the work ethic was broken by the ingenious "disability freeze amendments," first proposed in 1952. In this form disability status merely protected a Social Security contributor's subsequent rights to his or her Social Security pension; that is, upon being determined to be disabled, a worker no longer needed to contribute to the Social Security pension scheme to maintain benefit levels that had been earned up to the time of disablement. Eligibility was "frozen" and would not be lost by subsequent nonparticipation in the work force and noncontribution of FICA taxes. The proposal failed in the 1952 bill, but it succeeded in 1954. Indeed, although the AMA fought it, the provision was very difficult to oppose: a similar freeze was common in private health insurance, the proposal seemed eminently fair, and it cost very little.

The logical next step, of course, was cash benefits. If claimants were completely disabled and their inability to work was an excuse for failure to make FICA payments, why should they not be given a pension to replace their lost income? Yet logic does not control political choice. Indeed, in this case the major factor facilitating passage seems to have been party politics. A Democratic congress seeking to gain legislative initiative from the Eisenhower administration put disability cash payments into the 1956 Social Security amendments over the protests of the administration. The contest was heated and the amendments passed by only a one-vote margin in the Senate.

Although social insurance ideology had "triumphed," the inclusion of this essential building block in the edifice of American Social Security hardly forgot about the difficulties of maintaining work incentives that had troubled Congress all along. In the 1956 act, disability cash benefits were available only to workers over fifty years of age; it was an early retirement system. Moreover, the criteria for eligibility were quite severe: disability had to result from clinically determinable medical causes; the claimant had to be unable to do any job available in substantial numbers in the national economy; the disability had to be one that would lead to death or was of indefinite duration; the worker had to have very recent attachment to the work force; there was a six-month waiting period before benefits could begin; administration was by state rehabilitation services, which were thought to have a strong rehabilitation-for-work bias; and the SSA was given the power to veto any award of benefits by a state agency that it viewed as too generous.

The post-1956 disability program has thus sought to fuse or to harmonize the ethical structure of social insurance with that of a market economy. Adequate and comprehensive coverage competes with the desire to eliminate free tickets out of the work force. Moreover, this tension between goals must often be resolved through the administration of the program. Political pressure for either restraint or generosity sometimes focuses on legislative amendment of the program. More often, however, the pressures are brought to bear on the administrative level of operation. The politics of disability insurance is a micropolitics in which ideologically charged issues of social insurance adequacy versus market incentives may be transformed into technical issues of implementation.

Equally important, the institutional structure of implementation is as heavily weighted toward generous provision and rights protection for social insurance beneficiaries as it is toward managerial control of a potentially unruly program. This institutional orientation begins with state agency administration. First, although state agencies originally may have had a rehabilitation orientation, it was unlikely that they would fail to notice over time they were spending 100 percent federal dollars to support claimants who might otherwise qualify for state-funded assistance programs. Second, claimants may appeal denials at the state agency level to an "independent" administrative law judge, whose tenure and salary are fixed by the Office of Personnel Management not the ssa; the government, by contrast, has no appeal from a state agency award. Third, denials by administrative law judges may be appealed to the federal judiciary. Finally, an initially cautious Congress was unlikely not to perceive the bountiful opportunities for casework for constituents provided by Social Security claims. Every congressional office can, and usually does, become an ombudsman seeking to protect the rights of rejected disability applicants. This cast of institutional characters virtually assures that ssa will be the "heavy" whenever fiscal restraint is on an administration's political agenda.

With this understanding of the fundamental character of the disability program and the forces for constraint and expansion built into it, let us survey two distinct periods in the program's operation. First, I will describe briefly the era of expansion from 1956 through about 1974. Then I will focus on the period from 1975 to 1985 and the increasingly acrimonious political struggles over the administration of the disability insurance program during a decade filled with calls for federal fiscal restraint.

A Brief Survey of the Politics of Expansion

From 1956 to roughly 1975 disability insurance and related programs steadily expanded.[3] In part this expansion resulted from a series of legis-

[3] The legislative and statutory history of the disability program is chronicled in U.S. Con-

lative amendments. In 1958 the requirements for recent attachment to the work force were relaxed, and cash benefits for the dependents of disabled workers were added. In 1960 the limitation of the disability insurance program's coverage to persons over age fifty was dropped, and in 1965 the requirement that a disability be expected to continue indefinitely or to result in death was replaced by the requirement that the disability only be expected to continue for twelve months or longer. In 1972 the waiting period for the receipt of benefits was reduced and the grant-in-aid program for the permanently and totally disabled who were also impoverished was federalized under the Supplemental Security Income (SSI) program. (SSI employs the same definition of disability as the disability insurance [DI] program.) There were other minor expansionary amendments, but by 1972 the combined DI and SSI programs provided virtually universal coverage against the risk of disablement.

Perhaps only two episodes could be viewed as congressional retrenchment during this period. The first was the reaction of an expansionist Congress to the even more beneficent inclinations of the judiciary. Originating in the case of *Kerner v. Fleming*,[4] hence called the *Kerner* doctrine, the federal courts of appeals insisted that once a claimant had established by substantial evidence an inability to perform his or her previous job, the burden then shifted to the secretary of Health and Human Services, the nominal defendant in Social Security litigation, to show by substantial evidence that alternative jobs that could be performed by the claimant were available. Thus stated, the *Kerner* doctrine was not resisted by the SSA or by Congress, although the doctrine required establishment of a large and expensive program of vocational experts who could be called to testify in hearings whenever a claimant was likely to be able to demonstrate incapacity to perform a prior job.[5]

The real problem arose from further elaboration of the secretary's burden of proof by the lower courts. For, in *Kerner*, Judge Henry Friendly had not indicated exactly what the secretary was required to prove; he simply stated that "mere theoretical ability to engage in substantial gainful activity is not enough if no reasonable opportunity for this is available." The lower courts took this holding to mean that claimants could be denied only on a finding that they would actually be hired for a job available in their locality of residence. In short, the secretary had to prove the claimant employable in a concrete context. The administration re-

---

gress, House, Committee on Ways and Means, *Committee Staff Report on the Disability Insurance Program* (Washington, D.C.: Government Printing Office, 1974), pp. 107–24.

[4] See 283 F.2d (2d Cir. 1960).

[5] See Jerry Mashaw, Charles Goetz, Frank Goodman, Warren Schwartz, Paul Verkuil and Milton Carrow, *Social Security Hearings and Appeals* (Lexington: National Center for Administrative Reform: Lexington Books, 1978), pp. 74–85.

sisted this interpretation of the statute, and in 1967 Congress amended the definition of disability to make clear that it intended the more "theoretical" national economy test.[6]

The second episode involves the black lung program enacted in 1969. Arguably an expansion of the disability program—because it provided a specific vocational disability program for miners—the black lung statute was also a reaction to expansive interpretations of the disability insurance statute. As the soft coal mining industry went bad in Virginia, West Virginia, Kentucky, Ohio, Pennsylvania and Tennessee, unemployed miners filed thousands of claims for disability benefits with the SSA. Although the SSA resisted many of these claims on the ground that they were essentially vocational disability or residual unemployment claims, the district courts, the courts of appeals, and ultimately the administrative law judges in the fourth and sixth circuits were much more responsive. Thus, one interpretation of the genesis of the black lung program is that its design protected the disability program from a situation which made it politically impossible to administer the statute as drafted.[7] If the whole program were not to be enormously expanded through the ripple effects of the precedents developed to make awards to coal miners, then the miners' disability problem, which in many cases involved loss of pulmonary function, had to be carved out for separate treatment.

Notwithstanding these two essentially defensive attempts by Congress to maintain the integrity of the disability program in the face of expansionist attack by the judiciary, the general tenor of congressional action until the mid-1970s encouraged a generous attitude by the SSA as well. The tone of congressional oversight was set for a decade and a half by a major inquiry into the administration of the disability insurance program in 1960, sometimes called the Harrison Report (after the name of the chairman of the subcommittee which undertook the inquiry.)[8]

The Harrison Subcommittee began its investigation because of persistent reports of "strict interpretation" of the act by the SSA. Its hearings and its final report reflected both the proclaimants' rights attitude of Congress and the concern that the administration administer a strict statutory standard in a "reasonable" fashion. Indeed, at one point in its final report, the Harrison Subcommittee virtually instructs the SSA to relax the statutory standard to include some notion of job availability. The proclaimant stance of the post-*Kerner* judiciary obviously was not com-

[6] See *Committee Staff Report*, pp. 116–17.

[7] For a graphic of the shift from mining coal to mining welfare, see Harry M. Caudill, *Night Comes to the Cumberlands* (Boston: Little, Brown, 1963).

[8] U.S. Congress, House, Committee on Ways and Means, *Administration of the Social Security Disability Insurance Program*, Report to the Subcommittee on the Administration of the Social Security Laws (Washington, D.C.: Government Printing Office, 1960).

pletely off-base in its reading of congressional intent. Throughout its report the Harrison Subcommittee devoted most of its attention to the question of how claimants could be assisted and informed to better pursue their claims at all levels of the administrative process. The SSA's development of medical criteria which, if satisfied, led to an immediate finding of disability was applauded by the subcommittee, whose only concern was that these criteria be immediately put into regulatory form so that they would be generally available to claimants, their physicians, and their representatives. Moreover, the subcommittee urged the administration to develop vocational criteria to guide the determination of disability in situations where claimants were not qualified on the basis of the medical criteria alone.

Far from being concerned with whether state agencies might be too generous in dispensing federal funds, the subcommittee's concerns were rather that state agency processing might be too slow and that the statutory provision allowing the federal administration to reverse state agency awards but not denials might skew administration toward stringency. The subcommittee was mollified by the SSA's assurance that it in fact reviewed denials as well as awards and recommended redetermination to state agencies in situations where it thought the state agency had applied the standard too strictly. Finally, although aware of the district courts' persistent attempts to enlarge disability coverage by redetermining the cases submitted to them on appeal, the subcommittee responded that any problem with the courts probably resulted from the SSA's failure to convince them that it had provided the claimants with a full and fair hearing.

The administrative results of the political environment created by both congressional amendment and congressional oversight were not surprising. First, the number of disability beneficiaries and the cost of the program increased rapidly. In 1957 the program had supported roughly one hundred fifty thousand workers at a cost of $57 million; by 1973 it was supporting roughly two million disabled workers and making payments in excess of $5.7 billion.

Closely associated with program growth was not only expansionist legislative amendment, but also an alteration in the bases for administrative determinations. When the Harrison Subcommittee examined the disability program in 1960, 70 percent of all persons gaining disability awards obtained their awards because of medical impairments so severe that they met the medical criteria for disability without even considering the claimant's age, education, or prior work experience. Only 30 percent of awards were based on the more judgmental bases either that the claimant had multiple impairments equal in severity to some per se basis of eligibility under the medical listings or that the claimant should obtain an award because of adverse "vocational factors." Indeed, the latter and most judgmental category accounted for only 10 percent of awards in 1960.

By 1975 this situation was all but reversed. Less than 30 percent of awards were premised on medical impairments severe enough to meet the medical listings. Vocational factors accounted for 26 percent of the awards, and nearly 45 percent were founded on the judgmental basis that the claimant's impairments could be taken to equal in severity the medical criteria, although the claimant had no ailment that in fact met any of those listings. Moreover, the behavior of the upper levels of the adjudicatory process was increasingly generous. In particular, administrative law judges, who had granted only about 20 percent of the claims presented to them in the early years of the program, were by 1973 granting nearly 50 percent of the appeals that went to hearing.

The judiciary was also showing an increased willingness to overturn denials, but the change was not nearly as dramatic as with the administrative law judge corps. Statistics revealed a judiciary apparently prepared to respond to episodic pressures on the program but to retreat in the face of congressional action. Although the combined impact of the *Kerner* doctrine and the soft-coal crisis pushed judicial reversals from 20 percent in 1963 to a whopping 58.6 percent in 1967, the 1967 amendments, combined with the black lung program, produced a steady decline in the percentage of judicial reversals thereafter. Thus, by 1973 the courts had returned to reversing the SSA in only about 30 percent of appealed cases.

The Politics of Retrenchment

It was, of course, predictable that at some point this statistical experience would become troublesome. And, indeed, the troubles of retrenchment are the major story from the mid-1970s until the present. We can get some appreciation of the difference between the political perspectives of the 1980s and those of the early 1970s by recalling that, far from instructing the SSA to purge the roles of ineligibles, as late as 1974 the General Accounting Office, at congressional request, was studying whether the SSA should routinely reexamine denied claimants to determine whether they might subsequently have become eligible. The central concerns of disability insurance not only shifted, they shifted rapidly.

The Fiscal Crunch. The first indications of real worry came in 1974 in a staff report to the House Ways and Means Committee.[9] This was the first major inquiry into the administration of the disability insurance program since the Harrison Subcommittee's report in 1960. The stated occasion

---

[9] *Committee Staff Report.*

for this inquiry contrasts starkly with that of the Harrison Report. The cause for concern, if not alarm, was the "adverse actuarial experience" of the DI program in the late 1960s and early 1970s: between 1968 and 1973 the actuarial estimates of the future costs of the DI program had doubled. Moreover, because of the similarly unhappy projections for revenues and expenditures in other Social Security programs, principally pensions and medical care, it seemed that interfund borrowing could not cover the disability insurance shortfalls. Without increased taxes or decreased expenditures the program was projected to be "bankrupt" in about 1979. The committee staff was charged to determine the cause of this adverse experience and to provide a basis for corrective action. (One should probably imagine that implicit in the staff's instructions were directions to find corrective actions other than raising taxes or curtailing benefits, if at all possible.)

Although it constituted an imposing document, crammed with statistical and other information about the disability insurance system, the 1974 staff report was unable to arrive at a conclusion about the cause of the dramatic rise in disability insurance applications and payments. Possibly increases resulted simply from congressional expansion of the program; this was certainly a contributing cause, but it was inadequate as a complete explanation. The major legislative expansions had occurred nearly ten years prior to the dramatic increases in caseloads. And possibly the experience of the disability program was a simple function of unemployment rates. Everyone knowledgeable about disability systems understood that unemployment put heavy pressure on such programs. Workers with some medical impairments were highly likely to be more at risk than the general population in hard economic times. As unemployment benefits expired and jobs remained unavailable, these workers were likely to turn to the disability programs as a source of income. Yet, the unemployment pressure explanation was also inadequate. Rising and prolonged unemployment might explain application rates, but why should award rates be a simple function of applications? This latter question, of course, focused attention directly on disability adjudication. For, if the program were appropriately structured and managed it should be able to resist the pressure of applicants to turn it into a residual unemployment program.

Thus, like the Harrison Committee of 1960, the House Ways and Means Committee in the mid-1970s focused attention on the management of the adjudicatory apparatus of the DI program. The 1974 Staff Report, and further congressional inquiries in the mid-1970s, identified an interrelated set of managerial and adjudicatory issues that might help explain explosive disability program growth. Those issues can be grouped under two general headings. First was "lax management" of the state agency adjudicatory process. Pursuant to a request by Congressman

James Burke, chairman of the Subcommittee on Social Security of the House Ways and Means Committee, the General Accounting Office (GAO) studied state agency adjudication and the role of the SSA in assuring the integrity of the state adjudicatory process. The GAO report, "The Social Security Administration Should Provide More Management and Leadership in Determining Who is Eligible for Disability Benefits,"[10] was highly critical of the SSA's managerial performance. Although the report stressed problems of lack of uniformity and efficiency in case processing, it was clear that the inquiry was occasioned by dramatic increases in cost. The study recommended that the SSA take control of the disability adjudication process by issuing revised adjudicatory criteria and instructions and by closely monitoring state agency performance through its quality assurance program.

The second major administrative issue identified by the 1974 Staff Report, and pursued in various hearings and studies thereafter, was the increasing propensity of the upper levels of the decision process—namely, the administrative law judges—to grant claims. Moreover, it was clear that the Bureau of Hearings and Appeals (now the Office of Hearings and Appeals [OHA], the administrative office that manages the appeals process in Social Security) had placed its major efforts in the early 1970s on expediting the processing of appeals cases. The influx of SSI and black lung claims in that period, combined with increasing numbers of claims in the DI program itself, had produced massive backlogs at the administrative law judge (ALJ) hearing level. Congressmen were inundated with inquiries from constituents who feared their claims had been lost somewhere in the vast bureaucracy of the SSA. And Congress, both in hearings and through tens of thousands of inquiries concerning individual claims, put significant pressure on the SSA to speed up the hearing process.

This emphasis on speed tended to result in generosity. Because an administrative law judge who grants a claim need not write an extensive opinion justifying the result in the case and because judicial review will not be sought by claimants who are granted benefits, one way for the judges to increase their productivity was to grant marginal cases. Also, the Appeals Council, which hears claims that proceed beyond the administrative law judge stage, and which had historically reviewed administrative law judge awards on its "own motion," abandoned own motion review in order to delegate much of its staff to hearing offices around the country to assist in speeding up the hearing process. Thus, the only ad-

---

[10] Controller General of the United States, *The Social Security Administration Should Provide More Management and Leadership in Determining Who is Eligible for Disability Benefits* (Washington, D.C.: Government Printing Office, 1976).

ministrative check on administrative law judge "generosity" had been abandoned.

Finally, as applications and awards rose in the 1970s, so did the absolute number of final denials from which appeals might be taken to the federal judiciary. And, as petitions for review mounted in the federal courts, so did the number of judicial reversals of administrative law judge denials. Judicial review added additional pressure tending to tilt the hearing process toward the granting of doubtful claims.

Nevertheless, the possible profligacy of the upper levels of the hearing process was not a cause of major congressional concern. The number of claims granted at the hearing level and beyond was dwarfed by the scale of awards in the state agency process. Moreover, the imagery of the hearing process as the major bulwark protecting claimants' rights against error or maladministration at the state agency level remains strong. Far from an inviting political target, the ALJ hearing tended to reinforce the position of those who believed, as the Harrison Subcommittee had in 1960, that the major underlying problem with the disability insurance scheme was its strict standard of eligibility. That administrative law judges disagreed with the state agency decision in 50 percent of the claims that went to hearing was for many a ground for criticizing the state agency process, not the ALJ hearing.

Legislative Retrenchment. Concerns about fiscal strain, lax management, and the role of the ALJ hearing process punctuated congressional attention to the disability program throughout the second half of the 1970s.[11] A multitude of hearings, debates, reports, and proposals culminated in the Social Security disability amendments of 1980.[12] Here, for the first time since the program's inception in 1954, was comprehensive legislation designed to constrain the size of the population being supported by disability benefits.

The legislation had two major parts. The first dealt with a series of program characteristics which tended to reduce work incentives. Congress was convinced that for some workers, particularly younger workers and low-wage earners, the disability benefits structure made benefits too competitive with work. Indeed, for some workers Social Security benefits provided a greater net income than their prior employment. To handle this problem Congress capped the replacement rate of Social Security disability benefits with respect to prior earnings and also made technical changes to reduce the replacement rate generally for younger disabled

[11] See, e.g., U.S. Congress, House, Committee on Ways and Means, *Possible Areas of Subcommittee Action*, Subcommittee on Social Security, Disability Insurance (Washington, D.C.: Government Printing Office, 1978).

[12] Social Security Disability Amendments of 1980, P.L. 96–265, 94 Stat. 441.

workers. Congress further recognized that certain features of the program, such as the waiting period for the resumption of both benefits and Medicare coverage should a worker attempt to go back to work but be unsuccessful, limited the incentives of current beneficiaries to return to work. The 1980 amendments thus contained a series of provisions that might ease the transition of workers who attempted to leave the disability rolls.

The second major set of provisions in the 1980 statute addressed the bevy of administrative problems previously identified. The statute mandated stepped-up federal review of state agency determinations. Phased in over three years, the SSA was instructed ultimately to review at least 65 percent of all favorable state agency decisions prior to their effectuation. The SSA was also ordered to reinstitute own motion review by the Appeals Council of favorable administrative law judge determinations. Finally, and most importantly for the subsequent development of disability politics, the SSA was ordered to reinvestigate at least every three years the eligibility of beneficiaries not under a "permanent" disability. (All beneficiaries were to be reinvestigated at intervals to be determined by the secretary.) The 1980 amendments also confirmed a position long held by the SSA: the SSA had the power by regulation to specify methods of administration by state agencies and to take over administration directly if a state were found to be seriously out of compliance with SSA guidelines.

Administrative Stringency. While these legislative changes would have dramatic effects in the next several years, they were in some sense a belated recognition of a retrenchment that had already taken effect at the level of administration. Responding to continuous criticism of its lax administration and an obvious congressional interest in "adverse actuarial experience," the SSA had made significant progress already in gaining control over program growth.[13]

Between 1975 and 1980 the SSA had moved on a number of fronts simultaneously.[14] First, it began to take an almost uniformly restrictive view of its own directives. Virtually all of the SSA's policy advice to state agencies over the period of the late 1970s was in the direction of tightening the eligibility standard. Second, the SSA reverted to a stricter standard for the continuation of benefits for beneficiaries subjected to a reinvestigation of their status; this policy shift meant that each continuing disability investigation (CDI) would be a de novo decision on current dis-

[13] See generally, U.S. Congress, House Committee on Ways and Means, *Actuarial Condition of Disability Insurance—1978.* Report to the Subcommittee on Social Security (Washington, D.C.: Government Printing Office, 1979).

[14] See generally, Jerry Mashaw, *Bureaucratic Justice; Managing Social Security Disability Claims* (New Haven: Yale University Press, 1983), pp. 103–70, 173–80.

ability. Previously the SSA had reinvestigated beneficiaries only to determine whether improvement in their condition would justify a cessation of benefits. The change in the CDI policy, combined with an increasingly stringent approach to eligibility, was by 1980 having dramatic effects. In that year 71,500 persons were removed from the benefit rolls pursuant to CDI review. Projecting forward to the time when reviews reached the levels specified by the 1980 amendments, the SSA estimated that CDIs would effect 360,000 terminations annually.

The SSA also cracked down on state awards, in part through the quality assurance review. During the late 1970s the central office reviewing staff was finding nearly three times as many errors in state awards as in state denials of benefits. This pattern of errors skewed in the direction of awards was consistent with neither the historic pattern of error identification at the central office nor with the similar quality assurance reviews carried on in regional offices. Indeed, the regional offices were at the same time finding 20 percent more errors in state denials than in state awards of benefits. Obviously, the climate at the central office was more stringent than that obtained in the field. Moreover, to the extent that SSA specifically investigated state agency administration through what were called "100 percent disciplinary reviews," those reviews occurred only in states with high allowance rates. These 100 percent reviews consistently found problems with state awards in much greater numbers than with state denials. The purpose of these disciplinary reviews, as well as quality assurance returns generally, was to make state Disability Determination Service (DDS) examiners "feel the pulse of the adjudicative climate" at the federal level.

By 1980 SSA administrative actions had produced significant shifts in the program's statistics. Whereas state agencies were granting 50 percent of the claims submitted to them in 1975, by 1980 the award rate had dropped to 33 percent. Moreover, most awards were now being made on the basis of the medical criteria in the "listings." Awards made on the more discretionary or "judgmental" basis of the vocational criteria had been reduced to less than 20 percent of all awards. Indeed, the ratio of beneficiaries to covered workers under the program had dropped in 1980 from its 1975 all-time high (7.1 workers per 1,000) to its 1964 all-time low (4.1 workers per 1,000). The cumulative effect of these administrative shifts was a stable or slightly declining beneficiary population in the face of rapidly increasing applications.

The 1980 amendments thus added fuel to an administrative fire that was already burning brightly. The addition of the fiscally conservative Reagan administration, whose operatives were armed with oxygen tanks rather than fire extinguishers, transformed a political bonfire into a political firestorm.

TABLE 6.1   Disabled Workers' Applications, Awards, and Ratio of Awards to Applications, and Awards per 1,000 Insured Workers, Selected Years, 1960–1985

Year	Number of Applications (in thousands)	Total Awards	Total Awards Divided by Total Applications (%)	Awards per 1,000 Insured Workers
1960	418.6	207,805	50	4.5
1965	532.9	253,499	48	4.7
1970	868.2	350,384	40	4.8
1975	1,285.3	592,049	46	7.1
1980	1,262.3	396,559	31	4.0
1981	1,161.3	345,254	30	3.4
1982	1,020.0	298,531	29	2.9
1983	1,017.7	311,491	31	3.0
1984	1,035.7	357,141	34	3.4
1985	1,066.2	377,371	35	3.5

SOURCE: Committee on Ways and Means, *Background Material and Data on Programs within the Jurisdiction of the Committee on Ways and Means* (Washington, D.C.: Government Printing Office, 1987), p. 44, Table 7.

Retrenchment Plus Stringency Equals Outrage. As might be expected, the disbeneficiaries of administrative stringency and legislative retrenchment were outraged, individually and collectively, at the shift from generosity to stringency in the late 1970s (see Table 6.1). Moreover, in the Social Security system displeasure can be translated into legal action.[15] In 1975, roughly when the shift toward stringency began, disability appeals to administrative law judges were running at about 150,000 a year. By 1984 that figure was nearly 275,000, down from a peak of 364,000 appeals in 1983. Moreover, administrative law judges were making awards in 53 percent of the cases in 1984 compared with only 42 percent of the cases in 1975.

Even more dramatic change was reflected in statistics for the United States District courts. Those courts had received just over 5,000 DI appeals in 1975; in 1984, the number was 28,000. The shift in reversal rates was equally staggering. Whereas in 1975 the SSA's denials of benefits had

[15] See generally, U.S. Department of Health and Human Services, Social Security Administration, Office of Hearings and Appeals, *Operational Report* (Washington, D.C.: Government Printing Office, 1984).

been reversed or remanded by district courts in only 19 percent of the cases filed, in 1984 courts were sending cases back to ssa, or reversing them outright, a whopping 62 percent of the time.

As might be imagined, the enormous increase in the level of legal conflict at the hearing and review stages of the disability process produced general political conflict as well. Still chafing from administrative actions in the early 1970s designed to increase productivity, administrative law judges were now being subjected to Appeals Council own motion review of their determinations pursuant to the 1980 amendments. Moreover, the ssa targeted for special review over 100 administrative law judges who had higher than normal award rates. Although the ssa viewed this as sensible—given both the political impetus for the 1980 amendments and their own quality assurance statistics, which revealed a high correlation between errors and abnormally high award rates—the administrative law judge corps viewed the action as an attempt to destroy its independence as guaranteed by the Administrative Procedure Act. Picking up allies from among the organized bar and elsewhere, the administrative law judges immediately counterattacked both in congressional hearings[16] and in lawsuits against the OHA.[17]

Meanwhile, the federal judiciary, inundated with poignant claims for relief from terminated disability beneficiaries, used a wide array of techniques for reversing denials and terminations. Most distressing to the ssa were numerous cases advancing novel and expansive interpretations of the Social Security Act. Courts not only held that the ssa could not engage in a de novo redetermination of existing beneficiaries, but they also overturned long-standing administrative interpretations concerning the necessary levels of proof to sustain a disability claim.[18] The administration's refusal to follow these judicial interpretations, even in the circuits in which they were rendered, generated a political controversy of constitutional dimensions.[19] For many the administration's attitude seemed to indicate a complete breakdown in the rule of law.

[16] See, U.S. Congress, Senate, Committee on Governmental Affairs, *The Role of the Administrative Law Judge in the Title II Social Security Disability Insurance Program*, Hearing before the Subcommittee on Oversight of Government Management, Social Security Disability Reviews (Washington, D.C.: Government Printing Office, 1983).

[17] See, e.g., *Nash v. Califano*, 613 F.2d 10 (2d Cir. 1980).

[18] See generally, Don D. Crawford "Judicial Review of Social Security Disability Decisions, A Proposal for Change," *Texas Tech. Law Review* 11 (Winter 1980), pp. 215–48; Heaney, "Why the High Rate in Reversals in Social Security Disability Cases?" *Hamilton Law Review* 7 (1984): 1.

[19] See generally, U.S. Congress, House, Select Committee on Aging, *Social Security Disability Reviews; A Costly Constitutional Crisis* (Washington, D.C.: Government Printing Office, 1984). Perhaps the most important principle developed, ultimately subscribed to by virtually every circuit court, was the idea that a recipient could be removed from the rolls

As the continuing disability investigation program proceeded, it also met increasing resistance by states.[20] The states' interest was not difficult to fathom; terminated disability insurance recipients often turned to state welfare programs for subsistence. From the state perspective the CDI program thus seemed simply a means for shifting recipients from the federal to state budget. In state after state governors first protested the new policy and then, citing judicial opinions in support of their actions, simply announced their refusal to apply it. By the end of 1984, twenty-nine of the fifty states had ceased operating the CDI process in accordance with SSA instructions. The whole administrative structure from the state agencies to the federal judiciary now seemed in open revolt against the policy of retrenchment.

At the fiftieth anniversary of the Social Security Act, celebrants could hardly fail to notice that the politics of Social Security had shifted radically, at least in the disability program. The pre-1974 politics of expansion had given way to the politics of retrenchment. In that process, an administrative agency which had for forty years maintained both high public esteem and astute political control over its programs found itself embattled on multiple fronts. It was also playing the unaccustomed role of bureaucratic villain. Moreover, if the ingredients of Social Security politics were historically as Martha Derthick described them—that is, a politics featuring narrow participation and limited debate over issues of imposing technicality—those ingredients too had changed. Disability politics in the 1980s involved a diverse array of groups and interests, ever-widening debate about alternatives, and concerns about issues that bear on the fundamentals of political and institutional organization. But to appreciate the changed complexion of Social Security disability politics we must look more closely at group and institutional activity between 1981 and 1985. Amid the din of political rhetoric we may hear the echo of a French proverb, *plus ça change.* . . . Retrenchment is giving way to expansion.

---

only on a demonstration that there had been a medical improvement sufficient to make the recipient capable of doing work in the national economy. The Social Security Administration hotly contested this interpretation of the statute. In its view each redetermination was essentially de novo. Indeed, the SSA viewed de novo review as essential if the errors of the overly generous growth years of the early 1970s were to be rectified. The SSA recognized that it was evaluating people under standards different from those that had resulted in their initial eligibility. However, its view was that the current group of applicants and recipients were all entitled to the application of the same standard. For these and perhaps other reasons the SSA issued a ruling in which it declined to accept the circuit court's insistence on a "medical recovery" standard for CDI review.

[20] See generally, U.S. Congress, House, Select Committee on Aging, *Social Security Disability Reviews: A Federally Created State Problem* (Washington, D.C.: Government Printing Office, 1983).

The Actors and the Issues
in the Retrenchment Debate

Congress and its committees and subcommittees remained both important actors in the Social Security debate and an important forum within which other actors made their arguments. But the shift in tone of congressional presentation of disability issues and inquiries into disability administration between the late 1970s and the early 1980s is quite marked. To provide a sense of the changed character of the debate one need only compare congressional interest in the DI program in 1979 with its interest in that program in 1983–1984.

The printed congressional documents concerning disability insurance issued in 1979 (hearings, staff studies, and legislative proposals) necessarily provided the groundwork for Congress's attempts to reduce the disability rolls via the 1980 amendments. A staff analysis of the actuarial condition of the disability insurance program at the end of 1978 (published in February of 1979) reflects the dominant mode of discourse. The SSA (although, of course, the real culprit may be the Office of Management and Budget) was being chastised for its failure to request larger increases in its administrative budget for the fiscal year 1979. In the introduction to the staff survey, the author noted:

> In the staff's survey and study, reference is made to a situation which, if allowed to continue, might have the tendency to reverse the favorable actuarial experience which has been developing in the last three years. Both the state agencies and the Commissioner point to better documentation of claims and an improved system of quality assurance as one of the reasons for the reduction in allowances. Actions by the Social Security Administration, however, had prevented some of the states from being able to purchase medical evidence necessary to meet federally established documentational requirements. It now appears that no additional funds were requested in fiscal 1979 by the Social Security Administration to implement the new quality assurance requirements imposed on the state agencies. This is true even though the Ways and Means Committee, in its budget transmittal of March 15, 1978, had pointed to this specific area.[21]

Congress was prepared to support benefit reductions ("favorable actuarial experience" is the euphemism) by insisting that SSA take more money for administration than it had requested.

A review of congressional documents for 1983, just four years later, reveals a strikingly different perspective on disability policy and politics.

[21] U.S. Congress, House, Committee on Ways and Means, *Actuarial Condition of Disability Insurance—1978*, p. 1.

On January 12, 1983, for example, Congress enacted Public Law 97–455, which made major changes in the procedure for continuing disability reviews.[22] First, Congress inserted a provision permitting the secretary of HHS to waive the requirement under the 1980 amendments (on a state-by-state basis) that disability cases be reviewed at least every three years. Second, beneficiaries who had been initially determined no longer qualified after a CDI were given the option to have their benefits continued through the reconsideration and hearing stages of the adjudicatory process. Finally, Congress required that any reconsideration decision with respect to a terminated recipient be made only after a face-to-face evidentiary hearing. A Congress committed to retrenchment in the 1980 amendments was by 1983 finding the political fallout of that retrenchment difficult to withstand.

Indeed the congressional documents for 1983 and 1984 reveal a Congress preoccupied with the impact of the CDI program. Special hearings were held in nine states and the District of Columbia to ventilate complaints from a variety of interested parties. Moreover, the issue had sufficient political salience that committees other than the House Ways and Means Committee's Subcommittee on Social Security wanted to get in on the act. The Senate Select Committee on Aging, the Senate Subcommittee on Oversight of Government Management, the Select Committee on Aging of the House of Representatives, and the Subcommittee on Public Assistance and Unemployment Compensation, all held hearings or initiated inquiries. Even the Subcommittee on Civil Service, Post Office, and General Services held hearings—"Oversight of Social Security Continuing Reviews: Effect and Impact on Administrative Law Judges and Individual Beneficiaries." Congressional hearings also began to be printed under titles that reflected the tone of the testimony: "Social Security Disability Reviews: A Federally Created State Problem" is a mild example; another series of hearings adopted the more provocative title "Social Security Disability Reviews: The Human Cost."

In 1984 a major set of amendments were adopted consolidating and extending the developments in the 1983 amendments.[23] Most importantly, Congress for the first time specified in detail the evidentiary requirements for terminating existing recipients. Rejecting the SSA's position that the CDI process should take a de novo look at eligibility, the 1984 amendments require a showing by SSA that a recipient has improved or that changes in medical technology or the marketplace make a previously unemployable person capable of substantial gainful employment.

[22] 96 Stat. 2497 (1983).
[23] Social Security Disability Benefits Reform Act of 1984, P.L. 98–460, 98 Stat. 1794 (1984).

The 1980–1984 congressional hearings, leading to the 1984 amendments, also reveal the breadth of the participation in contemporary disability debates. The historical participants—SSA officials, the AMA, the insurance industry, and the AFL-CIO—were still in evidence. But their participation was dwarfed, at least in terms of numbers of appearances, by the activities of claimants' advocacy organizations and organizations representing the interests of Division of Disability Services personnel and administrative law judges. Many such organizations operate at the state level, but they also maintain national umbrella groups in Washington to represent their positions expertly and vigorously, both before Congress and in continuous contacts with the SSA. Their concerted efforts during the early 1980s had a clear and direct influence in moderating the policies of retrenchment that were developed in the late 1970s and embodied in the 1980 amendments.

Perhaps most striking to a reader of congressional documents from a prior era, including most of the disability insurance program's history up until the 1980s, is the democratization of the legislative politics that contemporary hearing transcripts portray. The conversation is not one among specialists from inside Congress, the administration, and a few major interest groups; it is between congressional committees and a range of organizations, many of which did not exist in the early 1970s. Thus, although Wilbur Cohen, Martha Derthick's consummate insider, is still present at major hearings, he no longer represents SSA or testifies as a professor or as a former HEW secretary, now he speaks for Save Our Security, an umbrella group of more than two hundred grassroots organizations seeking to protect Social Security benefits.

The participation of state governments has likewise been transformed. To be sure the heads of state disability determination services testify with respect to particular issues of administration, but Congress now also listens to organizations representing the DDS line adjudicators whose views may diverge from the "official" state position. More important, states have recently adopted a technique long used in the arena of veterans' benefits; they have created state organizations whose sole purpose is to advocate the position of the state's disabled or handicapped population.

Democratization of the disability policy process is of obvious significance in attempting to understand the likely future direction of the disability insurance system. "Mr. Inside" has become "Mr. Outside," but he is still taking the same basic position: the necessity to protect, rationalize, and hence expand social insurance coverage. At least equally important is the new role of lawyers and lawyers' organizations in shaping the content of the contemporary debate. In 1975 few lawyers could be found who understood the disability program. Today the National Association of Disability Claimants Representatives publishes a sophisticated monthly journal and participates in every major congressional or administrative decision. Legal Services Organizations and projects on the legal rights of the elderly and the handicapped have developed a small army of disability specialists who both litigate disability test cases and participate in state and federal policy processes.

The role of these lawyers, moreover, has been qualitatively distinct from the contributions of others in the broadened policy debate about disability benefits. Legal objections to congressional and administrative policies of increased stringency have transformed congressional administrative policy debates into disputes about broader issues of due process and the rule of law. The SSA has been excoriated by the federal courts[24] and the leaders of the American Bar Association[25] in terms reminiscent of those employed to describe the mélange of "Watergate" abuses of executive power. The legal, indeed constitutional, conflict that has raged over the SSA's nonacquiescence policy has been widely reported in the press.[26]

Legal disputes erupting around public policy controversies are hardly new to the American political experience. The interesting wrinkle here is that the bar, the press, the governors, and presumably the general public all viewed the administration as clearly in the wrong, when it had at least as good a case legally as had its opponents. For example, the only decisional body that addressed the administrative law judges' claims on the merits, the Merit System Protection Board, held in a series of removal actions that the SSA was justified in its exercise of managerial supervision over its administrative law judges.[27] Indeed, the board held that an administrative law judge's refusal to abide by those management directives could constitute "good cause" for removal under the civil service statutes. The SSA actions, insisting on standards for both productivity and accuracy, were described in these decisions as essential to the protection of disability beneficiaries' rights to timely and proper decisionmaking by administrative law judges. Those findings hardly settle the issue, but they certainly throw a different light on the true nature of the dispute.

Furthermore, many legal scholars feel that the separation of powers

[24] See, e.g., *New York Times*, August 29, 1984, p. 1, col. 5.

[25] In his annual survey of administration law cases for the committee on administrative law of the American Bar Association, Professor Bernard Schwartz described the SSA nonacquiescence policy (i.e., refusal to follow judicial interpretations with which it disagreed) as the most significant development in administrative law for the year. Moreover, he described the policy as "contrary to the very foundations of the rule of law." Bernard Schwartz, "Administrative Law Cases During 1984," *Administrative Law Review* 37 (1985): 133.

[26] The *New York Times* index for 1984, for example, contains thirty-nine entries related to legal disputes over social security disability benefits.

[27] See, for example, SSA v. *Goodman*, 58 Ad. L. 2d 780 (1984); SSA v. *Brennan*, 58 Ad. L. 2d 792 (1984); SSA v. *Manion*, 58 Ad. L. 2d 796 (1984).

enshrined in the Constitution and the vision of judicial supremacy enunciated and adhered to in American constitutional law since *Marbury v. Madison* do not require that administrative agencies acquiesce in, and thereby adopt as policy, the statutory interpretations of reviewing courts.[28] Of course, it is necessary to follow the court's decision in the particular case in which the interpretation is being given. The SSA has never denied that responsibility. But the administration did deny the responsibility to generalize a circuit court's determinations across either the whole of its caseload or all cases arising within that circuit when the administration believed the judicial construction of the act was erroneous.

The legal justification for the SSA position would lead us into a dense constitutional thicket of sometimes arcane arguments from history, principle, and policy. Suffice it to say that on the *legal* question, the SSA position seems at least as good as that of its opponents. The real problem with the position is political. Post-Watergate America is not likely to see the commissioner of Social Security as a valiant defender of the integrity of the Social Security Act against the depredations of the federal judiciary. To the contrary, the public is likely to perceive, indeed almost surely will, a lawless administrator seeking to impose heartless fiscal constraints, heedless of legal or human consequences.

1985 and Beyond

Ultimately, Congress adopted the 1984 amendments mandating a revised approach to certain interpretive issues and a significant alteration in the process of continuing disability review.[29] Arguably, by mandating a "recovery" standard and a face-to-face hearing before termination Congress has given up much of the policy it apparently supported in the 1980 amendments. In addition, the 1984 amendments' approach to other issues—such as the evaluation of pain and multiple impairments, the evaluation of psychiatric disorders, and the necessity for regulatory prescription of all SSA policy—also supports the historically more generous approach of the administrative law judge corps and the federal courts to disability adjudication as against the greater caution of the state agency process. How much the 1984 amendments mark a return to an emphasis on benevolence and expansiveness, and simultaneously an abandonment of caution and fiscal constraint, one cannot currently determine. As always, the real effects of high-level political decisions will be observable

[28] See generally, Paul Brest and Sanford Levinson, *Processes of Constitutional Decisionmaking*, 2d ed. (Boston: Little, Brown, 1983), p. 915.
[29] Disability Reform Act of 1984.

only in the pattern of administration over time. But two observations seem in order.

First, disability policy is and has been remarkably responsive to informal legislative direction. This was as true in the growth years from 1960 to 1975 as in the retrenchment years from 1975 to 1985 (see Table 6.1). Because Congress is, to say the least, quite permeable to public opinion, there is every reason to believe both that the disability insurance program is systematically subject to democratic supervision and that "we the people," to use the constitutional vernacular, favor a relatively generous provision for the disabled. The program can get into political trouble by courting fiscal disaster, but those troubles pale beside the ones that lie in wait for the administration that takes restraint too seriously. One would therefore expect the long-term trend line of disability policy to reflect expansionary rather than restrictive incremental change.[30]

Second, and partially supporting the first observation, disability politics reflects a strong ideological commitment to the idea of social insurance entitlements. When retrenchment-oriented policies begin to have bite, policy talk switches quite easily to rights talk. This issue transformation is embedded in the institutional structure of a program that uses administrative law *judges* to adjudicate contested claims and federal court *judges* to guarantee the legitimacy of the administrative law judges' determinations. Unlike the paternalistic institutional imagery of the U.S. veterans' benefits programs (which exclude lawyers and courts in favor of informal, "fraternal" negotiation with claims representatives supplied largely by veterans' organizations), the class accommodation flavor of labor-management adjudicatory boards in some Western European disability schemes, or the therapeutic orientation of other plans (which premise awards on medical evaluation by physicians who also decide the claims),[31] the American scheme features adjudicators who, by definition, determine legal rights. Although it is not literally true in our constitutional system that legal rights once given in the form of social insurance entitlements cannot be repealed or constrained (see Chapter 3 for full discussion), the idea that rights have been conferred operates as a political ratchet. The ideology of entitlement holds the current political purchase, while the lever of public opinion and interest group demand is repositioned to move the system to the next level of benevolence.

The administration and Congress have apparently learned a political lesson from the "juridification" of the disability debate, and I suspect that lesson will shape the politics of the program for the indefinite future.

---

[30] For the view that this may be true of all disability schemes, however organized, see Deborah Stone, *The Disabled State* (Philadelphia: Temple University Press, 1984).

[31] For more on disability insurance in Europe, see, for example, *ibid.*

Broadly stated the lesson is that substantial retrenchments in social insurance benefits are legally suspect and, therefore, politically unacceptable. Stringency in a social insurance program is easily equated with lawlessness. When that perception arises, the whole of the legal community rallies to the cause of disappointed claimants. This lesson may, of course, be an overreading of recent experience, but so is much that passes for political education.

7

Coping with a Creeping Crisis: Medicare at Twenty

THEODORE R. MARMOR

In 1985, Medicare marked its twentieth birthday. But, like the rest of American medicine, Medicare is in trouble. Program costs have risen sharply during the past two decades and continue to outpace the general cost of living and government revenues. Coverage has eroded to a certain degree, and the present benefits leave millions of the elderly confused, disappointed, and at risk of facing the catastrophic financial burden of both acute and chronic illness.

At a present cost of over $70 billion a year, Medicare pays less than half the medical expenses of this nation's elderly citizens. Since 1981, the program has been a candidate for budget reductions, although Congress has resisted the administration's most severe proposed cutbacks. With the federal deficit dominating public policy, Medicare has returned to center stage. And the future, cloaked in changing estimates of Medicare's impending "bankruptcy," frightens millions of present and future beneficiaries.

In 1965, when only 56 percent of Americans over age sixty-five had hospital insurance,[1] Medicare was viewed as a way to bring the elderly into the mainstream of American medicine. With the passage of time, however, the emphasis has shifted dramatically. Today the policy focuses on how Medicare can be used as a mechanism both to influence the nature of American medicine and to control the costs of health to the federal government. By examining Medicare's origins, its history, and its evolution, this chapter attempts to explain how and why this dramatic change occurred and what that implies for Medicare's future.

[1] Marian Gornick, Jay N. Greenberg, Paul W. Eggers, and Allen Dobson, "Twenty Years of Medicare and Medicaid: Covered Populations, Use of Benefits, and Program Expenditures," Annual Supplement, *Health Care Financing Review* (1985): 13–59.

The Origins of Medicare

Medicare, enacted in 1965 and fully operational in 1966, has complicated historical origins that are difficult to understand in the political environment of the late 1980s. Perhaps the best way to understand Medicare is to appreciate how peculiar the program is from an international perspective. No other industrial democracy has compulsory health insurance for its elderly citizens alone, and none started its program with such a beneficiary group. Almost all other nations started with coverage of their work force, or, as in the case of Canada, went from special programs for the poor to universal programs for one service (hospitals) and then to another (physicians).[2] This means that peculiarly American circumstances, rather than some common feature of modern societies, explain why it is that compulsory government health insurance began in the United States with the recipients of Social Security cash pensions.

The roots of this particular history lie in the United States's distinctive rejection of national health insurance in the twentieth century. First cited in the years before World War I, national health insurance fell out of favor in the 1920s. When the Great Depression made economic insecurity a pressing concern, the social security blueprint of 1935 broached both health and disability insurance as controversial items of social insurance that should be included in a more complete scheme of protection. From 1936 to the late 1940s, liberals recurrently called for incorporating universal health insurance within America's nascent welfare state. But the conservative coalition in Congress, despite wide public support, defeated this expansionist aim.[3]

The original leaders of Social Security, well aware of this frustrating opposition, reassessed their strategy of expansion during Harry Truman's last term of office. By 1952, they had formulated a plan of incremental expansion of government health insurance. Looking back to the 1942 proposal that medical insurance be extended to Social Security contributors, the proponents of what became known as Medicare shifted the category of beneficiaries while retaining the link to social insurance. Medicare became a proposal to provide retirees with limited hospitalization insurance—a partial plan for the segment of the population whose financial fears of illness were as well-grounded as their difficulty in purchasing health insurance at modest cost. And the long battle to turn a proposal acceptable to the nation into one passable in Congress began.[4]

[2] Theodore R. Marmor, "Can the U.S. Learn from Canada?" in *National Health Insurance: Can We Learn from Canada?*, ed. Spyros Andreopoulos (New York: Wiley, 1975).

[3] Theodore R. Marmor, *The Politics of Medicare* (New York: Aldine, 1973).

[4] For the history of the battle, see Daniel Hirshfield, *The Lost Reform* (Cambridge: Harvard University Press, 1970); Starr, *Social Transformation of American Medicine*; Ronald

These origins have much to do with the initial design of the Medicare program and the expectations of how it was to develop over time. The incrementalist strategy assumed that hospitalization coverage was the first step in benefits and that more would follow under a common pattern of Social Security financing. Likewise, the strategy's proponents assumed that eligibility would be gradually expanded to take in most if not all of the population, extending first, perhaps, to children and pregnant women. All the Medicare enthusiasts took for granted that the rhetoric of enactment should emphasize the expansion of access, not the regulation and reform of American medicine. The clear aim was to reduce the risks of financial disaster, for the elderly and their families, and the clear understanding was that Congress would demand a largely hands-off posture toward the doctors and hospitals providing the care that Medicare would finance. Twenty years after the program's enactment, that vision seems odd; it is now taken for granted that how one pays for medical care affects the care given. But in the build-up to enactment in 1965, no such presumption existed.

The incrementalist strategy of the fifties and early sixties assumed not only that public concern about the health insurance problems of the aged was widespread. But it also took for granted that social insurance programs enjoyed vastly greater public acceptance than did means-tested assistance programs. Social insurance in the United States was acceptable to the extent that it sharply differentiated its programs from the demeaning world of public assistance. "On welfare," in American parlance, is a term of failure, and the leaders within Social Security made sure that Medicare fell firmly within the tradition of benefits that are "earned," not given. The aged could be presumed to be both needy and deserving because, through no fault of their own, they had lower earning capacity and higher medical expenses than any other age group. The Medicare proposal avoided a means test by restricting eligibility to persons over age sixty-five (and their spouses) who had contributed to the Social Security system during their working life. The initial plan limited benefits to sixty days of hospital care; physician services were originally excluded in hopes of softening the medical profession's hostility to the program.

Once this incrementalist proposal was outlined, who and what shaped its fate? The debate itself was cast in terms of class conflict: socialized medicine versus the voluntary "American way," private enterprise and local control versus the octopus of the federal government. The parties to the debate were numerous and varied, representing broad strata of the American population. Though the program would most immediately af-

L. Numbers, *Almost Persuaded: American Physicians and Compulsory Health Insurance* (Baltimore: Johns Hopkins University Press, 1987); and Marmor, *Politics of Medicare.*

fect the aged, physicians, and hospitals, it would also involve (directly or indirectly) the families of the aged, all Social Security contributors, and the entire health care industry.

Medicare's principal antagonists and their adversarial methods illustrated a familiar form of ideological politics in the United States. The dispute over Medicare recreated the polarization that had characterized earlier fights over national health insurance. The most prominent adversaries—national business, health, and labor organizations—engaged in open, hostile communication and brought into their opposing camps many groups whose interests were not directly affected by the Medicare outcome. Both the contest and the contestants over Medicare remained remarkably stable from 1952 to 1964; two well-defined camps with opposing views reigned, and few individuals remained impartial or uncommitted.[5] Beneath the public rhetoric, though, was much division of interest and opinion, particularly in the health world. Blue Cross and the American Hospital Association, for example, had much to gain from Medicare's coverage of the high-risk aged, but their public testimony gave little hint of the extent to which they differed from the American Medical Association (AMA).

The stereotypical, static quality of the fight over Medicare is also understandable in light of the size and character of the major parties to the dispute. Large national associations like the AMA and the AFL-CIO have widely dispersed component parts; they function in part as Washington lobbyists for issues affecting the interests of disparate members. Such groups must seek common denominators of sentiment that will satisfy the organization's leading actors without antagonizing more passive members. These large organizations have specialized lobbying units, with full-time staffs devoted to preparing responses to public policy questions when the occasion arises and in the direction dictated by past organizational attitudes. Their attitudes, slow to change, help account for the predictable way in which sides were taken on various Medicare proposals over time. It is therefore not surprising that the debate during this period was stable; mutually incompatible positions on health insurance arose in part from the needs of large-scale organizations and their leaders to maintain their members' loyalty and a clear organizational identity.

The particular features of the political environment in 1965 explain details of the original Medicare program that seem problematic twenty years later. The overwhelming Democratic victory of 1964 seemed to guarantee that hospitalization insurance for the aged would pass in 1965.

---

[5] A more extensive discussion of the debate over Medicare can be found in Marmor, *Politics of Medicare*, and Theodore R. Marmor with James A. Morone, "The Health Programs of the Kennedy-Johnson Years: An Overview," in Marmor, *Political Analysis and Medical Care: Essays* (New York: Cambridge University Press, 1983).

President Johnson's commitment to Medicare was plain in the electoral campaign, and the new Congress of 1965 acted to prevent further delays in the Great Society's agenda. The result was far more complex than expected. The certainty that some Medicare bill would be enacted transformed the fight from a polemic over Medicare's wisdom to a strategy game about exactly what the program would do. Out of that game came the beneficiary benefits, financing, and administrative design of the operational Medicare program.

Outside government, national pressure groups made enormous and costly efforts to shape the discussion of Medicare. The AMA, for instance, spent nearly a million dollars in 1965 attacking Medicare's "omissions," its dependence on Social Security financing, and its failure to protect comprehensively the aged who "really needed help." The AFL-CIO used its considerable resources to counter this last ditch AMA effort.[6]

The Medicare proposals sent to Congress reflected the continuing attempts of those within the government bureaucracy to articulate and balance the pressure groups' rival claims. Consultation between government and pressure groups was sometimes explicit and detailed: the AFL-CIO and the Blue Cross Association, for example, met regularly with officials of the Department of Health, Education, and Welfare (HEW) during the early 1960s. In other instances, consideration of group interests was tacit and intermittent, particularly in the case of the AMA. Government leaders of Medicare, for example, took into account presumed AMA objections to the program by excluding doctors' services from the bill sent to Congress in January 1965. When Congressman Wilbur Mills insisted that Medicare include a separate component covering physician services, these same leaders anticipated AMA objections to a fee schedule and wrote into the legislation a commitment to pay doctors their "customary" charges. Behind-the-scenes bargaining between government leaders and the hospital industry resulted in the proposal's adoption of Blue Cross's "reasonable cost" method of hospital reimbursement.[7]

The ideological polarization elicited by Medicare shaped the behavior of all the interested pressure groups. For instance, public conflict between the American Hospital Association (certain to be assisted by Medicare's underwriting of the hospital expenses of the aged) and the AMA (violently opposed to Medicare, despite its members' short-run economic interests)

[6] See Marmor, *Politics of Medicare*; Sheri I. David, *With Dignity: The Search for Medicare and Medicaid* (Westport, Conn.: Greenwood Press, 1985); and Max J. Skidmore, *Medicare and the American Rhetoric of Reconciliation* (University: University of Alabama Press, 1970).

[7] See Judith M. Feder, *Medicare: The Politics of Federal Hospital Insurance* (Lexington, Mass: Lexington Books, 1977); Herman M. Somers and Anne R. Somers, *Medicare and the Hospitals: Issues and Prospects* (Washington, D.C.: Brookings Institution, 1967).

TABLE 7.1   Outline of Medicare Legislation

Medicare Part A: Hospital Insurance
(the Johnson administration's proposal, H.R. 1 and S. 1)

Beneficiaries	all Social Security eligibles over 65
Benefits	sixty days of hospital coverage per benefit period; post-hospital skilled nursing home services
Financing	payroll tax on current workers and their employers
Administration	federal (Social Security Administration), through fiscal intermediaries

Medicare Part B: Supplemental Medical Insurance
(adaptation of Republican proposal to expand benefits)

Beneficiaries	persons eligible for Medicare who pay monthly premiums
Benefits	physician services (excluding physical check-ups)
Financing	premiums, general revenues, patient cost-sharing
Administration	federal (Social Security Administration), through fiscal intermediaries

Medicaid (federal-state grant program for poor families
and the medically indigent)

was muted throughout most of the fight over Medicare. American Hospital Association officials felt constrained to take the "health industry's position" against Medicare, although in private discussions and in meetings with HEW their willingness to go along with the legislation was clear.

The bargaining over Medicare that took place, however, should not be allowed to obscure the vital fact that the election of 1964 had given all the actors less to bargain about. The outcome of that election reallocated congressional power in such a way that Medicare's opponents were overruled. What remained at issue was not the wisdom of Medicare itself but the detailed features of the program; the legislation that emerged from that bargaining is outlined in Table 7.1.

The form adopted—Social Security financing and eligibility for hospital care and premiums plus general revenues for physician expenses—had a political explanation, not a philosophical rationale. Moreover, the structure of the benefits themselves, providing acute hospital care and intermittent physician treatment, was not tightly linked to the special circumstances of the elderly as a group. Left out were provisions that addressed the problems of the chronically sick elderly—medical conditions that would not dramatically improve and the need to maintain independent function rather than triumph over discrete illness and injury. Viewed as a first step, of course, the Medicare strategy made sense. But after twenty years, with essentially no serious restructuring of the benefits, Medicare seems philosophically and practically at sea.

There is another problem beyond the mismatch between Medicare's benefits and the health circumstances of the elderly. If Medicare's social insurance rationale provided a statutory basis for the "right" to insurance coverage, what precisely then is the character of that right and the extent of protection it assures? It is here that the absence of a guiding philosophy becomes most apparent. One interpretation of this right to medical care emphasizes equality of opportunity. For the elderly, circumstances of income, housing, illness and family all differ, sometimes profoundly. Protection from medical care expenses, from this point of view, would simply mean that equally ill elderly would receive the same treatment and that their ability to pay for care would be irrelevant to the care they would justly receive. The right to such treatment would place a corresponding obligation on the guarantors of the right to make other considerations irrelevant to the treatment deemed appropriate. Note that this conception does not require heroic treatment of any particular class of ailments; it requires instead that whatever treatment is otherwise appropriate be provided free of the impediments of class, region, race, and the like. Equal opportunity in this context means equal treatment, not luxurious treatment, heroic treatment, or unlimited treatment. Ascetic equality is justified just as luxurious equality of treatment might be. Considerations other than equality of opportunity would bear on the extent of treatment equally available.

Medicare's development does not express a clear commitment to this conception of the right to medical care. Were it the dominant conception, we would have followed Canada's example and discouraged the independent insuring of medical expenses that Medicare does not bear.[8] Consider, for instance, the way supplementary insurance for the elderly has developed. Medicare has a variety of cost-sharing devices to restrain use and thus to redistribute the costs of care to the ill among the elderly. There is, as noted earlier, a hospital deductible approximating the average cost of one day of American hospital care; there is a deductible for physician services and a coinsurance rate of 20 percent on charges Medicare deems "reasonable." Since the incomes of the elderly are unequal, the imposition of equal dollar deductibles or coinsurance in and of itself produces unequal burdens on the financial circumstances of differently situ-

[8] Theodore R. Marmor and Rudolf Klein, "Cost vs. Care: America's Health Dilemma Wrongly Considered," *Health Matrix*, 4 (Spring 1986): 25–34, and Robert G. Evans, "The Spurious Dilemma: Reconciling Medical Progress and Cost Control," *Health Matrix* 4 (Spring 1986): 19–24.

ated older Americans. But this situation is compounded by our permitting supplementary insurance to cover these and other medical expenses. These tax-subsidized insurance policies pay for the care Medicare will not finance. More than half the elderly have purchased such coverage, with the uncovered disproportionately located among lower-income older Americans.[9] The necessary consequence of this is that older Americans face quite different net prices for the care of similar medical conditions. A right to health care, properly understood, would proscribe such inequalities.[10] A policy that expressed such an understanding would either bar the purchase of insurance protection for expenses Medicare does not cover or pay completely for the care deemed medically necessary and fiscally sensible.[11]

Medicare's Implementation

Once under way, Medicare proved far more complex to administer than its parent pension programs within the SSA. Medicare expenditures varied with the use the elderly made of the program and with the charges and costs providers submitted. Technological changes in medicine added costs unpredictably, whereas pensions were based on a formula that related present benefits to past social insurance payments. Medicare had to accommodate both providers and beneficiaries; the pension program could focus on recipients and internal administration.[12] These differences in organizational tasks, coupled with the program's two-part insurance hybrid, produced a historically unprecedented level of complexity for Social Security's administrative elite.

Medicare's administrative structure reflected strong provider resistance to the program at the time of its enactment. To hasten the program's implementation in the face of this resistance, Medicare's designers and first administrators sought consensus in their negotiations with providers. This spirit of accommodation led to the adoption of benefit and payment arrangements, as well as other policies, that were to exert inflationary pressure and hinder government's ability to control future program costs increases. Vague definitions of key legislative terms—"reasonable costs" and "customary charges," in particular—proved significant loopholes

---

[9] Karen Davis, "Access to Health Care: A Matter of Fairness," *Health Care: How to Improve It and Pay for It* (Washington, D.C.: Center for National Policy, 1985), p. 50.

[10] Marmor and Morone, "Kennedy-Johnson Years," pp. 131–51.

[11] For a more extended discussion of Medicare's philosophical premises—at its origin and currently—see Theodore R. Marmor, "Reflections on Medicare," *Journal of Medicine & Philosophy* 13 (1988): 5–29.

[12] Lawrence D. Brown, "Technocratic Corporatism and Administrative Reform in Medicine," *Journal of Health Politics, Policy and Law* 10 (Fall 1985): 582.

that allowed energetic gaming strategies on the part of providers. Unusual allowances for depreciation and capital costs (such costs were taken into account in determining provider reimbursement rates) contributed a built-in inflationary impetus. The use of private insurance companies as intermediaries preserved physician and hospital autonomy and weakened government controls on reimbursement. It was left to these intermediaries, who had closer than arm's length relationships with many providers, to determine the reasonableness of hospital costs under Part A and physician charges under Part B.

The truth is that in the early years of Medicare's implementation, the program's administrators were not organizationally disposed to face the confrontations with providers necessary to restrain costs. SSA administrators prided themselves on their history of successful implementation of social insurance. They needed the cooperation of all parties for Medicare's implementation to proceed as smoothly, and vigorous efforts at Medicare cost control threatened this cooperative disposition. Medicare's designers, aware early on of the need to build cost-control mechanisms into the program, were reluctant to make strong cost-control efforts for fear of enraging Medicare providers.[13]

With the benefit of hindsight, it is easy to criticize the accommodationist posture of Medicare's early administrators. At the time of the program's enactment, however, Medicare's legislative mandate was to protect the nation's elderly from the economic burden of illness *without* interfering significantly with the traditional organization of American medicine. With this aim in mind the original Medicare administrators sought to accommodate providers and thereby ensure a smooth, speedy start for the program. Not until later did Medicare come to be seen as a powerful means to control the costs and delivery of health care.[14]

The late 1960s witnessed efficient administration of an inflationary design, with predictable results. Medicare expenditures swelled, as did the health outlays of the nation as a whole. In the first year of Medicare's operation, the average daily service charge in American hospitals increased by an unprecedented 21.9 percent.[15] The average compound rate of growth in this figure over the next five years was 13 percent.[16] Medicare's definition of "reasonable charges" paved the way for steep in-

[13] See Brown, "Technocratic Corporatism," and Feder, *Medicare*, pp. 2–3.

[14] Robert M. Ball, "Assignment of the Commissioner of Social Security," Mimeo, December 18, 1972, pp. 47–48, and Theodore R. Marmor, "Entrepreneurship in Public Management," in *Leadership and Innovation: A Biographical Perspective on Entrepreneurs in Government*, ed. J. Doig and E. Hargrove (Baltimore: Johns Hopkins University Press, 1987), p. 280, n. 41.

[15] Marmor, *Politics of Medicare*, p. 87.

[16] Ibid., p. 88, Table 4.

creases in physician fees. In the eleven months between the time Medicare was enacted and the time it took effect, the rate of increase in physician fees more than doubled, from 3.8 percent in 1965 to 7.8 percent in 1966.[17] The average compound rate of growth in physician fees remained a high 6.8 percent over the next five years.[18] In the first five full years of Medicare's operation, total Medicare reimbursements rose 72 percent, from $4.6 billion in 1967 to $7.9 billion in 1971.[19] Over the same period, the number of Medicare enrollees rose only 6 percent, from 19.5 million in 1967 to 20.7 million in 1971.[20]

The 1970s: Ineffectual Reforms and Intellectual Progress

By 1970, there was bipartisan consensus that the United States faced a cost crisis in medicine. Although partly stimulated by critiques of Medicare, health care policy initiatives in the early 1970s focused on reforming American medicine, not Medicare. Recognition of this cost crisis spawned two separate lines of policy developments aimed at controlling health costs.

The first line of development was a reawakening of the drive for national health insurance, which reached its apex in the 1974 competition over which plan—Nixon's Comprehensive Health Insurance Plan, the Kennedy–Mills bill, or the Long–Ribicoff catastrophic scheme—would pass.[21] Medicare reform in that setting was subordinated to grander designs. The second line consisted of more limited, fragmentary initiatives that addressed the conventional topics of health policy and management. Originating outside Medicare's administration (and, in fact, viewed with hostility by some Medicare administrators) and relying on state and local initiatives, the new programs were intended to circumvent the "protectiveness and particularism" of program specialists.[22] The Social Security Amendments of 1972 (P.L. 92–603) established professional standards review organizations to review the care received by federally funded patients, encouraged use of health maintenance organizations (HMOs) in Medicare, required states to review capital spending projects for hospitals, and authorized federal support for state experiments with prospec-

[17] Ibid., p. 86, Table 1.
[18] Ibid., p. 92, Table 3.
[19] Gornick et al., "Twenty Years," p. 43, Table 25.
[20] Ibid., p. 36, Table 17.
[21] For a detailed discussion of these proposals, see Judith Feder, John Holahan, and Theodore R. Marmor, eds., *National Health Insurance: Conflicting Goals and Policy Choices* (Washington, D.C.: The Urban Institute Press, 1980).
[22] Brown, "Technocratic Corporatism," p. 589.

tive payment systems. In 1974, Congress enacted the Health Planning and Resources Development Act (P.L. 93–641), which created hundreds of health systems agencies to oversee area-wide health care planning across the nation.

These measures were part of a broader scheme that ultimately failed to materialize. When proposals for national health insurance failed to pass Congress, the new programs became incomplete alternatives to systematic reform and, because of their contribution to the diffusion of federal political power, deflected centralized reform.[23] Most importantly, these reforms were almost destined to fail at controlling Medicare costs because they left the basic inflationary structure—retrospective payment, pluralistic financing, and intermediary administration—intact.

The adoption of these fragmentary initiatives revealed two features of health politics in the United States that are important to understanding how Medicare has reached its present circumstances. First, no matter how large the public subsidies and how substantial the public interest in the distribution, financing, and quality of services dominated by private actors, the American impulse is to disperse authority, finance, and control. In an industry like medical care, this reluctance to consolidate authority is a recipe for inflation, as the past two decades have demonstrated. Second, the initiatives of the early 1970s illustrate policy makers' adherence to a theory of medical care that had slowly emerged throughout the post-World War II period. This widely held theory, sometimes referred to as hierarchical regionalism, held that "more medical care for individuals distributed by regional hierarchies [of providers] would lead to better health for populations." On the basis of that conviction, governments acted to subsidize "research and professional education, increase the supply of professionals and facilities, establish and encourage regional hierarchies, and reduce the direct costs of care to patients."[24]

As prospects for national health insurance faded, legislative interest shifted from new programs consistent with national health insurance to a renewed emphasis on overall cost control, similarly broad in approach. As the decade progressed, though, there was little programmatic progress on this front. In 1977, the Carter administration, alarmed by rising hospital costs, concluded that "clearly, the time has come—indeed it has been here for a long time—to bite the bullet on hospital costs."[25] The Carter administration's attempts to secure passage of hospital cost containment

[23] Ibid., p. 587.

[24] Daniel M. Fox, *Health Policies, Health Politics: The British and American Experience, 1911–1965* (Princeton: Princeton University Press, 1986), p. 208.

[25] Walter Mondale, "The Case for Hospital Cost Containment Act," in *Controlling Health Care Costs: A National Leadership Conference* (Washington, D.C.: The Government Research Corporation, 1978), p. 67.

legislation failed, however, although its efforts in this area did succeed in putting the hospital industry on the defensive and resulted in the industry's adoption of a "voluntary effort" to control spending. And, in 1977, a new Health Care Financing Administration (HCFA) was created within HEW to administer both Medicare and Medicaid, thereby releasing Medicare from the SSA's managerial ethos and bureaucratic style. Medicare became "one element in the broader universe of federal health care financing programs,"[26] rather than a freestanding component of the nation's social insurance system. With this change, Medicare administrators, now within HCFA's Bureau of Medicare, became more concerned with health policy than with social insurance. Also in 1977, Congress enacted the Medicaid Anti-Fraud and Abuse Amendments (P.L. 95–142), which enabled HCFA to collect and analyze hospital cost data. This legislation and the shift in administrative outlook and emphasis accompanying HCFA's establishment ultimately led to the crucial reform of Medicare's payment system, reform that recognized and was compatible with Medicare's peculiar organizational character.

By the end of the decade, the piecemeal reform of the early 1970s was in disarray. From one side came the charge that such fragmented measures had predictably led to disproportionately high levels of inflation in the health industry. From the other side came the criticism that piecemeal change had left some thirty million American citizens uninsured for illness and both Medicare and Medicaid in precarious financial condition. Medicare's release from Social Security in the late 1970s did prompt hope for the program's reform. At the same time, however, this administrative shift obscured the program's need for changes that addressed the fundamental sources of medical inflation, the erosion of benefits, and the confusion experienced by beneficiaries.

Unreconstructed, Medicare continued to be subject to large annual increases in expenditures as the decade came to a close. Nevertheless, it was still viewed as social insurance and, because of popular support, escaped severe budget cuts. By 1981, annual increases in overall health spending had reached crisis proportions. The rapid growth of expenditures on medical care far exceeded the rate of inflation in the general economy throughout most of the 1970s and, with the exception of 1979 and 1980, has maintained this inflationary pattern (see Figure 7.1). The result is that medical care spending consumes an increasing proportion of the gross national product (GNP) (see Table 7.2). National health expenditures in 1981 represented 9.8 percent of GNP, up from 6.4 percent in 1967; Medicare alone constituted about 16 percent of this total health care bill, up

---

[26] Brown, "Technocratic Corporatism," p. 591.

Percent Annual
Change

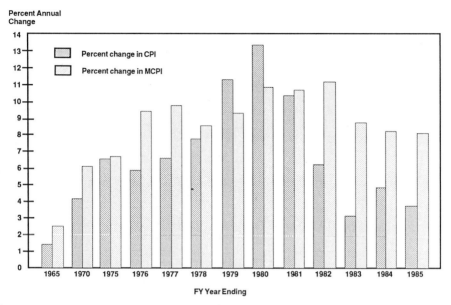

FIGURE 7.1. Change in MCPI vs. Change in CPI, 1965–1985
Source: U.S. Department of Health and Human Services, Public Health Service, *Health, United States, 1986* (Washington, D.C.: Government Printing Office, 1986), p. 180, Table 86.

from 9 percent in 1967.[27] Medicare payments for hospital care alone rose 22 percent from 1979 to 1980 and 21 percent from 1980 to 1981. Payments for physician services increased at a comparable rate, rising 22 percent from 1979 to 1980 and 23 percent from 1980 to 1981.[28] Medicare, and all health care, was consuming a larger and larger piece of the economic pie, seeming to crowd out spending on other goods and services.

During the 1970s, despite the rapid rate of growth in program expenditures, the elderly experienced significant erosion in their Medicare benefits. From 1965 to 1975, during Medicare's first decade, the fraction of income spent by beneficiaries on health care (including long-term care) declined from 15 percent to 12 percent. By the end of Medicare's second decade, however, this pattern had been reversed. The elderly as a group now spend the same proportion of their income on health care as they did before Medicare's enactment and by 1990, that proportion is projected to be close to 20 percent.[29] In addition, the proportion of income going

[27] Gornick et al., "Twenty Years," p. 50, Table 33.
[28] Ross H. Arnett, III, David R. McKusick, Sally T. Sonnefeld, and Carol S. Crowell, "Health Spending Trends in the 1980s: Adjusting to Financial Incentives," *Health Care Financing Review* 6 (Spring 1985): 6, Table 4.

TABLE 7.2   Medicare Expenditures as Percentage of Total National Health
Expenditures, Selected Calendar Years, 1967–1984

Year	Health Expenditures ($ billion)	Health Expenditures as Percent of GNP	Medicare[a] ($ billion)	Medicare Percentage of National Health Expenditures
1967	51.1	6.4	4.7	9.2
1970	75.0	7.6	7.5	10.0
1975	132.7	8.6	16.3	12.3
1980	247.5	9.4	36.8	14.9
1981	285.2	9.6	44.7	15.7
1982	321.2	10.5	52.4	16.3
1983	355.1	10.7	58.8	16.6
1984	387.4	10.6	64.6	16.7
ACRG[b]	12.6	—	16.7	—

SOURCE: Health Care Financing Administration, Office of the Actuary: Data from the
Division of National Cost Estimates. Arnett et al., "Projections of health care spending to
1990," *Health Care Financing Review* 7, no. 3 (1986): Table 7, p. 9.
   [a] Includes administrative expenses.
   [b] Annual compound rate of growth 1967–1984.

for Medicare copayments has nearly tripled, from 2.5 percent in 1968 to
6.4 percent in 1984 (see Figure 7.2).

The answer to Medicare's fiscal problems does not lie in higher copayments and deductibles. The incomes of the elderly vary widely. Although
Social Security pensions have diminished the rate of poverty among the
elderly to where it is roughly equivalent to that of the rest of the population, nearly 60 percent of Medicare beneficiaries have incomes below
$15,000.[30] Of Medicare beneficiaries with incomes under $9,000, nearly
two-thirds have neither private supplemental health insurance (Medigap)
nor Medicaid eligibility to pay for some of the care Medicare does not
finance.[31] Increases in Medicare Part B premiums and, especially, in out-

   [29] Mark Schlesinger and Pamela Drumheller, "Beneficiary Cost Sharing in the Medicare
Program," in *Renewing the Promise: Medicare, Its History and Reform*, ed. David Blumenthal, Mark Schlesinger, and Pamela Drumheller (New York: Oxford University Press,
1988), Table 3.4, and p. 17.
   [30] U.S. Congress, House, Committee on Ways and Means, *Background Material and
Data on Programs within the Jurisdiction of the Committee on Ways and Means* (Washington, D.C.: Government Printing Office, 1987), p. 199. See Figure 2.1 for an illustration of
the relationship between the elderly poverty rate and that of the nation as a whole.
   [31] Ibid.

Percent of
Income

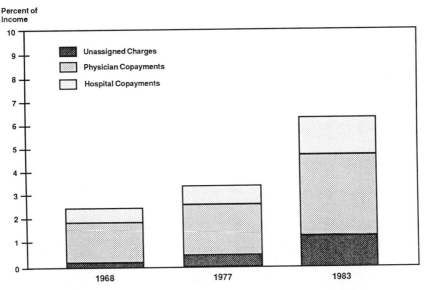

FIGURE 7.2. Medicare Copayments as Portion of Income, Changes 1968–1983
   Source: Medicare: Coming of Age, A Proposal for Reform, Harvard Medicare Project,
Division of Health Policy Research and Education, Harvard University, 1986, p. 9.

of-pocket copayments for care, which rise as fast as medical care prices, disproportionately affect these elderly, who, as Figure 7.3 illustrates, spend over one-quarter of their income on health care.

In its original form, the Medicare program produced a degree of confusion for elderly citizens that has persisted and, arguably, worsened over time. The separate coverage of hospital and physician services, borrowed wholesale from the conventional Blue Cross and Blue Shield plans, was easy enough for Congress to stitch together in the bargaining of 1965. For the elderly, though, it meant two different programs, each with its own fiscal intermediary, each with different deductibles, coinsurance provisions, and forms. Part A was financed by past social insurance taxes; Part B drew financing from both individual monthly premiums and general revenues. To this mix was added the additional complexity of supplementary policies sold by major commercial and nonprofit health insurers, the so-called Medigap plans. Since the supplementary plans took Medicare as their base, their benefits were typically expressed as partial coverage of the already noncomprehensive Parts A and B. Imagine the sick, elderly person recovering from major surgery who has to negotiate in such an environment. Deductibles, coinsurance, and excluded items are confusing enough. But adding to this confusion and compounding its complexity are the supplementary plans, bought by at least half the eld-

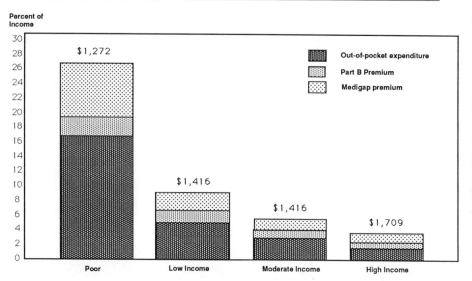

FIGURE 7.3. Per Capita Health Care Costs for Elders by Income Level (1984 dollars)
   Source: Mark Schlesinger and Pamela Drumheller, "Beneficiary Cost Sharing in the Med-icare Program," in *Renewing the Promise: Medicare, Its History and Reform*, ed. D. Blumenthal, M. Schlesinger, and P. Drumheller (New York: Oxford University Press, 1988), Table 3.2.
   Notes:
   poor and near-poor: incomes less than 125% of the poverty line
   low income: between 125 and 200% of the poverty line
   moderate income: between 200 and 300% of the poverty line
   high income: over 300% of the poverty line
Part B premiums were $172.80 annually for all enrollees. The difference in average expend-itures across income classes reflects the extent to which Medicaid covers the costs of these premiums. For Medigap premiums, it is assumed that poor and low income have the same average premiums; the differences in average expenditure reflect differences in the extent to which elders purchase Medigap policies.

erly population on average. If Medicare Part B pays 80 percent of the doctor's charge as defined by Medicare, the supplementary policy might pay 80 percent of the remainder. But that payment ignores the charges in excess of the Medicare-defined charge, so the 80 percent of the 80 percent is nowhere near what the beneficiary thought would be reimbursed. Such experiences occur yearly for millions of sick, older Americans.

   What was initially confusing has become only more so over time. With the reorganization of Medicare's administration in HCFA, Social Security offices throughout the country ceased to regard Medicare's administra-tive matters as their business. For the elderly, this change has meant less assistance with the delays, complicated documents, and requests for clar-ification about services received. Beneficiaries are left to cope with this administrative jungle largely on their own; their only links to Medicare are the toll-free telephone numbers of the insurance companies that act as the program's fiscal intermediaries. It is this lonely confusion that constitutes a depressing legacy of both the incremental strategy of Medicare's founders and the subsequent administrative adjustments made during the 1970s in the interests of cost containment and federal convenience.

The 1980s: Medicare in the Reagan Era

Medicare, after nearly fifteen years of quiet controversy in the specialized politics of health finance, has acquired a greater salience in the Reagan era. Always of interest to those in the now $450 billion health-care industry, Medicare was a second-order topic in the mass politics of the late 1960s and the 1970s. The oil crisis of the 1973–1974 period and the consequent stagflation joined with Social Security finance as the other high-priority items on the national agenda. This is not to say that Medicare was uneventful, but simply that it was a program of ordinary interest group politics, specially protected under the mantle of social insurance entitlement theories and the elderly's reputed political influence.[32] That protected status was what the 1980s were to challenge.

The challenge came in two forms. The first was inclusion of Medicare cutbacks in the grand design of the Reagan–Stockman fiscal policy of 1981. The second was the bold departure in reimbursement policy that the DRG (diagnosis-related group) reform of 1983 represented.

The Reagan administration, like others, lamented medical inflation and the budget implications of Medicare's rapidly increasing expenditures, but the administration approached cost control from a distinctive viewpoint. It was preoccupied with restraining the costs of public programs, not with reducing medical inflation. This preoccupation meant that Medicare policy was really budget-reduction politics. As a result, Reagan health policy has been marked by four themes: reducing public medical budgets; cutting benefits, in particular through increased cost sharing for Medicare and Medicaid recipients; claiming that excessive health insurance causes medical inflation; and restricting payments to Medicare providers.

In 1981 and 1982, Congress accepted this budget-cutting approach to the extent that it reduced Medicare spending $22 billion below what it otherwise would have been.[33] According to Congressional Budget Office

---

[32] For a discussion of the contrast between Medicare's protected status and Medicaid's vulnerability, see Theodore R. Marmor, "Welfare Medicine: How Success Can Be a Failure," in Marmor, *Essays.*

[33] U.S. Congress, House, Committee on Ways and Means, *Background Material and*

estimates, one-third of these cuts came at the expense of the elderly and a disproportionate amount came from families with annual incomes of less than $20,000.[34] The administration requested an additional $20 billion in cuts over the 1984–1988 period, placing fully 87 percent of the burden on beneficiaries.[35] Congress, however, balked at the more severe administration proposals.

The insistence that the elderly pay higher premiums and deductibles for physician services reflected the belief that cost sharing by the elderly effectively controls inflation. Yet Medicare patients already face substantial cost sharing; the elderly now are reimbursed by Medicare for only 45 percent of their medical expenses.[36] If cost sharing were such a powerful constraint, its dampening effect on Medicare's budgetary growth would already have become clear.[37] Instead, Medicare costs have skyrocketed. In 1983, they increased 13 percent, more than three times the rate of general inflation,[38] largely because of price increases by physicians, hospitals, and nursing homes rather than increased use.[39]

Data on Programs within the Jurisdiction of the Committee on Ways and Means (Washington, D.C.: Government Printing Office, 1983), p. 11, Table 9.

[34] U.S. Congressional Budget Office, "Major Legislative Changes," Mimeo, August 1983, p. 75, Table 10.

[35] U.S. Department of Health and Human Services, Social Security Administration, "Briefing," Photocopied document, February 1, 1984; and U.S. Senate, Task Force on Medicare and Medical Cost Control, Mimeo, 1984, p. 3.

[36] U.S. Congress, Senate, Special Committee on Aging, *Medicare and the Health Costs of Older Americans* (Washington, D.C.: Government Printing Office, 1984), p. 2, Table 1.

[37] There is some evidence that making patients pay more at point of use, through higher deductibles or coinsurance, will reduce total medical costs with few negative consequences in the short run. See Joseph Newhouse et al., "Some Interim Results from a Controlled Trial of Cost Sharing in Health Insurance," *New England Journal of Medicine* 305 (17 October 1981): 1501–7, and Robert M. Brook et al., "Does Free Care Improve Adults' Health?" *New England Journal of Medicine* 309 (8 December 1983): 1426–33. It should be pointed out that this Rand study did not include the elderly; it limited the maximum financial risk to 15 percent of the family income or $1,000, whichever was less; 70 percent of the sample participated for only three years, and the rest participated for only five. For data supporting an alternative—and, I think, compelling—view of the financial consequences of cost sharing, see M. L. Barer, R. G. Evans, and G. L. Stoddart, *Controlling Health Care Costs by Direct Charges to Patients: Snare or Delusion?* (Toronto: Ontario Economic Council, 1979). Even if one assumes that the Rand findings apply to the elderly, the already high out-of-pocket burden on the elderly would have to be drastically increased to reap those theoretically achievable savings. As noted above, the Rand study limited the maximum possible expenditure to at most 15 percent of the family's income. Since the average Medicare beneficiary is already paying slightly more than that, there is little room left for increasing cost sharing without putting an unacceptable financial burden on the elderly.

[38] U.S. Congress, House, Committee on Ways and Means, *Background Material and Data on Programs within the Jurisdiction of the Committee on Ways and Means* (Washington, D.C.: Government Printing Office, February 21, 1985), p. 119, Table 7; and Robert Pear, "Increase in Health Care Cost Fund Slowing," *New York Times*, January 29, 1984.

[39] Kenneth R. Wing, "American Health Policy in the 1980s," *Case Western Reserve Law*

The Reagan administration theory that medical inflation is driven by excessive insurance, which leads to overutilization of medical services, is inconsistent with evidence that demonstrates the small role that increased utilization has played in driving up health care costs.[40] Proponents of this theory overlook how crucial the decisions of providers are to the medical inflation problem. Moreover, the theory's strong advocacy of cost sharing is dangerous encouragement of practices that can prevent early diagnosis and useful care.

By the late 1980s more than half the elderly purchase supplemental insurance to protect themselves from Medicare's incomplete coverage. Since the poorest beneficiaries are the least likely to buy supplemental insurance, increasing Medicare deductibles and coinsurance would hit hardest the people least likely or able to bear the additional burden. At the same time, unless supplemental insurance is outlawed, the hypothesized financial savings are unlikely to materialize. Most patients would still not face the financial consequences of seeking and receiving care and thus would not reduce their use of services. But even outlawing supplemental insurance would not produce the full cost savings proponents claim. Over 30 percent of Medicare expenditures are for financially "catastrophic" episodes. Once the Medicare deductible and coinsurance were paid, there would be no further financial constraint on the patient to limit care. Other controls would still be required to restrain the very large costs resulting from catastrophic episodes.

Federal reimbursement policies toward Medicare's hospital charges changed dramatically in 1983 when Congress adopted the administration's prospective hospital payment method for Medicare. Under this new form of payment, based on a set of diagnosis-related groups (DRGs), with which New Jersey has experimented for some years, the Medicare program now pays fixed prospective rates for specific diagnoses (e.g., diabetes mellitus, arteriosclerosis).

There are three difficulties with this much heralded policy. First, restricting prospective rates to Medicare alone has created incentives for hospitals to shift costs to privately financed patients. Cost shifting by hospitals, to the extent it occurs, reduces Medicare's expenditures, without effecting medical cost inflation. Second, to the degree that hospitals are unable to shift Medicare's costs to other payers, Medicare patients are

---

Review 6 (1985–86): 608–85. Fifteen percent of the increase in hospital prices from 1973 to 1983 was the result of hospital price inflation over and above general inflation. For 1983, this figure rose to 25 percent (pp. 633–34). In 1983, physician fees rose 7.7 percent, while the Consumer Price Index, adjusted to exclude the effects of medical care increases, rose 2.9 percent (p. 638). Wing points out that, in the case of nursing homes, increased utilization, largely due to predictable demographic shifts, played a more important role in increased spending than it did in the other sectors of the health field (p. 643).

[40] Ibid.

likely to be less welcome. As a result, the elderly's access to hospitals may be restricted as Medicare's prospective payments to the nation's hospitals tighten. The problem of restricted access is likely to be most severe for the sickest patients with the most complex medical problems; in fact, restrictive payments by Medicaid have already reduced many poor Americans' access to health services.[41] Restricting Medicare or Medicaid program expenditures alone is no substitute for the containment of medical care costs overall. Third, even efficient hospitals may be placed in financial jeopardy if they serve large numbers of government-sponsored or indigent patients.

Current administration policies do not offer long-run solutions to projected deficits in the Medicare Hospital Insurance Trust Fund or to the problematic continuation of increased premiums. Even if all the proposed 1984 Medicare cuts had been enacted, Medicare insolvency would have been delayed less than one year. As it is, Medicare spending is expected to rise from $64.6 billion in 1984 to $118.6 billion in 1990, an increase of more than 10 percent each year,[42] while Social Security cost-of-living adjustments, which should help the elderly pay for Medicare's rising out-of-pocket costs, are estimated to increase at only about 5 percent each year.

The politics of Medicare in the 1980s is unintelligible if viewed simply as technical policy adjustments in an era of fiscal strain. The changes from the period of enactment to the present are environmental as much as programmatic. On the one hand, the combination of increased defense spending and sharply reduced tax revenues has put all social spending in a political vice. Social Security escaped that vice through the 1983 changes and the consequent insulation from the automatic cut requirements of the 1985 Gramm–Rudman legislation (see the Introduction and Chapter 1), but Medicare remains within the vulnerable set of programs. On the other hand, the world of American medicine is very different, both politically and institutionally, from that of twenty years ago. No one of political significance is advocating universal health insurance. The deficits of the first Reagan administration dominate political discourse and set severe limits on what seems sensible to discuss. Intellectually, we are living with the debris of the ambitious designs of Medicare's early promoters. In that environment, celebrators of market reform in medicine have had an unusually great effect.

Attracted by the goldmine of funds flowing through a system of retrospective, cost-based reimbursement, the captains of American capitalism

---

[41] N. Lurie, N. B. Ward, M. F. Shapiro, and R. H. Brook, "Termination from Medi-Cal: Does it Affect Health?" *New England Journal of Medicine* 311 (16 August 1984): 480–84.

[42] Arnett et al., "Health Spending Trends," p. 9, Table 7.

came to see opportunity where politicians had found causes for complaint.[43] In the hospital world, small chains of for-profit companies—the Humanas and the Hospital Corporations of America, to name the most prominent examples—grew into large corporations during the disappointing regulatory decade of the 1970s. Industrial giants, like Baxter-Travenol and American Hospital Supply, took their conventional plans for competitive growth and extended them to vertical and horizontal integration. A glut of doctors came into practice, weakening the traditional power of physicians to determine their terms of work.

All these changes in the structure of American medicine took place within the context of increasingly antiregulatory and anti-Washington rhetoric. Both Democrats and Republicans were influenced by a generation of policy analysts, mostly economists, who ridiculed the costliness and captured quality of the decisions taken by independent regulatory agencies in Washington. The Civil Aeronautics Board and the airlines industry came to symbolize the distortions likely when government regulates industry; and, with time, the convention of describing any set of related activities with economic significance as an "industry" demythologized medicine as well. So, even before the Reagan administration took office, the time was ripe for celebrating competition in medicine, getting government off the industry's back, and letting the fresh air of deregulation solve the problems of access, cost, and quality.

The irony is that the most consequential health initiative of the Reagan period—Medicare's prospective payment method, the DRG system—is an exceedingly sophisticated, highly regulatory form of administered prices that change the incentives facing hospitals. The further irony is that medical inflation declined somewhat from the high levels of the early 1980s (see 1983–1984 detail, Figure 7.1) just at the time that the federal deficit makes unthinkable a direct attack on the problem of thirty million people who lack anything resembling decent health insurance, let alone reforms to improve the scope of Medicare's benefits.[44] Fifteen years after a seem-

---

[43] Theodore R. Marmor, Mark Schlesinger, and Richard Smithey, "A New Look at Nonprofits: Health Care Policy in a Competitive Age," *Yale Journal on Regulation* 3 (1986): 313–49.

[44] At the time of this writing (June 1987), Congress was for the first time in twenty-two years considering major legislative changes that would expand Medicare's benefits. This development, interesting in its own right, has both a complicated explanation and the promise of serious disappointment. The first step was an administration proposal—strongly urged by HHS Secretary Bowen but furiously resisted by the Office of Management and Budget—to protect Medicare beneficiaries against "catastrophic" expenses. In fact, both the administration's proposal and the bills favored by the finance committees of the Congress do not provide full protection for such fears. Long-term care is not insured in any substantial way, and there is no provision for an overall limit on out-of-pocket medical outlays—the key element in any satisfactory protection against financial catastrophe. In the bidding battle

ing consensus on the crisis in medicine, the relative rate of medical inflation is still twice that of general inflation, and truly extraordinary changes
in the rules of the professional game are taking place as American capitalism flexes its muscles on the $400 billion industry we used to call med-
icine.[45]

Medicare, like disability coverage, was an unfinished item from the social insurance blueprint of the New Deal. Its politics involved fundamental, but recognizable conflicts over the shape of the American welfare
state, a struggle between liberals and conservatives that the electoral land-
slide of Lyndon Johnson in 1964 settled. Medicare's implementation
stressed accommodation to the medical world of the 1960s. Medicare's
objective was to keep the economic burden of illness from overwhelming
old people and their children; its early administrators worked on the
premises that Medicare required a smooth start and that accommodation
to American medicine's rules was congressionally demanded.

Twenty years later, the setting is radically altered. The difficulties of
Medicare are those of American medicine, not the program itself. The
remedial proposals for it are substantially broader than the tinkering with
Social Security's cash programs discussed elsewhere in this book. The politics of the program have thus diverged from those of retirement and disability pensions; this divergence is the consequence of differences in administering a program of third-party payment instead of pension checks,
the pace of change in the world of medical care, and the continued strain
of medical inflation. The result is that Medicare is now more vulnerable
to change than other parts of the nation's social insurance system. More
confusing to the elderly, it is also administratively divorced from the social insurance roots that gave it initial legitimacy. Moreover, Medicare is
unsettled and likely to remain so in the stalemated politics of budget deficits.

This state of affairs has both opportunities and risks. There is the
chance to recover the reasons why the nation agreed that medical care
should be especially protected from the influence of personal wealth and
the accidents of health. There is the opportunity, in the health industry,
to obtain more appropriate care without paying more for it. Unlike pensions, where increased benefits mean paying more, in medicine the real-
location of funds freed up by reduced payments for unnecessary or harm-

between the Republican administration and the Democratic Congress, the presumption of
improved benefits has emerged, but it has become mislabelled in the process. For more on
this development, see Lynn Etheredge, Testimony before the House Ways and Means Committee, March 4, 1987.

[45] For varied discussions of these new elements in American medicine, see Jeffrey Goldsmith, "Death of a Paradigm: The Challenge of Competition," *Health Affairs* (Fall 1984):
7–19; Starr, *Social Transformation*; and Marmor et al., "New Look at Nonprofits."

ful care holds out the possibility of improved performance. But with promise come risks. Suggestions abound that would worsen the circumstances of older citizens in the name of competition, rationalization, and reform. Cost containment can easily become the withdrawal of needed care. There are already examples of cases in which incentives of the DRG system have induced hospitals to discharge older patients prematurely.[46] Cost containment, when applied to Medicare alone, can simply shift costs to others or make Medicare patients less welcome as patients. Providing vouchers for HMOs to Medicare beneficiaries can as easily prompt providers to search for the healthier old as it can result in the provision of more efficient medical care to beneficiaries. And concentration on budgetary aggregates can obscure the reality that millions of older Americans, despite Medicare's $70 billion of expenditures, are without effective protection from the catastrophic consequences of prolonged chronic illness.[47] The mantle of social insurance, so crucial to Medicare's origins, provides no protection from these risks. Only a more informed and humane health policy will address the problems Medicare shares with other citizens and their programs for health insurance.

[46] U.S. Congress, Senate, Special Committee on Aging, Staff Report, *Impact of Medicare's Prospective Payment System on the Quality of Care Received by Medicare Beneficiaries* (Washington, D.C.: Government Printing Office, 1985).

[47] See note 44.

IV

8

Defusing the Crisis of the
Welfare State: A New Interpretation

RUDOLF KLEIN AND
MICHAEL O'HIGGINS

Assertions of crisis in the welfare state raise questions about what, if anything, has changed, why, and what the implications of these changes actually are for policy and politics in the future social welfare arena. Currently fashionable answers reflect a variety of ideological preconceptions. The apocalyptic right argues that the people have risen against the overreaching state and are reimposing the primacy of the individual and the market; the resource-constrained incrementalist center argues that the strains are a natural consequence of the decade of economic disruption and periodic recession since the oil price shocks of the mid-1970s but can be expected to decline with the resumption of economic growth; the neo-Marxist left sees the strains as symptomatic of the internal contradictions of capitalism, or, as Offe has put it, "the machinery of class compromise has itself become the object of class conflict."[1]

There is some truth in each interpretation. Citizens have reacted against high tax rates; low economic growth exacerbates the problems of financing welfare provisions; and the pressure to maintain the consumption power of vulnerable groups in the population may absorb resources that could otherwise be directed toward industrial or technological investment. They also beg questions. Why have people reacted against taxes now? Would the difficulties vanish or be significantly reduced if consistent economic growth resumed? In fact, are all these tensions explicable as aspects of the consequences of recession?

In answering these questions and dissenting from the simpler forms of the underlying explanations, we want to point out an apparent paradox:

We are grateful for the helpful comments of Ted Marmor.
[1] Claus Offe, *Contradictions of the Welfare State* (London: Hutchinson, 1984).

the size of the welfare state is both its strength and its weakness in this political debate. Despite the political rhetoric of rollback and the extent of economic disruption, the attack on social policies has, in most countries, been largely blunted. In many, expenditure on social programs has continued to rise; in others, the programs where cuts would have been necessary if conservative administrations were to effect any significant inroads into government spending, such as Social Security pensions in the United States, have been broadly protected. Initial assaults appear to have been repelled, reflecting a fact ignored in the rhetoric comparing current events to the 1930s or even the 1830s. The debate is now taking on what Therborn calls "a terrain largely shaped by the welfare state."[2] In other words, a wide range of programs now exists, has existed for several decades, and is a part of the day-to-day reality and expectation of the population. In the arguments about the establishment of the National Health Service (NHS) in the United Kingdom or Social Security pensions in the United States, the prospective beneficiaries were precisely that—prospective. They now exist as major blocks of the population, whose influence is important not only because of their mechanistic voting power but also because their existence affects the perception of normality held by the remainder of the population. The major social programs now *are* the status quo, with all the resistance to change that implies.

To abolish or severely restrict such programs means and requires discussing where the responsibility would lie in their absence—on the individual, family, community, voluntary groups. This does not mean that changes are impossible, simply more difficult. In particular, changes premised on broad ideological opposition, as distinct from dissatisfactions with the current workings of a system of provision, confront the apparently mundane and therefore much stronger interests of those who wonder what they will now do instead. Such consumers are not necessarily confined to the poorer and less powerful in society. The irony of the welfare state is that what some see as its distributional failures are part of the reason for its political success. It is precisely because the middle classes benefit from so many of the welfare programs that their distribution impact is often weaker than expected by the Left and their political base wider than anticipated by governments of the Right.[3] In the case of Britain, for example, public support for the heartland programs of the welfare state, such as pensions and the NHS, cuts across both social class and political loyalties.[4]

---

[2] Goren Therborn, "The Prospects of Labour and the Transformation of Advanced Capitalism," *New Left Review* 145 (1984): 1–38.

[3] Julian Le Grand, "The Future of the Welfare State," *New Society*, June 7, 1984. This theme is further developed in Robert E. Goodin and Julian Le Grand, *Not Only the Poor* (London: Allen and Unwin, 1987).

[4] Peter Taylor-Gooby, "The Politics of Welfare: Public Attitudes and Behaviour," in *The*

Such a widespread distribution of benefits is the basis of a sometimes unrecognized conflict between short-term and longer-term rationality in social policy. Rational allocation suggests directing limited resources toward those most in need. Thus, it may be argued that any increments in NHS resources should be concentrated on the underfinanced services for the elderly and chronically ill, where need is clearly greatest. Similarly, it may be argued that it is wasteful to increase by any equal percentage all Social Security pensions in the United States, surely the resources could be better directed. But to do so may weaken the commitment of middle-income groups to these services, causing them to shift their political loyalties. Longer-term political rationality may point in a different direction from short-term resource rationality.

In addition to this consumer self-interest, the institutionalized self-interest of the welfare service providers—professionals and workers in health, education, and the social services—helps account for the difficulties experienced by governments apparently dedicated to rolling back the welfare state. This constituency for the preservation of the welfare state is both the product of its growth and an important factor in explaining its continued ability to resist political onslaughts.

But if the size of the welfare state and the pragmatic self-interest of large sections of the population aid it in resisting assault, they are also among the factors that will prevent it from again experiencing a phase of relative growth similar to that experienced in the three decades after World War II. As Heclo has argued, after "the peculiar and unsustainable quality" of postwar welfare state development, social policies are in a period not of "crisis" but of reformulation.[5] Our political language, our mental images, and our analytic tools are all drawn from the era of the establishment, growth, and consolidation of the welfare state, yet we now confront mature institutions that require a different set of analytical tools and categories. In the mid-1970s, the management of retrenchment became briefly fashionable, but this was really merely the reverse of the previous ideas. We now need a new set of ideas to allow us to consider problems of adaptation and change in mature institutions.

Toward a New Perspective

What difference does it make if we begin to treat the welfare state as a mature social institution? How does this affect or enlighten our perception of whether or not it is in crisis? On the economic side, this treatment

---

Future of Welfare, ed. Rudolf Klein and Michael O'Higgins (Oxford: Basil Blackwell, 1985).

[5] Hugh Heclo, "Toward a New Welfare State," in *The Development of Welfare States in Europe and America*, ed. Peter Flora and Arnold Heidenheimer (New Brunswick, N.J.: Transaction Books, 1982).

asserts that the rate of growth in spending on social programs is unlikely to be consistently more rapid than the level of economic growth in a society, as was the case throughout the period of expansion after World War II, although this does not mean that particular needs will not lead to specific expansions. This assertion is based neither on the perhaps ephemeral political hostility in a range of countries toward taxing and government spending nor on any belief that we have in some sense adequately provided for the major social needs of the population. Rather the assertion is based on two related aspects of the fiscal implications of rapid relative growth in social spending by mature welfare systems.

First, the opportunity costs of relative expansion in larger programs are much greater than in the case of smaller programs. If social spending accounts for 10 percent of an economy that is growing at 2 percent annually, the 4 percent annual growth in social spending still allows other spending to grow at 1.8 percent each year. However, if social spending is 25 percent, this growth would allow the remainder to grow at only 1.3 percent; and if social spending accounts for 30 percent, the remaining possible growth is reduced to 1.1 percent. The salience of this point is indicated by the fact that in 1960 the average ratio of public social expenditure to Gross Domestic Product (GDP) in the seven major Organization for Economic Cooperation and Development (OECD)[6] countries was 13.7 percent; by 1981 it had grown to 24.8 percent.[7] Formally, these opportunity costs only apply to the purchase of goods and services by the government since transfer spending simply redistributes private consumption power. But, of course, both goods and services are subject to the tax cost constraint.

Second, the expansion of social spending has increasingly been financed by taxes that stretch further and further down the income distribution, thus generating some social problems in the pursuit of solutions to others. For example, Social Security contributions are now the major tax falling on low-income earners in both the United Kingdom and the United States. Similarly, if more ludicrously, income tax is payable by some in the United Kingdom at income levels that entitle them to apply for income-conditioned cash transfers to supplement their resources. This is not simply due to (or remediable by reversing) regressiveness in the distribution of the tax burden. The increase in the tax burden in most countries has been of a magnitude that could not realistically have been

[6] Organization for Economic Cooperation and Development. The seven major countries are: Canada, France, Germany, Italy, Japan, United Kingdom, United States. The ten smaller member countries are: Australia, Austria, Belgium, Finland, Greece, Ireland, Netherlands, Norway, Sweden, and New Zealand.

[7] Organization for Economic Cooperation and Development (OECD), *Economic Survey: Sweden* (Paris: Organization for Economic Cooperation and Development, 1981).

financed without making the distribution of taxes less progressive. For example, in Britain in 1959 the top 10 percent of the income distribution paid 65 percent of the total amount paid in income tax; by 1976–1977 this had declined to 40 percent. But because the average tax burden had risen from 10 to 20 percent of income, their tax burden rose 23 to 31 percent of their income; for them to have paid their 1959 *share* of taxes, their *average* tax burden would have had to increase to 51 percent of their income.[8] Although some progressive shift could take place in the distribution of taxes in both countries, particularly after the regressive shifts of recent years, this provides scope for one-time increases in spending rather than for renewed relative growth.

Although conservative administrations have generally been unsuccessful in effecting major cuts in social programs, they have been notably, if less noticeably, successful in shifting the burden of paying for social programs onto lower-income groups—a sort of "if we can't get rid of them, we can at least pay less for them" approach to social programs.[9] Thus, the net effect of social spending is now less advantageous to low-income groups than had previously been the case. Although this switch allows social spending to increase, thus appeasing political opposition to service or benefit cuts, it means that the evaluation of the desirability of increases in such spending needs to consider much more than hitherto the tax costs to the less well-off.

On the political side, mature welfare institutions face the same problems of rigidities, inflexibilities, and employee self-interest that characterize other large geriatric bureaucracies. Although these may protect programs from sharp contraction, they also reduce the degree to which welfare state institutions are likely to generate significant support for further expansion. Therefore, these factors help both to explain the survival of the welfare state and to underline the need to focus debate on problems of change and adaptation. If our assumption of continuing fiscal constraints on renewed spending growth of the pre-1975 type is correct, and if demographic, social, and economic changes (most obviously an aging population) will continue to make new demands on social welfare services, then it follows that resources will have to be shifted between pro-

[8] Michael O'Higgins, "Income Distribution and Social Policy: An Assessment After the Royal Commission on the Distribution of Income and Wealth," in *The Yearbook of Social Policy in Britain 1979*, ed. M. Brown and S. Baldwin (London: Routledge and Kegan Paul, 1980): Table 5.5.

[9] For data on the regressive shifts in the tax burden in the United States and the United Kingdom, see Marilyn Moon and Isabel Sawhill, "Income Distribution and Social Policy: An Assessment After the Royal Commission on the Distribution of Income and Wealth," in Brown and Baldwin, eds., *Yearbook*; and Michael O'Higgins, "Inequality, Redistribution and Recession: The British Experience 1976–1982," *Journal of Social Policy* 14 (July): 279–307.

grams. From this perspective, any crisis is less fiscal in character than one of institutionalized *immobilisme*.

The economic and political sides of the mature social programs perspective therefore point in the same direction when thinking about the nature of the strains facing social policy. Although consistent economic growth would ease the strains by both increasing resources and reducing the pressures of unemployment on budgets, the era of *sustained relative growth* is over. Now better ways are required to achieve change within priorities, to meet new or maturing commitments by collapsing or finishing older ones, and to generate flexibility and responsiveness in bureaucratic agencies.

Country Variations and Program Themes

In the previous section, we sought to unpackage some different ideas encapsulated in the general notion of the "crisis of the welfare state." In this section, we turn to disaggregating—both between different countries and between different policy areas—the actual post-oil shock experiences of the advanced industrialized nations of the West. To do so, we use the most recently published OECD analysis of social expenditure trends from 1960 to 1981.[10] Although this has the advantage of bringing the data together in a convenient, comparable form, it also has the disadvantages of imposing its own form of presentation on the analysis and ending the analysis in 1981 with the end of the time series. Furthermore, by treating the periods from 1960 to 1975 and from 1975 to 1981 as though each were homogeneous, the study may suggest conclusions that would not be borne out if the focus of analysis were on trends within each period. In particular, the form of presentation begs the question of whether, in the words of the OECD report, "the passage of time would probably have seen some automatic moderation as the major social programmes approached maturity."[11]

Two other difficulties with the OECD data must be noted. First, social expenditure is defined to be spending on education, health care, pensions, and unemployment compensation. Therefore, it excludes spending on means-tested social assistance and ignores possible substitution effects between different types of program. So, for example, Sweden was spending only 0.5 percent of GDP on unemployment compensation at the beginning of the 1980s; however, if we also consider the various active labor market policies adopted to preserve jobs and maintain people in work, the figure

[10] OECD, *Social Expenditure 1960–1990: Problems of Growth and Control* (Paris: Organization for Economic Co-operation and Development, 1985).

[11] OECD, *Social Expenditure*, 9.

rises to about 5 percent, well over the OECD average.[12] In effect, Sweden was using public spending to control the social effects of economic recession, while other countries were concentrating on trying to control the public expenditure effects of the extra demands for social support generated by economic recession.

Second, the OECD figures ignore tax expenditures, yet some of the most significant shifts in public policy, particularly in terms of their distributional effects, have taken the form of tilting the balance between direct and tax spending. Thus, in the United Kingdom under the Thatcher government, tax spending on the elderly, as a proportion of public expenditure on this group, rose from 10.4 percent in 1978–1979 to 14.4 percent in 1982–1983.[13]

The picture presented by the OECD data is therefore incomplete, and the analysis that follows must be read with this in mind. Despite these reservations, a number of apparently robust conclusions emerge from the OECD data. First, all the OECD nations reacted to the new economic climate after 1975 by reducing the growth rates of social spending, but none actually reduced real total social expenditure. In short, they all demonstrated a steering capacity. Second, the reactions of different countries varied both in scale and direction—that is, they varied both in the extent to which they reduced spending growth and in the priorities accorded different spending programs.

The experience between 1975 and 1981 thus demonstrates the way in which a common economic crisis was translated into very different social spending responses by national political systems. It invites an analysis of the impact of politics and policies on welfare state spending[14] and puts a large question mark against the conceptualization of the "crisis of the welfare state" as some systemic affliction common to all advanced capitalist countries, independent of national political ideology or institutions. In what follows, we elaborate on these propositions.

Over the OECD as a whole, the average annual growth rate of real social spending fell by 3.6 percentage points between the periods 1960–1975 and 1975–1981, from 8.4 percent to 4.8 percent (compared to economic growth figures of 4.6 percent and 2.6 percent respectively).[15] The national reductions, however, varied by a factor of eight—from 1.1 percent in France to 8.8 percent in the Netherlands. Such differences might reflect

---

[12] OECD, *Economic Survey: Sweden.*

[13] Rudolf Klein, "Privatization and the Welfare State," *Lloyds Bank Review* (January 1984): 12–29.

[14] Francis G. Castles, ed., *Impact of Parties* (London: Sage, 1982); Harold L. Wilensky, Gregory M. Luebbert, Susan Reed Hahn, and Adrienne M. Jamieson, *Comparative Social Policy* (Berkeley: Institute of International Studies, 1985).

[15] OECD, *Social Expenditures*, Table 1: 21.

either the degree of maturity reached by different welfare states by the mid-1970s or different degrees of economic difficulty, as well as different political responses.

We investigated the general relationships between social spending growth and the economic and maturity variables by regression analysis on the cross-sectional data. If S is annual percent growth in social spending since 1975, M is the 1975 share of social spending in GDP (as a proxy for maturity), and G is annual average growth in GDP since 1975, then analysis across the fourteen countries for whom adequate data are available yields the equation:

$$S = 4.92 - 0.126M + 0.855G^* \; ; N = 14, R = 0.44$$
$$[1.62] \; [2.25]$$

(T-statistics are in brackets; * = significant at 5 percent)

The results do indeed suggest some general patterns of association between the variables, with the rate of growth of social spending negatively linked to the 1975 spending share but positively related to subsequent economic growth rates. Thus, system maturity and economic performance seem to have the hypothesized effects.

The overall pattern suggested by the regression equation may of course conceal differences between individual countries. Figures 8.1 and 8.2 present the relationships between the average annual growth rates of social spending in various OECD countries since 1975 and, respectively, the average annual economic growth rates and the relative level of social expenditure in 1975. The figures emphasize that although most countries follow the general pattern, there are still important differences between countries that reflect different political responses. Sweden and the United Kingdom, for example, with similar levels of economic growth, have very different rates of growth of social spending. In Figure 8.2, interestingly, one group of countries seems to be different. The major English-speaking countries—the United Kingdom, the United States, and Canada—had lower spending growth after 1975 than might have been predicted on the basis of their low relative spending in 1975. Therefore, a case may exist for considering the possibility of Anglo-Saxon exceptionalism, whether in terms of ideology or of institutions.

Table 8.1 presents data on the relationship between changes in social spending policies by individual programs and the changes in the economic environment in individual countries. The data set out the annual rates of change of GDP and of real spending on education, health, and pensions in each period, 1960–1975 and 1975–1981. For each of these program areas the final three columns show the ratios of the elasticity of spending growth to GDP growth in the later period to the corresponding elasticities in the earlier period. Thus, a relative elasticity of 1.0 indicates

TABLE 8.1   Annual Growth in GDP and in Social Spending in 14 OECD Countries, 1960–1975 and 1975–1981

Country	Years	GDP	Average annual real change in spending on			Relative elasticity of spending on		
			Educ.	Health	Pensions	Educ.	Health	Pensions
New Zealand	60–75	4.0	5.2	3.5	5.2			
	75–81	0.4	−0.9	0.9	7.7	−1.7	2.6	14.8
Sweden	60–75	4.0	3.4	11.3	8.7			
	75–81	1.0	2.1	3.4	6.9	2.5	1.2	3.2
United Kingdom	60–75	2.6	5.0	3.4	5.9			
	75–81	1.0	−2.0	2.0	4.5	−1.0	1.5	2.0
Netherlands	60–75	4.5	4.3	11.4	10.3			
	75–81	2.0	1.1	4.4	5.2	0.6	0.9	1.1
Australia	60–75	5.2	8.9	9.1	8.5			
	75–81	2.4	1.2	−0.5	4.0	0.3	−0.1	1.0
Japan	60–75	8.6	5.7	12.2	12.7			
	75–81	4.7	4.1	6.6	13.7	1.3	1.0	2.0
France	60–75	5.0	n.a.	10.9	7.7			
	75–81	2.8	1.0	6.3	8.7	—	1.0	2.0
Finland	60–75	4.5	3.0	11.9	11.1			
	75–81	2.9	1.7	3.9	5.5	0.9	0.5	0.8
Canada	60–75	5.1	8.4	13.0	8.3			
	75–81	3.3	1.0	3.0	6.8	0.2	0.4	1.3
Italy	60–75	4.6	4.6	6.7	9.6			
	75–81	3.2	3.9	0.1	7.7	1.2	0.0	1.2
Germany	60–75	3.8	7.2	6.6	6.3			
	75–81	3.0	1.6	2.1	2.1	0.3	0.4	0.4
Ireland	60–75	4.3	7.4	7.7	8.2			
	75–81	3.5	4.5	6.3	6.6	0.8	1.0	1.0
United States	60–75	3.4	6.1	10.3	7.2			
	75–81	3.2	0.4	3.8	4.4	0.1	0.4	0.7
Norway	60–75	4.3	6.9	9.0	12.1			
	75–81	4.1	3.6	5.2	4.6	0.6	0.6	0.4

SOURCE: The relative elasticity data derived from the GDP and spending data, which are from OECD (1985) Tables 1, 6a–6g and A1–A7.

NOTES: The real spending data have been deflated both by the GDP deflator and by the service-specific relative price effect. The relative elasticity data are calculated by dividing the ratio of the rate of growth of the particular spending item to the rate of growth of GDP in the 1975–1981 period by the corresponding ratio for the 1960–1975 period.

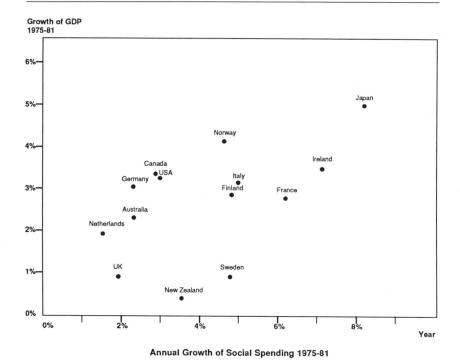

Annual Growth of Social Spending 1975-81

FIGURE 8.1. Relationship Between Growth of GDP and Social Expenditures, 1975–1981
Source: Organization for Economic Cooperation and Development, *Social Expenditures 1960–1990* (Paris: OECD, 1985).

that spending growth was reduced by the same proportion as economic growth between the two periods, but a figure of greater (less) than 1.0 indicates that spending growth was decreased by a lesser (greater) amount than economic growth. To facilitate interpretation, the countries are listed in order of the relative magnitudes of the drop in economic growth, from those where the relative fall was greatest (New Zealand and Sweden) to those where it was smallest (Norway and the United States).

The data in Table 8.1 demonstrate in detail both the similarities and the divergences in countries' social spending behavior. In almost all cases, real program spending growth was lower after 1975 than before. Of the forty-one examples in the table the spending growth rate increased in only three cases (pensions in New Zealand, Japan, and France). On the other hand, real spending was cut in only three instances. In most cases the rate of growth of social spending was reduced in response to the less favorable economic climate.

The relative elasticity data, however, demonstrate the variability of the

**Social Expenditures
(% GDP) 1975**

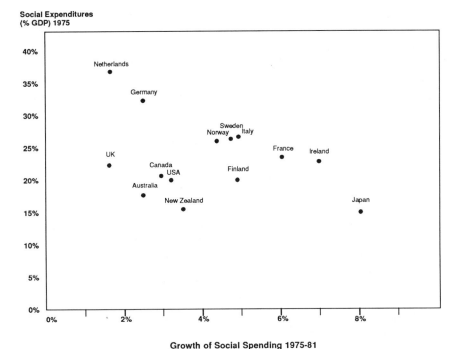

Growth of Social Spending 1975-81

FIGURE 8.2. Relationship between Growth of Social Expenditures, 1975–1981, and Social Spending Share of GDP in 1975

Source: Organization for Economic Cooperation and Development, *Social Expenditures 1960–1990* (Paris: OECD, 1985).

individual responses.[16] In more than half the cases the response was an "overreaction"—the relative elasticity is less than 1.0—but in a third of the instances spending was cut by proportionately less than the fall in growth. This variety is reflected when the patterns of response are examined for each country. Four of the fourteen countries fall consistently, across all three programs, into the "overreacting" category, ranging from Norway, usually grouped with the Scandinavian, Social Democrat high welfare spenders to the United States, the prototype low spender. Two countries, Ireland and Australia, either "overreact" or react proportionately in all three program areas, while Canada and the Netherlands fall into the "overreacting" category for two of the three programs. Four countries reduced the relative rates of economic growth: New Zealand and the United Kingdom, among the worst economic performers in our

---

[16] Rudolf Klein and Ellie Scrivens, "The Welfare State: From Crisis to Uncertainty," *Journal of Public Policy* 5 (May 1985): 141–53.

group of countries, and Japan and Italy, who maintained reasonable levels of economic growth. Only Sweden falls into the "underreacting" category for all three programs.

The cases of the United States and Norway are particularly interesting because, despite their very different political traditions, they are two of the strongest overreactors. The result in each case reflects a combination of a lower fall in economic growth than the OECD average (0.2 for both countries against an OECD average of 2.0) and a greater fall in spending growth (4.8 and 5.5 points respectively, against an average of 3.6). These data suggest that national perceptions and definitions of fiscal crisis are more important than economic statistics.

Table 8.1 also shows significant national variations between program categories. While ten countries "overreacted" in the case of education, and eight in the case of health, only four countries did so for pensions. Indeed, in twelve of the fourteen countries the relative elasticity of pension spending was greater than that of either health or education. This reflects the fact that the patterns of spending growth vary between different programs over time. In the period 1960–1975, spending on health care grew fastest. In the seven largest OECD economies, real spending for health care grew by an average of 9 percent, as compared to 8.2 percent for pensions and 6.2 percent for education. In the period 1975–1981, the growth rates for health care and education fell to 3.4 percent and 1.4 percent respectively, while that for pensions came down only to 6.8 percent. These data suggest, therefore, some scope, given flexibility and adaptiveness, for accommodating new demands (such as those created by the aging of the population) by holding back the growth rates of other programs and changing public spending priorities.

The OECD data on education provide an interesting illustration of how different countries reacted to a "demographic bonus"—that is, to a decline in the size of the population requiring a particular service. New Zealand and the United Kingdom used this not only to cut the real level of program spending, as shown in Table 8.1, but also to reduce the level of real benefits or inputs per head.[17] In contrast, Norway and the Netherlands managed to increase the level of real education benefits while reducing the spending growth rate by more than the relative decline in economic growth. And Italy and Sweden increased real benefits while reducing the growth rate of spending by proportionately less than the decline in economic growth.

In this respect, as in others, the OECD data are more useful for setting up interesting puzzles, highly relevant for future policy making, than for providing answers. If the level of inputs per head goes up while the school

---

[17] OECD, *Social Expenditure*, Tables 6f and A5.

population is falling, this could mean a deliberate political decision to increase resources to improve standards. On the other hand, it could indicate a political acceptance of institutional rigidities and of the veto power of the teaching profession. If institutional rigidities are indeed one disease of the middle-aged welfare state, as the OECD report argues, then it would be useful to know whether and how some countries have managed to devise techniques for dealing with them.

The experience from 1975 to 1981 indicates that the constituencies for the status quo in services like health and education are generally able to resist real cuts without necessarily or universally being strong enough to generate continuing priority in growth. The political institutions and ideological contexts of the particular countries again seem to be crucial variables. There is both a differential political ability and willingness to accommodate higher spending, and a differential capacity to pursue incremental strategies for reducing the rate of expansion. It is tempting to conclude, therefore, that if in good times changes in social spending tend to be a function of economic growth,[18] in bad times they tend to be a function of political institutions and ideology.

BRITISH THEMES AND VARIATIONS

This is not the place to attempt an evaluation of the Thatcher impact on social policy in Britain. Nonetheless, having pointed to the importance of national political institutions and circumstances in interpreting the different experiences of OECD countries, it may be useful to flesh out this experience in slightly more detail for the country we know best. The apparent similarity of ideological approach between the Reagan and Thatcher administrations may also give such a discussion more salience for an American audience.

In terms of three major factors—spending cuts, popular support, and shifting responsibilities from the state—the Thatcher administrations have failed in the light of their original intentions. Real public spending has grown by an average of between 1.5 percent and 2 percent annually since the Conservatives came to office in 1979, and the social spending share of this rising total has itself increased slightly. Following their reelection in 1983, a reasserted, if somewhat diluted, pledge was made to hold real government spending constant during their second term of office. This also went awry, and program spending rose a further 10 percent over the term of that parliament.[19]

[18] But see Castles, *Impact*, and Wilensky et al., *Comparative Social Policy*.

[19] Michael O'Higgins, "Social Policy Needs and Resources: The Prospects for the 1990s," in *Challenges to Social Policy*, ed. R. Berthoud (Aldershot, England: Gower, 1985).

Part of this can be attributed to the failure of the government's macro-economic policies to check rising unemployment. But it is also due to the government's unwillingness or inability to make the other cuts that would have been necessary to follow the intentions. Spending on the NHS has grown, albeit in the face of rising need, and the government now boasts of having increased the resources going into the health service. The real value of pensions, which account for half the income support budget, has been maintained. Even where some real cuts have been made, in the education and housing budgets, they have been partly offset by consequential increases in the employment services and income support budgets.

These failures accurately reflect the government's inability to maintain popular support for reductions in social responsibility. After a mild decline at the end of the 1970s, data on public opinion on social welfare clearly chart a renewal of widespread support for increased spending on health, education, and transfers.[20] The "blip" in popular support appears to have signaled either a temporary dissatisfaction or desire for a slight shift in priorities, rather than a fundamental change in popular views.

Similarly there has been only limited success in privatizing social responsibilities. While the program of privatizing state-owned industry is being carried through, there has been no equivalent widespread success in social policy. Two-thirds of a million local authority housing units have been bought by their previous tenants, with significant political gains to the government, but at the expense of large discounts on the market selling price of each housing unit. Employers, in place of the social insurance system, are now responsible for paying benefits in the early weeks of sickness, but in the negotiations to persuade them to do so the government was forced to suggest five different schemes for compensating employers. The effect of the scheme finally adopted is that the government's loss from tax revenue forgone is significantly greater than its gain from public spending saved, with employers being the beneficiaries.[21]

Just as the spending failures of the first parliamentary term are being repeated in the second, so also are shifting responsibilities. After a plethora of pre- and post-election talk of a major review of the welfare state—and in particular whether its projected future costs were sustainable—the government announced a series of ministerial studies of aspects of the income support system. The reports of these studies in general concentrated on proposing major changes to minor parts of the system, with

[20] Taylor-Gooby, "Politics of Welfare."

[21] Klein, "Privatization"; Michael O'Higgins, "Privatization and Social Security," *Political Quarterly* 55 (April 1984): 129–39; Michael O'Higgins, "Social Welfare and Privatization: The British Experience," in *Privatization and the Welfare State*, ed. A. Kahn and S. Kamerman (Princeton: Princeton University Press, 1988).

some cost cutting; the exception to this was in respect to earnings-related pensions.

The Social Security (Pensions) Act of 1975, passed with bipartisan support after almost twenty years of abortive attempts to legislate for an effective scheme of earnings-related pensions, provides that, in addition to contributing to the basic (flat-rate) social insurance pension scheme, each employee must be covered by an acceptable earnings-related scheme. This scheme may be an occupational pension (subject to its satisfying certain criteria) or the State Earnings-Related Pension Scheme (SERPS). SERPS benefits became payable from 1979, full SERPS pensions will be payable from 1998, and the scheme will reach full maturity after 2020, when the elderly population is projected to be increasing again. The scheme involves a complex interaction between public and private sectors, one which seems to be potentially both inequitable and expensive.[22] In recent years a powerful academic critique has developed, emphasizing both its unplanned effects and its unforeseen expense.[23] Against this background, some government action was not surprising.

The government proposed abolishing SERPS, while maintaining the rights of older employees currently registered within it. In place of a requirement to be in SERPS or a private sector scheme of equivalent quality, younger and future employees were to face a requirement to make a minimum earnings-related contribution to a private pensions saving scheme, and the government would act to increase transferability in private pension provisions. These proposals would have constituted a major shift of provision out of the public sector, albeit in the very long term.

However, the government, despite its large majority in parliament, was forced to withdraw the original proposals and replace them with proposals for modification of some of the more expensive and anomalous aspects of SERPS, proposals that essentially reflected much of the informed critique of the previous years. Two features of this political retreat are of interest here: (1) the reasons for the retreat and their implications for the possibility of major changes to social provision structures; and (2) the political response to the second set of proposals.

Why did the government retreat? Informed and interested reaction was hostile to the original plans, some 98 percent of formal responses opposed it, including most sectors of industry and finance. From the viewpoint of the private pension industry, this may have been because they already had the bulk of the market they sought—the majority of affluent employees who are contracted-out of SERPS. Those who are contracted-in are gen-

---

[22] Michael O'Higgins, "Public-Private Interaction in Social Policy."

[23] John Kay, "Income for the Elderly: The Future of State Provision," in *Challenges to Social Policy*, ed. R. Berthoud (Aldershot, England: Gower, 1985).

erally less well-paid and work in smaller companies, thus being a less attractive prospect for coverage. The informed opposition may also reflect an awareness of the double burden costs of transition. The more affluent, younger members of the workforce were to be required to contribute to the considerable costs of the residual (pay-as-you-go) SERPS scheme, while also paying to build up their own future funded entitlement.

A more political explanation focuses less on informed than on perceived mass opinion: the government was seen to be proposing to reduce pension benefits. Since the savings were long-term, there were no compensating tax cuts to offer the electorate. The complexities of the issue became irrelevant to a perception of potentially suicidal political masochism. As Taylor-Gooby says in similar context, "the moral for policy makers is that they do best to work by deceit."[24] Modifications and technical amendments incur fewer short-term costs even if they bring lower long-term savings; even for a professedly radical conservative government, therefore, major restructuring is replaced by incremental reform.

The response of the main political opposition, the Labour party, to the second set of proposals is equally instructive. They opposed the reforms and have pledged to reverse them if returned to power, despite the probability that some modifications will be redistributive and that many reflect measures they themselves would likely have proposed, if in power, in response to the increasingly perceived defects of the original scheme. The original Conservative proposals, however, had changed the nature of the political debate possible. The revised proposals were seen not as justifiable or reasonable adaptations of a defective structure but as a second attempt to dismantle a part of social provision. By distancing themselves from a consensus about the broad structure of provision, the Conservatives have rendered it more difficult to achieve consensus on adapting that structure.

Turning to health policies, there is rather a different story to tell—a reminder that generalizations about the welfare state even within particular countries must be qualified by reference to the specific characteristics of individual policy arenas (one country's sacred cow may turn out to be another's sacrificial lamb.) If the Conservatives entered office in 1979 with the idea of carrying out a fundamental review of the NHS, it was soon abandoned. By the time of the 1983 general election all hints of such review and any suggestions that Britain might switch to an insurance-financed system had been abandoned.[25] Instead, the theme of the conser-

[24] Taylor-Gooby, "Politics of Welfare," p. 91.
[25] Rudolf Klein, "Why Britain's Conservatives Support a Socialist Health Care System," *Health Affairs* 4 (Spring 1985): 41–58.

vative manifest was "the NHS is safe with us." In other words, political competition by 1983 had reverted to the traditional post-1950 British pattern of each party trying to demonstrate that it was more committed to, more enthusiastic about, and more supportive of the NHS than its rivals.

This born-again commitment of the Conservatives to the NHS is hardly surprising. Financially, the NHS is the best-buy model for any government trying to control welfare state spending. It is the most effective cost containment mechanism yet invented. Politically, the NHS enjoys overwhelming, cross-party support among the voters, and a one million strong, highly unionized constituency of workers sensitive to any threats to their security.

Health policies have indeed had a high political profile, not because the Conservatives have threatened the principles or foundations of the NHS but rather because every incremental change—notably in the management structure of the service and in the relationship between the public and private sectors—has been exploited by the opposition to try the government's maleficent intentions. Just as the Conservatives have been forced to exaggerate the importance of their largely symbolic changes (as in mildly encouraging private provision) to satisfy their own party zealots, so the opposition has been forced to exaggerate the significance of government policies to try to persuade the voters that the NHS is under threat.

The contrast between pensions and the NHS during the Thatcher years suggests there are two alternative models of social policy making. In the case of pensions, the model is one of conflict *without* consensus; in the case of the NHS, it is one of conflict *within* consensus. In other words, in the former instance there is no built-in stabilizer, and each settlement is only the prelude to another round of change. However, in the latter instance the policy debate is constrained by overarching agreement about the framework. Although political controversy may be intense, it does not call fundamentals into question. This distinction, as we shall argue in our conclusions, helps not only to make sense of the divergent patterns of policy process in Britain but also to explain some of the differences between countries.

Policy Constraints and Options

The argument of this paper so far has been that, although the existing institutions of the welfare state limit policy options by creating a set of expectations and organized interest groups, they also leave scope for political decisionmaking and policy change within those constraints; that scope was demonstrated by the diversity of recent experience among the

OECD countries. If, therefore, we abandon the notion of crisis—and, with it, the idea that only a radical, dramatic change is an adequate response—we are able to address ourselves to what (in our view) will be the real agenda of the coming decade: a continual, gradual process of adaptation. This will be policy creep, not policy revolution. Such an agenda, itself a prediction, raises issues of both analysis and prescription.

The predictive aspect follows from both the evidence we have so far examined on what has been happening and our analysis of the economic and political constraints on social politics. It is illustrated by considering developments in different countries regarding the biggest time bomb in social policy—the future impact of the entitlements now being built up by an aging population. The example of Britain is unusual only in that the government appeared to consider "big-bang" change before being forced to do what others are doing—that is, to pursue a strategy of decremental creep. Savings are being achieved not by overt changes in the structure of pension schemes, a highly visible strategy where the political costs are carried by the present generation of politicians with the savings bequeathed to further generations thereof, but by changing the methods of calculating and adjusting benefits, a less visible strategy where both costs and savings fall on future generations.

The prescriptive aspect is directly related. If change is to be reformist rather than radical and if alterations are to be made in ways compatible with broader policy objectives rather than by attacks or defenses based on short-run expediency, then policy making must give higher priority to institutional adaptability and instrumental flexibility. In part, this implies, as we have previously argued, building in more short-term, self-terminating programs, whose birth, life, and death can be manipulated in line with wider exigencies—to take space when it is available, to make it when it is needed.[26]

It further implies the need for a conscious pluralism in the choice and construction of policy instruments. If there is a range of ways in which a policy may be pursued, perhaps the choice of which way to follow should be based not simply on which is most efficient in the context of the aims and prejudices of a particular administration but on which can accommodate the preferences of a range of possible governments, while still achieving an acceptable policy impact. In the British context this is best illustrated by the example of child benefits. Until the late 1970s, policy for assisting with the cost of rearing children had contained two components—a cash transfer and a tax relief. Because of the characteristic re-

---

[26] Rudolf Klein, "Public Expenditure in an Inflationary World," in *The Politics of Inflation and Economic Stagnation*, ed. Leon Lindberg and Charles S. Maier (Washington, D.C.: Brookings Institution, 1985), pp. 223–31.

gressiveness of tax relief, a campaign had developed, with all party support, to convert them into cash transfers.

This campaign, born of the era of program rationality in policy making, succeeded at precisely the wrong time in terms of the changing concerns of government. It was not that governments became antichild or antifamily, indeed families had returned to political fashion. But public spending went out of fashion and tax cuts came in, just as the possibility of helping families through tax cuts was eliminated; this left public spending as the only route to concentrate help on the family. Although the real value of child benefits was protected, though not increased, until 1985, it was then increased by 2 percent less than inflation, and all indications are that this was but the first of a series of erosions in its real value. Yet there can be little doubt that if child tax reliefs had still existed, the Conservative government would have delivered tax cuts to families to a degree which they have been unwilling to do through spending; tax cuts to families would be a political "two-fer," satisfying claims about both family aid and tax cutting at one time. The distributional impact might have been less satisfactory had the same resources been transferred through direct spending, but the amount of resources would have been considerably greater. Thus, a well-intentioned diminution in instrumental flexibility has had unanticipated negative consequences for policy impact.

These predictions and prescriptions are not regime-specific. They apply as much to progressive as to conservative administrations. The process of trimming programs slowly and at the edges is as likely for progressive governments trying to make space to meet new or growing commitments as for conservatives seeking ways to reduce the role of government. Expediency is as much likely to influence the choices made by one as the other. Yet two issues merit particular attention in the case of conservative administrations: the relationship between the distribution of the costs and the benefits of programs; and the longer-term implications of a gradual erosion of government responsibility in some areas of social policy.

We noted earlier the role played by relatively widespread benefits of welfare services in defending those services against attack, a redistributive role as long as the tax system is progressive. But we also noted the extent to which the Reagan and Thatcher administrations have reshaped the tax systems so as to reduce their progressiveness. The effect, given the aggregate size of the tax burden, is to increase the extent to which public programs represent transfers within income groups, rather than between them. If progressiveness is restored to the tax system then perhaps no great issue arises, but how likely is this? Even nonconservatives now agree that effects of social policy measures on economic performance cannot be ignored and that some attention must be paid to arguments about incentives and supply-side compatibility. Any restoration of nominal progressiveness may therefore be limited. The balance in the distribution of costs and benefits may need more attention in the evaluation of social programs than before; in particular, we must examine the extent to which administrations seek to avoid the political opposition which overt service cuts may generate by preserving services at the expense of shifting the distribution of costs toward lower-income groups.

Any strategy of decremental creep is also likely to involve transferring public into private costs. Such a strategy is often implicit in the rhetoric of community care and family responsibility, all too often a code for pushing more of the financial and psychic costs back onto the families (and, in particular, the women) concerned. Occasionally, as in the case of Individual Retirement Accounts in the United States, this may be accomplished by creating attractive alternative structures in the private sector. Equally, it may be accomplished simply by reducing the quality of the public services. Thus, "a gradually lower quality of public service, or a failure to raise service levels as private prosperity increased could be expected to lead to more people opting for private alternatives. In other words, the role of state services would diminish not because of governments depriving clients of their entitlements to access, but because of consumers choosing to take their custom elsewhere. A degree of remarketization or privatization would be accomplished by attrition rather than assault."[27]

The Great Transformation

To argue that the rhetoric of crisis diverts attention from what is really happening in a process of incremental adjustment is neither to adopt a posture of complacency nor to dismiss the significance of what has occurred during the past decade. On the contrary, it is to argue that the widespread perception of crisis, plus the characteristics of the mature welfare state, have subtly but importantly changed the currency of discussion about the relationship between institutions, programs, and policy objectives—between the means and the ends of social policies. This transformation affects the capacity and the manner in which different political systems cope both with the predictable strains, such as demographic trends, and the unpredictable demands that may be made on them in the coming decades. In conclusion, we therefore examine briefly, and in the light of previous chapters, some of the normative and analytic implications of this transformation.

[27] Patricia Ruggles and Michael O'Higgins, "Retrenchment and the New Right: A Comparative Analysis of the Reagan and Thatcher Administrations," in *Stagnation and Renewal in Social Policy: The Rise and Fall of Policy Regimes*, ed. G. Esping-Andersen, L. Rainwater, and M. Rein (Armonk, N.Y.: M. E. Sharpe, 1987).

If tinkering at the edges is likely to be the pattern of policy making, then this would suggest that our normative concern should be with asking questions about the extent to which incremental, discrete, and low-visibility changes may also be changing the character of the welfare state. So, for example, Paul Starr's chapter suggests that the marginal privatization of pensions in the United States may eventually erode support for the Social Security system, just as in Britain it is sometimes argued that even a marginal private sector of health care could eventually subvert the principle of a universal NHS. It is thus essential to recognize that policy incrementalism is shaped by ideology; indeed, this is both inevitable and desirable. To the extent that policy incrementalism is not just a stumbling adaptation to an uncertain environment but a purposive, if necessarily slow and halting, attempt to achieve certain goals over time, so an account of process cannot be divorced from arguments about objectives. But if the incentives to policy makers are to pursue low-visibility, covert policies with a distant horizon, so the academic analyst's responsibility is to make the implicit explicit and to draw attention to the long-term implications of policy creep.

This point also raises a complex set of questions about the relationship between welfare state institutions and welfare policy objectives. One characteristic of the crisis of the welfare state debate has been precisely, as we have argued, that it has conflated two very different kinds of argument; on the one hand, public expenditure on the welfare state was too high (and, in the view of some right-wing critics, undesirable anyway), and, on the other hand, the existing institutions of the welfare state were too bureaucratic, rigid, and unresponsive (a view to which many left-wing critics could subscribe).

The debate has thus had a double and somewhat confusing effect. It has created a realization that institutions and programs could be changed, and perhaps should be changed, without necessarily changing policy objectives. At the same time, however, it has also created the suspicion that governments like Reagan's or Thatcher's will use institutional or program change as a way of achieving their real objective of cutting the welfare state down to size; incrementalism will always speak with the same bias. The paradox, then, is that the institutions of the welfare state may be defended on political grounds in full awareness of their shortcomings. To the extent that existing organizations and programs represent a strong political constituency, often precisely because they are a large bureaucracy, so they represent a safeguard for the policy commitment they have come to institutionalize. Although economic uncertainty argues for institutional adaptability in pursuit of social policy goals, political uncertainty may push in the opposite direction.

This brings the argument of this chapter full circle. In our analysis of cross national expenditure trends, we stressed the importance of differences between countries. These differences, in turn, reflected differences in political ideology and political institutions. If these are crucial in helping explain why the "crisis" of the welfare state was so variously defined, perceived, and acted upon, they are also crucial in understanding the nature and limits of the current policy debate about options for the future, a debate to which this book is a contribution.

To outside observers, we would suggest, the United States debate is remarkable for a pervasive lack of confidence in the capacity of the country's political institutions. In other words, to exaggerate only a little, we would detect a crisis of national political institutions rather than a crisis of welfare state institutions. As argued in the preface, American "governmental institutions fragment attention in an already diverse polity, making regular incremental adjustment difficult, reassessment nearly impossible." To which we would add that the diverse nature of the polity, plus the need to mobilize an ad hoc coalition of interest groups, promotes a "big-bang" style of social policy making perhaps unique to the United States. That is, an impression of crisis has to be created, whether a crisis of social unrest or one of excessive spending, in order to get *any* change. As Tomasson argues, "a consequence of this low level of agreement [about the form and structure of Social Security] is an apparent incapacity of Congress to make even minor deliberalizations in the system without the presence of an imminent crisis from which there is no escape."[28]

This generalization needs to be qualified in one respect. The different characteristics of individual policy arenas, even within the same national polity, remain important. In the case of Britain, we noted the difference between the policy arenas for pensions and for health. In the former, we characterized the policy debate as representing conflict without consensus; in the latter, we described it as conflict within consensus. The same distinction, but in reverse, can perhaps be made in the United States. If health care is Britain's sacred cow, then the United States's is the Social Security system, where there appears to be nearly a general consensus about the underlying policy commitment maintaining a universal system of financial protection against the risks of old age. Within that consensus, there may be sharp differences about means; however, it may well be that the relative consensus creates the political confidence required to discuss alternative options, as James Tobin does in Chapter 2. Conversely, there appears to be no such underlying consensus in the case of health care in the United States, as Chapter 7 demonstrates; thus, there is not only conflict but also a lack of willingness to engage in debate about the various

[28] Richard Tomasson, "Government Old Age Pensions under Affluence and Austerity," *Research in Social Problems and Public Policy* 3 (1984): 217–72, especially 248.

options for achieving a given set of aims since there is no agreement about those aims. In short, the characteristics of different policy arenas are not defined by their substantive nature (for example, whether they are concerned with something called health or pensions) but by the way their political environments have developed over time in specific countries.

This should suggest at least some differences in the ways in which national policies have developed over the past decade, and more will continue to be evident in the ways in which countries adapt to the challenges of the coming decades. Just as countries with governmental systems capable of generating and sustaining consensus across time (for example, Sweden, Germany, and Austria) have managed to develop more extensive welfare states without damage to their economies, so, too, they are more likely to have the flexibility needed to adapt to change.[29] Social policy performance, like economic performance, may depend crucially on devising governmental institutions capable of generating the kind of overarching consensus needed to overcome the policy stasis created by the balance of conflicting interest groups.[30] Only within the framework of such a consensus, our own argument and the somewhat pessimistic tone of most chapters in this book would suggest, is it possible to explore fully the options for radical adaptations to the welfare state without risk that those arguments will be hijacked by those who want to renege on the societal commitments represented by the welfare state.

[29] Wilensky et al., *Comparative Social Policy*; Klein, "Public Expenditure."
[30] Mancur Olson, *The Rise and Decline of Nations* (New Haven: Yale University Press, 1982).

REFERENCES

Aaron, Henry. 1982. *The Economic Effects of Social Security*. Washington, D.C.: Brookings Institution.

Achenbaum, W. Andrew. 1986. *Social Security Visions and Revisions*. New York: Cambridge University Press.

Advisory Council on Social Security of 1937–1938. 1939. *Final Report*. Washington, D.C.: Government Printing Office.

Advisory Council on Social Security of 1947–1948. 1949. *Recommendations for Social Security Legislation, Reports to the Senate Committee on Finance*. Washington, D.C.: Government Printing Office.

Advisory Council on Social Security of 1965. 1965. *The Status of the Social Security Program and Recommendations for Its Improvement*. Washington, D.C.: Government Printing Office.

Advisory Council on Social Security of 1971. 1971. *Reports of the 1971 Council*. Washington, D.C.: Government Printing Office.

Advisory Council on Social Security of 1980. 1980. *Report of the Council*. Washington, D.C.: Government Printing Office.

Advisory Council on Social Security Financing. 1959. *Financing Old-Age, Survivors and Disability Insurance, A Report*. Washington, D.C.: Government Printing Office.

Altman-Lupu, Nancy. 1986. "Rethinking Retirement Income Policies: Nondiscrimination, Integration and the Quest for Worker Security." *Tax Law Review* 42 (Spring): 433–508.

American Enterprise Institute for Public Policy Research. 1981. *Public Opinion*. August–September.

Andreopoulos, Spyros, ed. 1975. *National Health Insurance: Can We Learn from Canada?* New York: Wiley.

Andrews, Emily S. 1985. *The Changing Profile of Pensions in America*. Washington, D.C.: Employee Benefit Research Institute.

Armstrong, Barbara N. 1932. *Insuring the Essentials: Minimum Wage Plus Social Insurance*. New York: Macmillan.

Arnett, Ross H., III, David R. McKusick, Sally T. Sonnefeld, and Carol S. Crowell. 1985. "Health Spending Trends in the 1980s: Adjusting to Financial Incentives." *Health Care Financing Review* 6 (Spring): 1–26.

Ball, Robert M. 1972. "Assignment of the Commissioner of Social Security." Mimeo. December 18.

Ball, Robert M. 1978. *Social Security: Today and Tomorrow*. New York: Columbia University Press.

———. 1982. "Social Security Today" Testimony Before the Task Force on Entitlements, Uncontrollables and Indexing, Committee on the Budget. Washington, D.C.: U.S. House of Representatives. March 1.

———. 1985. "The 1939 Amendments to the Social Security Act and What Followed." In *The Report of the Committee on Economic Security of 1935 and Other Basic Documents Relating to the Developments of the Social Security Act, Fiftieth Anniversary Edition*, ed. Alan Pifer and Forrest Chisman. Washington, D.C.: National Conference on Social Welfare.

Ballantyne, C. 1985. "Actuarial Status of the OASI and DI Trust Funds." *Social Security Bulletin* 44 (June): 27.

Bell, Daniel. 1976. *The Cultural Contradictions of Capitalism*. New York: Basic Books.

Bell, Donald, and Diane Hill. 1984. "How Social Security Payments Affect Private Pensions." *Monthly Labor Review* (May): 15–20.

Berkowitz, Edward D. 1983. "The First Social Security Crisis." *Prologue* (The Journal of the National Archives) 15 (Fall): 133–48.

Bernstein, Merton C., and Joan Brodshaug Bernstein, 1987. *Social Security: The System that Works*. New York: Basic Books.

Blinder, Alan S. 1982. "Private Pensions and Public Pensions: Theory and Fact." Working Paper No. 902, National Bureau of Economic Research. Cambridge, Mass. June.

Bodie, Zvi. 1981. "Investment Strategy in an Inflationary Environment." Working Paper No. 701, National Bureau of Economic Research. Cambridge, Mass. June.

Boskin, Michael J. 1986. *Too Many Promises: The Uncertain Future of Social Security*. Homewood, Ill.: Twentieth Century Fund Report, Dow Jones-Irwin.

Boskin, Michael J., Laurence J. Kotlikoff, and John P. Shoven, 1982. "Personal Security Accounts: A Proposal for Fundamental Social Security Reform." Paper presented to the National Commission on Social Security Reform, Washington, D.C. Revised version, September.

Break, George F. 1981. "The Economic Effects of the OASI Program." In *Social Security Financing*, ed. Felicity Skidmore. Cambridge, Mass.: MIT Press, pp. 45–88.

Brest, P., and S. Levinson. 1983. *Processes of Constitutional Decision-making*, 2d ed. Boston: Little, Brown.

Brook, Robert M., J. E. Ware, W. H. Rogers, E. B. Keeler, A. R. Davies, C. A. Donald, G. A. Goldberg, K. N. Lohr, P. C. Masthay, and J. P. Newhouse. 1983. "Does Free Care Improve Adults' Health?" *New England Journal of Medicine* 309(23): 1526–33.

Brooks, John Graham. 1895. *Compulsory Insurance in Germany, Fourth Special Report of the Commissioner of Labor.* Washington, D.C.: Government Printing Office.

Brown, Lawrence D. 1985. "Technocratic Corporatism and Administrative Reform in Medicine." *Journal of Health Politics, Policy and Law* 10 (Fall): 579–99.

Browning, Edgar K. 1986. "Tax Incidence, Indirect Taxes, and Transfers." *National Tax Journal* 37.

Burkhauser, Richard, and Karen Holden, eds. 1982. *A Challenge to Social Security.* New York: Academic Press.

Butler, Stuart and Peter Germanis. "Achieving a Political Strategy for Reform." *Social Security: Prospects for Real Reform*, ed. Peter J. Ferrara.

Castles, Francis G., ed. 1982. *Impact of Parties.* London: Sage.

Caudill, Harry M. 1963. *Night Comes to the Cumberlands.* Boston: Little, Brown.

Clark, Robert L. 1984. *Inflation and the Economic Well-Being of the Elderly.* Baltimore: Johns Hopkins University Press.

Cohen, William S. 1982. "Gambling with the Future." *New York Times.* August 12.

Committee on Economic Security. 1937. *Social Security in America, The Factual Background of the Social Security Act as Summarized from Staff Reports to the Committee on Economic Security.* 1937. Washington, D.C.: Government Printing Office.

Comptroller General of the United States. 1976. *The Social Security Administration Should Provide More Management and Leadership in Determining Who is Eligible for Disability Benefits.* Washington, D.C.: Government Printing Office.

Consultants on Social Security. 1953. *A Report to the Secretary of* HEW *on Extension of* OASI *to Additional Groups of Current Workers.* Washington, D.C.: Government Printing Office.

Council of Economic Advisors. 1985. *Economic Report of the President.* Washington, D.C.: Government Printing Office. Chapter 5.

Crawford, Don D. 1980. "Judicial Review of Social Security Disability Decisions: A Proposal for Change." *Texas Tech Law Review* 11: 215–48.

Crystal, Stephen. 1982. *America's Old Age Crisis.* New York: Basic Books.

Danziger, Sheldon, Robert Havemann, and Robert Plotnick. 1981. "How Income Transfer Programs Affect Work, Savings and the Income Distribution: A Critical Review." *Journal of Economic Literature* 19 (September): 975–1028.

Danziger, Sheldon, J. van der Gaag, E. Smolensky, and Michael K. Taus-

sig. 1982–1983. "The life-cycle hypothesis and the consumption behavior of the elderly." *Journal of Post Keynesian Economics* 5 (Winter): 208–27.

David, Sheri I. 1985. *With Dignity: The Search for Medicare and Medicaid*. Westport, Conn.: Greenwood Press.

Davis, Karen. 1985. "Access to Health Care: A Matter of Fairness,"
Health Care: How to Improve It and Pay for It. Washington, D.C.:
Center for National Policy, p. 50.

DeMagistris, Robin C., and Carl J. Palash, 1982–1983. "Impact of IRAS
on Saving." *Federal Reserve Bank of New York Quarterly Review*
(Winter): 24–30.

Derthick, Martha. 1979. *Policymaking for Social Security*. Washington,
D.C.: Brookings Institution.

Drucker, Peter F. 1976. *The Unseen Revolution: How Pension Fund Socialism Came to America*. New York: Harper and Row.

Employee Benefit Research Institute. 1986. Issue Brief No. 51. *Pension
Vesting Standards*. Washington, D.C.

———. 1986. Issue Brief No. 52. *Retirement Income and Individual Retirement Accounts*. March.

———. 1986. Issue Brief No. 54. *Tax Reform and Employee Benefits*.

Epstein, Abraham. 1933. *Insecurity: A Challenge to America*. New York:
Harrison Smith and Robert Haas.

Evans, Robert G. 1986. "The Spurious Dilemma: Reconciling Medical
Progress and Cost Control." *Health Matrix* 4 (Spring): 25–34.

Feder, Judith M. 1977. *Medicare: The Politics of Federal Hospital Insurance*. Lexington, Mass: Lexington Books.

Feder, Judith, John Holohan, and Theodore R. Marmor, eds. 1980. *National Health Insurance: Conflicting Goals and Policy Choices*.
Washington, D.C.: Urban Institute Press.

Federal Old-Age and Survivors Insurance and Disability Insurance Trust
Funds. Board of Trustees. 1985. *Annual Report*. Baltimore: Social
Security Administration.

Feldstein, Martin. 1974. "Social Security, Induced Retirement, and Aggregate Accumulation." *Journal of Political Economy* 82 (September–October): 905–26.

———. 1985. "The Social Security Explosion." *Public Interest* 81 (Fall):
94–106.

Ferrara, Peter J. 1980. *Social Security: The Inherent Contradiction*. San
Francisco: Cato Institute.

———. 1982. *Social Security: Averting the Crisis*. Washington, D.C.:
Cato Institute.

———. 1984. "Rebuilding Social Security: Part 2, Toward Lasting Reform." *Backgrounder*. No. 346. Washington, D.C.: Heritage Foundation. 25 April.

———, ed. 1985. *Social Security: Prospectus for Real Reform*. Washington, D.C.: Cato Institute.

Flora, Peter, and Arnold Heidenheimer. 1982. *The Development of Welfare States in Europe and America*. New Brunswick, N.J.: Transaction Books.

Fox, Daniel M. 1986. *Health Policies, Health Politics: The British and American Experience, 1911–1965*. Princeton: Princeton University Press.

Galper, Harvey, and Eugene Steuerle. 1983. "Tax Incentives for Saving." *The Brookings Review*. Winter 1983: 16–23.

Gallup Organization. 1984. *The 1984 Gallup Study of Eligible Non-Owners of Individual Retirement Accounts*. Vol. I: *Summary of Findings*. Princeton, N.J.: Gallup Organization. October.

Goldsmith, Jeffrey. 1984. "Death of a Paradigm: The Challenge of Competition." *Health Affairs* 3 (Fall): 7–19.

Goodin, Robert E., and Julian LeGrand. 1987. *Not Only the Poor*. London: Allen and Unwin.

Goodman, John C. 1985. "Private Alternatives to Social Security: The Experience of Other Countries." In *Social Security: Prospects for Real Reform*, ed. Peter J. Ferrara. Washington, D.C.: Cato Institute.

Goodwin, Leonard, and Joseph Tu. 1975. "The Social Psychological Basis for Public Acceptance of the Social Security System." *American Psychologist*. September.

Gornick, Marian, Jay N. Greenberg, Paul W. Eggers, and Allen Dobson. 1985. "Twenty Years of Medicare and Medicaid: Covered Populations, Use of Benefits, and Program Expenditures. *Health Care Financing Review*. Annual Supplement. Washington, D.C.: Government Printing Office.

Grad, Susan. 1984. "Incomes of the Aged and Nonaged, 1950–82." *Social Security Bulletin* 47 (June): 3–17.

Graetz, Michael J. 1987. "The Troubled Marriage of Retirement Security and Tax Policies." *University of Pennsylvania Law Review* 135 (Spring): 851–908.

Griswold, Erwin N., and Michael J. Graetz. 1976. *Federal Income Taxation: Principles and Policies*. Mineda, N.Y.: Foundation Press.

Gunsteren, Herman van, and Martin Rein. 1985. "The Dialectic of Public and Private Pensions." *Journal of Social Policy* 14: 129–49.

Halperin, Daniel I. 1986. "Interest in Disguise: Taxing the Time Value of Money." *Yale Law Journal* 95.

Halperin, Daniel I. 1987. Tax Policy and Retirement Income: A Rational Model for the 21st Century. In *Search for a National Retirement Security Policy*. J. Vanderhei, ed.

Harris, Louis J., & Associates, Inc. 1984. *Retirement and Income: A National Research Report of Behavior and Opinion Concerning Retirement, Pensions, and Social Security*. New York: Garland Publishing.

Heaney, Gerald W. 1984. "Why the High Rate in Reversals in Social Security Disability Cases?" *Hamilton Law Review* 7: 1–17.

Heclo, Hugh. 1982. "Toward a New Welfare State." In *The Development of Welfare States in Europe and America*, ed. Peter Flora and Arnold Heidenheimer. New Brunswick, N.J.: Transaction Books.

Heineman, Ben W., Jr., and Curtis A. Hessler. 1980. *Memorandum for the President: A Strategic Approach to Domestic Affairs in the 1980s*. New York: Random House.

Hirshfield, Daniel. 1970. *The Lost Reform*. Cambridge: Harvard University Press.

Internal Revenue Service, *Internal Revenue Code*, Sec. 32.

Hurd, Michael D., and John B. Shoven. 1985. "The Distributional Impact of Social Security." In *Pensions, Labor, and Individual Choice*, ed. David Wise. Chicago: University of Chicago Press for National Bureau of Economic Research.

"Joint Tax Committee Releases Estimates of Federal Tax Expenditures." 1985. *Tax Notes* 762 (19 November).

Kay, John. 1985. "Income for the Elderly: The Future of State Provision." In *Challenges to Social Policy*, ed. R. Berthoud. Aldershot, England: Gower.

Klein, Rudolf. 1984. "Privatization and the Welfare State." *Lloyds Bank Review* No. 151 (January): 12–29.

———. 1985. "Public Expenditure in an Inflationary World." In *The Politics of Inflation and Economic Stagnation*, ed. Leon Lindberg and Charles S. Maier. Washington, D.C.: Brookings Institution.

———. 1985. "Why Britain's Conservatives Support a Socialist Health Care System." *Health Affairs* 4 (Spring): 41–58.

Klein, Rudolf, and Michael O'Higgins. 1985. *The Future of Welfare*. Oxford: Basil Blackwell.

Klein, Rudolf, and Ellie Scrivens. 1985. "The Welfare State: From Crisis to Uncertainty." *Journal of Public Policy* 5 (May): 141–53.

Koite, David. Congressional Research Service. *The Projected Social Security Surplus*. HD 7094 (Washington, D.C.: Library of Congress). May 16, 1984.

Korczyk, Sophie M. 1984. *Retirement Security and Tax Policy*. Washington, D.C.: Employee Benefit Research Institute.

Kristol, Irving. 1985. "Skepticism, Meliorism, and *The Public Interest.*" *Public Interest.* 81 (Fall).

Latimer, Murray W. 1932. *Industrial Pension Systems in the United States and Canada.* 2 vols. New York: Industrial Relations Counselors, 1932.

Le Grand, Julian. 1984. "The Future of the Welfare State." *New Society.* 7 June.

Leimer, Dean R., and Selig D. Lesnoy. 1982. "Social Security and Private Saving: New Time-Series Evidence." *Journal of Political Economy* 90 (June): 606–29.

Leonard, Charles A. 1971. *A Search for a Judicial Philosophy: Mr. Justice Roberts and the Constitutional Revolution of 1937.* Port Washington, N.Y.: Kennikat Press.

Leonard, Herman B. 1986. *Checks Unbalanced: The Quiet Side of Public Spending.* New York: Basic Books.

Lesnoy, Selig D. 1984. "Private Alternatives to Social Security." Paper presented at Commissioner's Briefing, Social Security Administration. June 18. Washington, D.C.

Lesnoy, Selig D., and Dean R. Leimer. 1985. "Social Security and Private Savings: Theory and Historical Evidence." *Social Security Bulletin* 48 (January): 14–30.

Levy, Frank, and Robert Michel. 1985. "Are Baby Boomers Selfish?" *American Demographic Magazine.* 7 (April): 38–41.

Light, Paul. 1985. *Artful Work: The Politics of Social Security Reform.* New York: Random House.

Lowenstein, Louis. 1986. "Three New Reasons to Fear Junk Bonds." *New York Times.* 24 August.

Lurie, N., N. B. Ward, M. F. Shapiro, and R. H. Brook. 1984. "Termination from Medi-Cal: Does it Affect Health?" *New England Journal of Medicine* 311(7): 480–84.

Marmor, Theodore R. 1973. *The Politics of Medicare.* New York: Aldine.

———. 1975. "Can the U.S. Learn from Canada?" In *National Health Insurance: Can We Learn from Canada?*, ed. Spyros Andreapoulos. New York: Wiley.

———. 1983. *Political Analysis and Medical Care: Essays.* New York: Cambridge University Press.

———. 1983. "Welfare Medicine: How Success Can Be a Failure," In Marmor, *Political Analysis and Medical Care: Essays.* New York: Cambridge University Press.

———. 1987. "Entrepreneurship in Public Management." In *Leadership and Innovation: A Biographical Perspective on Entrepreneurs in*

Government, ed. J. Doig and E. Hargrove. Baltimore: Johns Hopkins University Press, 1987.

———. 1988. "Reflections on Medicare." *Journal of Medicine & Philosophy*. 13: 5–29.

Marmor, Theodore R., and Rudolf Klein. "Cost vs. Care: America's Health Dilemma Wrongly Considered." *Health Matrix* 4 (Spring): 19–24.

Marmor, Theodore R., with James A. Morone. 1983. "The Health Programs of the Kennedy-Johnson Years: An Overview." In *Political Analysis and Medical Care: Essays*. New York: Cambridge University Press.

Marmor, Theodore R., Mark Schlesinger, and Richard Smithey. 1986. "A New Look at Nonprofits: Health Care Policy in a Competitive Age." *Yale Journal on Regulation* 3(2): 313–49.

Martynas, A. Ycas, and Susan Grad. 1986. "Incomes of Retirement—Aged Persons in the United States." Paper delivered at a meeting of the International Social Security Association, Baltimore, May 6–8.

Mashaw, Jerry. 1983. *Bureaucratic Justice; Managing Social Security Disability Claims*. New Haven: Yale University Press.

Mashaw, Jerry, Charles Goetz, Frank Goodman, Warren Schwartz, Paul Verkuil, and Milton Carrow. *Social Security Hearings and Appeals* (National Center for Administrative Justice, Lexington: Lexington Books, 1978): 74–85.

Maxfield, Linda Drazga, and Virginia P. Reno. 1985. "Distribution of Income Sources of Recent Retirees: Findings from the New Beneficiary Survey." *Social Security Bulletin* 48 (January): 7–13.

Merrill, Sally R. 1984. "Home Equity and the Elderly." In *Retirement and Economic Behavior*, ed. H. Aaron and G. Burtless. Washington, D.C.: Brookings Institution. Pp. 197–227.

Mitchell, William C. 1976. *The Popularity of Social Security: A Paradox in Public Choice*. Washington, D.C.: American Enterprise Institute for Policy Research.

Mondale, Walter. 1978. "The Case for Hospital Cost Containment Act." In *Controlling Health Care Costs: A National Leadership Conference*. Washington, D.C.: The Government Research Corporation. Pp. 66–67.

Moon, Marilyn, and Isabel Sawhill. 1984. "Income Distribution and Social Policy: An Assessment After the Royal Commission on the Distribution of Income and Wealth." In *The Yearbook of Social Policy in Britain 1979*, ed. M. Brown and S. Baldwin. London: Routledge and Kegan Paul.

Munnell, Alicia. 1982. *The Economics of Private Pensions*. Washington, D.C.: Brookings Institution.

————. 1985. "The Current Status of Social Security Financing." Revised version of paper prepared for the Yale Faculty Seminar on Social Security. 19 December.

Munnell, Alicia H., and Lynn E. Blais. 1984. "Do We Want Large Social Security Surpluses?" *New England Economic Review*. (September–October): 5–21.

Musgrave, Richard A. 1981. "A Reappraisal of Social Security Financing." In *Social Security Financing*, ed. Felicity Skidmore. Cambridge: MIT Press.

Myers, Robert J. 1985. *Social Security*. 3d ed. Homewood, Ill.: Richard D. Irwin.

National Commission on Social Security Reform. 1983. *Report of the Commission*. Washington, D.C.: Government Printing Office.

Newhouse, Joseph, W. G. Manning, C. N. Morris, L. Orr, N. Duan, E. B. Keeler, A. Leibowitz, K. H. Marquis, M. S. Marquis, E. E. Phelps, and R. H. Brook. 1981. "Some Interim Results from a Controlled Trial of Cost Sharing in Health Insurance." *New England Journal of Medicine* 305(25): 1501–7.

1986 Annual Report of the Federal Old-Age and Survivors Insurance and Disability Insurance Trust Funds. 1986. Washington, D.C.: Government Printing Office.

Numbers, Ronald L. 1987. *Almost Persuaded: American Physicians and Compulsory Health Insurance*. Baltimore: Johns Hopkins University Press.

O'Donnell, Terrence. 1936. *History of Life Insurance in Its Formative Years*. Chicago: American Conservation Co.

Offe, Claus. 1984. *Contradictions of the Welfare State*. London: Hutchinson.

O'Higgins, Michael. 1980. "Income Distribution and Social Policy: An Assessment After the Royal Commission on the Distribution of Income and Wealth." In *The Yearbook of Social Policy in Britain 1979*, ed. M. Brown and S. Baldwin. London: Routledge and Kegan Paul.

————. 1984. "Privatisation and Social Security." *Political Quarterly 55* (April): 129–39.

————. 1985. "Inequality, Redistribution and Recession: The British Experience 1976–1982." *Journal of Social Policy* 14 (July): 279–307.

————. 1985. "Social Policy Needs and Resources: The Prospects for the 1990s." In *Challenges to Social Policy*, ed. R. Berthoud. Aldershot, England: Gower.

————. 1986. "Public-Private Interaction in Social Policy: A Comparative Study of Pensions Provision in Sweden, West Germany and the United Kingdom." In *The Public-Private Interplay in Social Protec-

tion: A Comparative Study, ed. Martin Rein and Lee Rainwater. Armonk, N.Y.: M. E. Sharpe.

————. 1988. "Social Welfare and Privatization: The British Experience." In *Privatization and the Welfare State*, ed. A. Kahn and S. Kamerman. Princeton: Princeton University Press.

Olson, Mancur. 1982. *The Rise and Decline of Nations*. New Haven: Yale University Press.

Organization for Economic Cooperation and Development. 1981. *Economic Survey: Sweden*. Paris: Organization for Economic Cooperation and Development.

————. 1985. *Social Expenditure 1960–1990: Problems of Growth and Control*. Paris: Organization for Economic Cooperation and Development.

Pear, Robert. 1984. "Increase in Health Care Cost Fund Slowing." *New York Times*. January 29.

Pechman, Joseph, ed. 1977. *What Should Be Taxed: Income or Expenditure?* Washington, D.C.: Brookings Institution.

Pechman, Joseph A., Henry J. Aaron, and Michael K. Taussig. 1968. *Social Security: Perspectives for Reform*. Washington, D.C.: Brookings Institution.

Pifer, Alan, and Forrest Chisman, eds. 1985. *The Report of the Committee on Economic Security of 1935 and Other Basic Documents, Fiftieth Anniversary Edition*. Washington, D.C.: National Conference on Social Welfare.

President's Commission on Pension Policy. 1981. "Dimensions of the Retirement Income Problem." In *Coming of Age: Toward a National Retirement Income Policy*. Washington, D.C.: Government Printing Office.

Preston, Samuel H. 1984. "Children and the Elderly in the U.S." *Scientific American* 251 (December): 44–49.

Quadrennial Advisory Council on Social Security. 1975. *Report of the Council*. Washington, D.C.: Government Printing Office.

Report to the President of the Committee on Economic Security. 1935. Washington, D.C.: Government Printing Office.

Ruggles, Patricia, and Michael O'Higgins. 1987. "Retrenchment and the New Right: A Comparative Analysis of the Reagan and Thatcher Administrations." In *Stagnation and Renewal in Social Policy: The Rise and Fall of Policy Regimes*, ed. G. Esping-Andersen, L. Rainwater, and M. Rein. Armonk, N.Y.: M. E. Sharpe.

Ruggles, Richard, and Nancy Ruggles. 1985. "The Integration of Macro and Micro Data for the Household Sector." Working Paper No. 1031. Institution for Social and Policy Studies. Yale University. October.

Salisbury, D. 1986. In "Age Conference Explores Adequacy of Private Pension System." *Tax Notes*. April 28: 335.

Schlesinger, Arthur M., Jr. 1960. *The Age of Roosevelt: The Politics of Upheaval*. Cambridge, Mass.: Riverside Press.

Schlesinger, Mark, and Pamela Drumheller. 1988. "Beneficiary Cost Sharing in the Medicare Program." In *Renewing the Promise: Medicare, Its History and Reform*, ed. David Blumenthal, Mark Schlesinger, and Pamela Drumheller. New York: Oxford University Press.

Schulz, James H., and Thomas D. Leavitt. 1983. *Pension Integration: Concepts, Issues and Proposals*. Washington, D.C.: Employee Benefit Research Institute.

Schwartz, Bernard. 1985. "Administrative Law Cases During 1984." *Administrative Law Review* 37: 133–61.

Skidmore, Felicity. 1981. *Social Security Financing*. Cambridge: MIT Press.

Skidmore, Max J. 1970. *Medicare and the American Rhetoric of Reconciliation*. University: University of Alabama Press.

Smith, Toulmin. 1870. *English Gilds*, published for the Early English Text Society. London: N. Trubner. 155–57.

"Social Security Insecurity." 1981. *Public Opinion*. 14 (August–September): 35–37.

"Social Security: Young and Old View the System's Prospects." 1985. *Public Opinion* (April–May): 21–24.

Somers, Herman M., and Anne R. Somers. 1967. *Medicare and the Hospitals: Issues and Prospects*. Washington, D.C.: Brookings Institution.

Starr, Paul. 1982. *The Social Transformation of American Medicine*. New York: Basic Books.

Steuerle, Eugene. 1985. *Taxes Loans and Inflation*. Washington, D.C.: Brookings Institution.

Stone, Deborah. 1984. *The Disabled State*. Philadelphia: Temple University Press.

Summers, Lawrence H. 1986. "I.R.A.'s Really Do Spark New Savings." *New York Times*. May 25.

Sweet, Stuart J. 1984. "A Looming Federal Surplus." *Wall Street Journal*. March 28.

Taylor-Gooby, Peter. 1985. "The Politics of Welfare: Public Attitudes and Behaviour." In *The Future of Welfare*, ed. Rudolf Klein and Michael O'Higgins. Oxford: Basil Blackwell.

Therborn, Goren. 1984. "The Prospects of Labour and the Transformation of Advanced Capitalism." *New Left Review* 145: 1–38.

Thompson, Lawrence H. 1983. "The Social Security Reform Debate." *Journal of Economic Literature* 21: 1425–67.

Tomasson, Richard. 1984. "Government Old Age Pensions under Affluence and Austerity." *Research in Social Problems and Public Policy*
3: 217–72.

"Tremors in the Pension System Finally Wake Congress Up." 1985. *Business Week*. November 18.

U.S. Congress. 1986. 1 Tax Reform Act of 1986. Conf. Rep. No. 841.
99th Cong., 2nd sess., Title XI.

U.S. Congress. Congressional Budget Office. 1982. *Financing Social Security*: Issues and Options for the Long Run. Washington, D.C.:
Government Printing Office. November.

———. 1983. "Major Legislative Changes." Mimeo, August, p. 75, table
10.

U.S. Congress. House. Committee on Government Operations. 1985.
*Work and Poverty: The Special Problems of the Working Poor:
Hearings Before the Subcommittee on Employment and Housing.*
99th Cong., 1st sess.

U.S. Congress. House Committee on Ways and Means. 1953. *Analysis of
the Social Security System: Hearings*. 83rd Cong., 1st sess.

———. 1960. *Administration of the Social Security Disability Insurance
Program*. Report to the Subcommittee on the Administration of the
Social Security Laws. Washington, D.C.: Government Printing Of-
fice.

———. 1974. *Staff Report on the Disability Insurance Program*. Washington, D.C.: Government Printing Office.

———. 1978. *Possible Areas of Subcommittee Action*. Report to the Subcommittee on Social Security, Disability Insurance. Washington,
D.C.: Government Printing Office.

———. 1979. *Actuarial Condition of Disability Insurance—1978*. Report to the Subcommittee on Social Security. Washington, D.C.:
Government Printing Office.

———. 1983. *Background Material and Data on Programs within the
Jurisdiction of the Committee on Ways and Means*. Washington,
D.C.: Government Printing Office. February.

———. 1985. *Background Material and Data on Programs within the
Jurisdiction of the Committee on Ways and Means*. Washington,
D.C.: Government Printing Office. February.

———. 1987. *Background Material and Data on Programs within the
Jurisdiction of the Committee on Ways and Means*. Washington,
D.C.: Government Printing Office. February.

———. 1984. *Federal Tax Treatment of Low Income Persons: Hearing
Before the Subcommittee on Oversight*. 98th Cong., 2nd sess.

———. 1985. *Distribution and Economics of Employer Provided Fringe*

Benefits: Hearings Before the Subcommittee on Social Security and on Select Revenue Measures. 99th Cong., 1st sess.

———. 1985. *Retirement Income Security in the United States: Hearings*. 99th Cong., 1st sess., Serial 50.

———. 1987. *Background Material and Data on Programs within the Jurisdiction of the Committee on Ways and Means*. Washington, D.C.: Government Printing Office.

U.S. Congress. House. Select Committee on Aging. 1983. *Pension Asset Raids; Hearing*. 98th Cong., 1st sess., 28 September. Comm. Pub. 98–438.

———. 1983. *Social Security Disability Reviews: A Federally Created State Problem* Washington, D.C.: Government Printing Office.

———. 1984. *Social Security Disability Reviews: A Costly Constitutional Crisis*. Washington, D.C.: Government Printing Office.

———. 1985. *The Black Elderly in Poverty: Hearing*. 99th Cong., 1st sess., 27 September.

———. 1985. *Taxes, Social Security and the Deficit: Hearings*. 99th Cong., 1st sess., 15 April.

U.S. Congress, House. Subcommittee on the Administration of the Social Security Laws. 1959. *Hearing on the Administration of the Social Security Insurance Program*. 86th Cong., 1st sess.

———. Joint Committee on Taxation. *Estimates of Federal Tax Expenditures for Fiscal Years 1987–1991*.

U.S. Congress. Senate. Committee on the Budget. 1986. *Tax Expenditures: Relationships to Spending Programs and Background Material on Individual Provisions*. 99th Cong., 2nd sess.

U.S. Congress. Senate. Committee on Governmental Affairs. 1983. *The Role of the Administrative Law Judge in the Title II Social Security Disability Insurance Program*. Hearing before the Subcommittee on Oversight of Government Management, Social Security Disability Reviews. Washington, D.C.: Government Printing Office.

U.S. Congress. Senate. Special Committee on Aging. 1984. *The Employee Retirement Security Act of 1974: The First Decade*. 98th Cong., 2nd sess.

———. 1984. *Medicare and the Health Costs of Older Americans*. Washington, D.C.: Government Printing Office.

———. Staff Report. 1985. *Impact of Medicare's Prospective Payment on the Quality of Care Received by Medical Beneficiaries*. Washington, D.C.: Government Printing Office.

U.S. Congress. Senate. Task Force on Medicare and Medical Cost Control. 1984. *Report*. Mimeo, p. 3.

U.S. Congress. Social Security Disability Benefits Reform Act of 1984. P.L. 98–460, 98 Stat. 1794 (1984).

U.S. Department of Commerce. Bureau of the Census. 1984. *Statistical Abstract of the United States*, Table 103, p. 69, and Table 33, p. 30.

U.S. Department of Health and Human Services, Social Security Administration, "Briefing." Photocopied document.

U.S. Department of Health and Human Services. Social Security Administration. 1984. *Social Security Bulletin* 47 (October).

U.S. Department of Health and Human Services, Social Security Administration. 1985. *Social Security Bulletin Annual Statistical Supplement*. Washington, D.C.: Government Printing Office. December.

————. 1986. "Long-Range Estimates of Social Security Trust Fund Operations in Dollars." Actuarial Note 127. Baltimore, Md.

U.S. Department of Health and Human Services. Social Security Administration. Office of Hearings and Appeals. 1984. *Operational Report*. Washington, D.C.: Government Printing Office. September 30.

U.S. Office of Management and Budget. 1986. *Special Analysis of the Budget of the U.S. Government 1986*. Washington, D.C.: Government Printing Office. Special Analysis G.

Vanderhei, J., ed. 1987. *Search for a National Retirement Security Policy*. Homewood, Ill.: R. D. Irwin.

Venti, Steven F., and David A. Wise. 1986. "IRAs and Saving." Working Paper No. 1879. National Bureau of Economic Research. Cambridge, Mass. April.

"Ways & Means Subcommittees Consider Retirement Income Security." 1985. *Tax Notes* 391 (22 July).

Wilensky, Harold L., Gregory M. Luebbert, Susan Reed Hahn, and Adrienne M. Jamieson. 1985. *Comparative Social Policy*, Berkeley: Institute of International Studies.

Williams, Winston. 1985. "Raking in Billions from the Company Pension Plan." *New York Times*. November 3.

Wing, Kenneth R. 1985–1986. "American Health Policy in the 1980s." *Case Western Reserve Law Review* 6(4): 608–85.

Yankelovich, Daniel. 1981. *New Rules: Searching for Self-Fulfillment in a World Turned Upside Down*. New York: Random House.

CONTRIBUTORS

ROBERT M. BALL, Visiting Scholar, Center for the Study of Social Policy, Suite 405, 236 Massachusetts Avenue, N.E., Washington, DC 20002

ROBERT M. COVER, deceased. At the time of his death, he was Chancellor Kent Professor of Law and Legal History, Yale University School of Law.

MICHAEL J. GRAETZ, Justus S. Hotchkiss Professor of Law, Yale University School of Law, 127 Wall Street, New Haven, CT 06520

RUDOLF KLEIN, Professor of Social Policy, School of Humanities and Social Science, University of Bath, Claverton Down, Bath BA2 7AY, England

THEODORE R. MARMOR, Professor of Public Management and Political Science, Yale University School of Organization and Management, 111 Prospect Street, New Haven, CT 06520

JERRY L. MASHAW, William Nelson Cromwell Professor of Law, Yale University School of Law, 127 Wall Street, New Haven, CT 06520

MICHAEL O'HIGGINS, consultant on social policy, formerly Reader in Social Policy, University of Bath.

PAUL E. STARR, Professor of Sociology, Princeton University, Princeton, NJ 08544

JAMES TOBIN, Sterling Professor of Economics, Yale University, 30 Hillhouse Avenue, New Haven, CT 06520

INDEX